DEATH, RITUAL, AND BEREAVEMENT

Death has become a taboo subject in our time. Previous generations, however, supported the dying and bereaved in ways that no longer exist but are now being uncovered by historians investigating the rituals and customs surrounding death and dying.

These new studies in the social history of death in England from 1500 to the 1930s focus on the death-bed, funerals, burials, mourning customs, and the expression of grief. They throw fresh light on developments which lie at the roots of present-day tendencies to minimize or conceal the most unpleasant aspects of death, among them the growing participation of doctors in the management of death-beds in the eighteenth century and the creation of extra-mural cemeteries, followed by the introduction of cremation, in the nineteenth. They also underline the importance of religious belief, which at the deepest level denied death, in helping the bereaved in past times. Half of the essays are concerned with the complex but fundamental changes of Victoria's reign – changes obscured by writers who have contrasted the 'Victorian' outlook with that of later generations.

Death, Ritual, and Bereavement is the first volume in a new series published by Routledge in association with the Social History Society of the UK. It is aimed primarily at teachers and students of social and family history, the history of medicine and religion, but its straightforward, readable style and its many colourful accounts will appear to a wider audience.

DEATH, RITUAL, AND BEREAVEMENT

EDITED BY RALPH HOULBROOKE

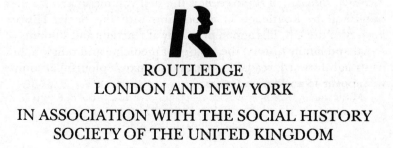

ROUTLEDGE
LONDON AND NEW YORK

IN ASSOCIATION WITH THE SOCIAL HISTORY
SOCIETY OF THE UNITED KINGDOM

First published 1989
by Routledge
11 New Fetter Lane, London EC4P 4EE
29 West 35th Street, New York, NY 10001

Typeset by LaserScript Ltd, Mitcham, Surrey
Printed in Great Britain by
TJ Press (Padstow) Ltd, Padstow, Cornwall

British Library Cataloguing in Publication Data

Death, ritual, and bereavement.
1. Great Britain. Death Customs, 1500–1940
I. Houlbrooke, Ralph A. (Ralph, Anthony)
393'.0941

ISBN 0 415 01165 5

Library of Congress Cataloging in Publication Data

Death, ritual, and bereavement / edited by Ralph Houlbrooke.
p. cm.
Bibliography: p.
Includes index.
1. Death – Social aspects – Great Britain – History. 2. Social history –
Modern, 1500- 3. Bereavement – History. I. Houlbrooke, Ralph A.
(Ralph Anthony)
HQ1073.5.G7D43 1989
306.9—dc19

CONTENTS

Foreword

Social history has been one of the great success stories of the academic world in the past generation. Historians have been recreating the past with a much greater emphasis on the way societies work and on how they are structured. This explosion of knowledge has brought great gains in understanding. We not only know far more about subjects previously considered inaccessible or 'unresearchable'; the techniques and insights of social historians have increasingly informed the work of political historians, such that it is now rare to come across a serious researcher uninterested in relating his work to its appropriate social context. It can no longer be claimed, as G.M. Trevelyan once asserted in a phrase frequently quoted out of context, that social history is 'history with the politics left out'.

The founding of a new society – the Social History Society of the United Kingdom – in 1976 bore testimony to the increasing importance of the subject. The Society has always been anxious to make its work accessible to the widest possible audience. To aid this objective, it has placed particular emphasis upon its annual conferences. These always centre around a research theme, selected by its Committee, in which new and sometimes experimental work is known to be actively in progress. In this way, social historians are able to obtain insights into exciting research developments at a formative stage.

The Society has always published abstracts of papers read at the annual Conference in its *Newsletter* but it was increasingly felt that the best work deserved both a wider audience and a more substantial format. The most appropriate vehicle for this was felt to be a volume of essays which would be lively and informative but which would also indicate the importance of the chosen theme and suggest how the new approaches might be further developed. The Society was delighted to learn that Routledge, a publishing house long known for its pioneer work in social history, was to participate in this venture.

Both Society and publishers take pride in launching this inaugural volume deriving from the conference on 'Death, Ritual, and Bereavement', held in Oxford in January 1987. It is edited by Ralph Houlbrooke, whose interest in these themes developed out of his well-known work on the family in early modern England. It will be the first in a series which makes exciting new research in social history available in accessible and attractive form.

1

INTRODUCTION

RALPH HOULBROOKE

'All that lives must die':[1] death is an inescapable fact of human existence whose essential nature does not alter in the course of time. But its causes and incidence, understanding of its physical aspects and beliefs about the after-life, the treatment of the dying and their comportment, the disposal of mortal remains and the ritual responses of survivors – all these have clearly changed, and the historian can study the process in a wealth of remaining evidence. This collection of essays is particularly concerned with the death-bed, the funeral, burial, grief, and mourning in England between the close of the Middle Ages and the early twentieth century. Funerary rites have long interested both historians and anthropologists, largely because of the great range of purposes they have been designed to fulfil in different cultures. Perhaps the most important has been to secure the happiness, or at least the tranquillity, of the departed, and if necessary prevent their return to earth to haunt the living. These rites have also served to repair the breaches in the fabric of society caused by the deaths of important people, to confirm the transfer of property and responsibilities to successors, reinforce the social hierarchy, and uphold traditions of hospitality. Mourning garb not only manifested respect for the memory of the dead, but also emphasized shared kinship and corporate solidarity.[2] Much less has been written about the death-bed, though the copious literature of the *ars moriendi*, the 'craft of dying' has attracted some attention.[3] Historians have shown themselves even more wary of getting to grips with the subject of grief.

Two subjects not directly addressed in the following essays are the demography of death and changing conceptions of the

1

hereafter. Yet so important are they to a proper understanding of the themes to be treated that something needs to be said about them at the outset. Before the twentieth century, death was much more obviously the companion of life than it is today, because infections and working conditions killed so many more people before they reached old age. Over the period between 1541 and 1871, the English expectation of life at birth fluctuated between about twenty-seven and forty-two years.[4] Within this band, there was a clear rising trend from the 1730s onwards, but the life expectancy of 1871 (41.31) was less than it had been nearly three hundred years before in 1581 (41.68), a good year in which to be born, in Elizabeth's reign. Not until the very end of the nineteenth century and the early decades of the twentieth did this pattern change dramatically; nearly twenty years had been added to the life expectancy of 1870 by 1930, and another ten by 1970.

The most important element in low life expectancy at birth was persistently high infant mortality; until the twentieth century a higher proportion of deaths occurred in the first than in any subsequent year of life. The United Kingdom infant mortality rate was about 150 per thousand as late as 1870. Not till just before 1900 did infant mortality begin to fall consistently, gradually at first, and then, during the first decade of the new century, much more rapidly, to drop below twenty per thousand by 1970. The later nineteenth and early twentieth centuries also saw substantial, though less striking, falls in mortality in childhood, youth, and middle age. Adult mortality started falling earlier than infant mortality. A man aged thirty, for example, could in 1810–11 expect to live another 32.5 years, perhaps three years longer than his counterparts between 1550 and 1649. Life expectancy for a man of this age was actually marginally less in 1840–1 than it had been thirty years earlier, but by 1890–1 it had grown by more than six years. Thereafter the rate of increase slowed: the biblical three score years and ten were what the man who was thirty years old on the eve of the First World War might expect to achieve. Adult mortality rates before old age were still comparatively high in the early nineteenth century. A quarter of all children lost one parent or both before their sixteenth birthday in the 1830s, while over a third of all marriages begun at the average age in the 1820s were terminated by death within twenty years. The impression given by these figures needs to be qualified in one important respect. They conceal wide variations in experience, and reflect above all what happened to the working classes who constituted the majority. The nobility, for example, experienced a sharp fall in mortality in the eighteenth century which was not shared by the population at large. Males born in this highest social group in the last quarter of the eighteenth century already enjoyed a life expectancy at birth rather better than that of the cohort of male babies born in England and Wales in 1875–6.[5]

Although it is clear that the most dramatic falls in mortality have taken place since the mid-nineteenth century, considerable changes occurred long before that in the patterns and causes of death. National mortality crises, when deaths leapt far above their normal levels, were far commoner before 1750 than they were after that date. In the sixteenth and seventeenth centuries, plague was the foremost epidemic killer, and its disappearance after 1665 was the biggest single reason for the long-term decline in crisis mortality. Plague was especially terrifying because of its capacity to kill off whole households and devastate urban parishes. Other diseases which reached epidemic proportions included smallpox, typhus, cholera, and influenza (which was responsible for the last great crisis of our period, in 1919). Background mortality remained at a high level even when crises became more infrequent. Smallpox succeeded plague as the chief killer of the young, and tuberculosis succeeded smallpox. Until the nineteenth century, the growth of towns and cities with their fumes, overcrowding, and problems of refuse disposal, produced a net deterioration in the environment in which English people lived. Until after the First World War, medicine played little part in reducing mortality: the one outstanding exception was the introduction of smallpox inoculation in the eighteenth century. More important were the diminishing virulence of particular diseases, preventative measures such as the quarantining of plague-stricken ships, improvements in water supply, sanitation, clothing and working conditions, and a rising standard of nutrition.[6]

Throughout the centuries of high mortality the prospect of an after-life offered the hope of compensation for the likely brevity of earthly existence and the disruption of human relationships by death. Most human societies have in varying measure denied mortality. Some have envisaged no more than a shadowy and somewhat tenuous existence for the departed, while others have accepted schemes laying out in some detail the geography and chronology of future states of existence. The Christian assertion of the immortality of the soul and the ultimate resurrection of the body constitutes the most fundamental denial of death. But during the centuries when the hold of Christianity was strongest, and its association with secular institutions at its closest, the churches also asserted uncompromisingly the reality of suffering in and after death. Their teaching emphasized the eternity of torment which awaited the damned, and, especially during the later Middle Ages and the first 150 years after the Reformation, the horrors of physical death itself. Yet rigour was followed by relaxation, almost as if by a process of natural reaction: each attempt to bring home to the faithful the bleaker implications of Christian doctrine was succeeded in the longer term by some accommodation. In the later Middle Ages a new emphasis on the awful prospect of a divine judgement exercised upon each individual was followed by the elaboration of the doctrine of purgatory, a place where repentant sinners might undergo a punishment made endurable by the knowledge that they were saved. Its effect was probably to lift the fear of damnation from the minds of the great majority. The Protestant reformers repudiated the doctrine of purgatory. But the centuries since 1700 have seen a gradually increasing reluctance among Christians themselves to recognize the inescapable reality of the eternity of pain which used to form the obverse of eternal happiness. Many in the age of reason could not accept what came to seem like cruelty and vindictiveness in God.[7]

During the Victorian period, despite the presence of an assertive and pervasive religiosity, doubt spread: rigorists complained that the clergy were increasingly reluctant to spell out the truth of damnation, while heterodox speculation about the after-life percolated downwards among the faithful. Perhaps this blurring of the outlines of doctrine has served in the long run to make more uncertain the prospect of the after-life itself. Some philosophers long ago contemplated with equanimity the extinction of the individual personality. In denying immortality, Lucretius the Epicurean (99?–55 BC) sought to free men from terror of the gods; annihilation and the cessation of all sensation meant that men had nothing to fear after death. Perhaps such ideas are increasingly acceptable in a society in which most people die old. The notion that a longer lifespan greatly reduces society's concern with death and the hereafter was aired as long ago as 1899, when the upper and middle classes were already experiencing big improvements in life expectancy which would soon be shared by the population at large. 'Thus on all sides death is losing its terrors. We are dying more frequently when our life's work is done, and it seems more natural to die.'[8] Yet our age has not achieved a new certainty or equanimity. It seems rather to face Hamlet's 'undiscover'd country' with a certain unease.

During the last twenty years the process by which death has supposedly been pushed to the margins of modern social experience has aroused considerable interest among sociologists and historians. The most important single stimulus has been provided by Geoffrey Gorer's *Death, Grief and Mourning in Contemporary Britain* (1965). Gorer claimed that the drastic simplification of funeral and mourning customs during the present century was symptomatic of a desire to ignore death. Grief itself, deprived of the supportive framework of mourning, was discouraged, while the terminally ill increasingly often died alone in hospital rather than at home surrounded by their families. Gorer's work has provoked a continuing debate about British attitudes to death during the last hundred years. It has also helped set in train an international discussion of the social history of death since the Middle Ages.

Gorer's call for more sympathetic treatment of the dying and the bereaved has been supported by a number of writers. But some historians have felt that his vision of the past was clouded by nostalgia. J. Morley, in his *Death, Heaven and the Victorians* (1971) described the extravagant panoply of funerary and mourning display in a tone of horrified fascination. In 1981 David Cannadine published a trenchant dismissal of the idea that Victorian mourning customs helped the bereaved to come to terms with their loss, arguing that the Victorian era 'was not so much a golden age of effective psychological support as a bonanza of commercial exploitation.'[9] The expense of funerals and mourning attire imposed a heavy financial burden on bereaved families. Moreover, many Victorians recognized this themselves, and long before the reign was out, a reaction was under way. (It is only fair to Gorer, incidentally, to point out that the years to which he looked back with some nostalgia were those immediately before the First World War, not the first half of Victoria's reign.) Over half the essays in this volume focus on the Victorian period. Three general points about them may be made at this juncture. First, they illustrate the great complexity of the cross-currents of opinion and feeling which flowed through the reign. Secondly, they underline the importance of the differences in sensibility between its first and second halves. Finally, they show that the roots of 'Victorian' attitudes must be sought in previous decades.

That recent changes in attitudes can only be properly understood if they are set in a much longer perspective than that afforded by the last 150 years is the conviction underlying the work of a number of other historians of death. In his three books on the subject, Philippe Ariès traced their origins back to the Middle Ages.[10] In seeking to explain why death, for centuries supposedly familiar and accepted, had become fearsome and unmentionable, he was guided by the hypothesis of 'a relationship between man's attitudes towards death and his awareness of self'. The roots of modern individual self awareness were, he believed, to be found in the later medieval centuries. A new sense of the uniqueness of loved ones developed later as an extension of individual self consciousness. Individualism, meaning a more acute sense both of one's own identity and of the irreplaceability of loved ones, made death harder to endure. Three other 'psychological themes', as he called them, came to seem important to Ariès: the defence of society against untamed nature, whether by collective ritual or the advances of science, belief in an after-life, and belief in the existence of evil. It nevertheless seems fair to assert that awareness of self remains the *leitmotiv* of his work. Ariès's writings on attitudes to death, though full of challenging insights and immensely impressive in their chronological sweep, are difficult to come to grips with. Distinctions between facts and hypotheses, the central and the less important parts of the argument, what is relevant to its main thread and what not: all these are sometimes hard to discern. The relationships between the changes he sought to document are often highly obscure, and the choice of 'individualism' as the main motor of change seems an arbitrary one. The idealized picture of the traditional death is unconvincing and rests on a few widely scattered examples.

In her *Death, Burial and the Individual in Early Modern England* (1984), the widest ranging recent study of the social history of death in England, Clare Gittings acknowledges her debt to Ariès's explanation.[11] But here, precisely because Gittings seeks to set out the links between 'individualism' and other elements in the developing situation in a clearer and more explicit fashion than Ariès, the difficulties involved in making it the most important cause of change become even more apparent. The Reformation, for example, whose influence on some aspects of funerary practice is well illustrated by Gittings, may have stimulated individualism (though this is far from clear), but it would be hard to argue that the growth of individualism played more than an indirect part in bringing it about. The nature and functions of the 'traditional group ties' whose gradual dissolution during her long period supposedly threw the 'burden of death' increasingly on the immediate relatives of the deceased are never fully defined. The core of Clare Gittings's work, an immensely valuable analysis of expenditure on funerals between the Reformation and the Interregnum, has been set in a much larger explanatory framework which does not really fit it. The basic problem with all theses which place a heavy burden of explanation on the 'rise of individualism' is that the sorts of evidence which enable us to detect its presence, such as 'the character drama or novel, the portrait and the biography or autobiography' can usually be equally or more plausibly attributed to other causes. And their non-existence or disappearance do not in themselves demonstrate its absence or weakness.

Various studies of other countries point to the eighteenth century, the age of the Enlightenment, as a critical phase in the development of attitudes to death. Michel Vovelle's study of Provençal wills led him to the conclusion that the decline of the devout clauses and provisions characteristic of 'baroque' piety was so marked in the second half of the eighteenth century that it was explicable only in terms of 'dechristianization' or secularization. Whether or not men were less assured of the hereafter in 1780 than in 1710, he could not say: but they had certainly decided not to reveal their assurance. In Paris, Pierre Chaunu discerned trends broadly similar to those discovered by Vovelle in Provence. Two features in his picture of the eighteenth century are perhaps especially important: the reaction against the fear of a severe judgement, and the decline of crisis mortality in the later seventeenth and early eighteenth centuries. Mortality of course remained at a far higher level than today's; but, Chaunu believed, the impact of death had become less terrifying. In his survey of changing attitudes to death in eighteenth-century France, John McManners assigned some weight to an improved expectation of life among the more fortunate classes; rather more to the influence of new notions about the hereafter; most of all to a supposedly new intensity of feeling within the nuclear family.[12]

More liberal theological currents also flowed in the eighteenth-century New England depicted by David Stannard, softening the austere face of inherited Puritanism. Whereas for the godly among the early settlers death had commonly been an ordeal rendered more terrible by uncertainties about their future state, their mid-eighteenth-century descendants were often comforted in their last hours by confidence of salvation. The reception of new ideas was facilitated by the growth of a more complex and worldly society, but, Stannard believed, the latter process was fraught with tension. One sign of this was the elaboration of previously starkly simple funeral rituals among the pious towards the end of the seventeenth century. Stannard attributed this to feelings of insecurity in a puritan group which found itself increasingly cut off from its English roots and under pressure within its own community. The growth of ceremony (or so he argued from anthropological studies of apparently analogous situations) was characteristic of groups and societies under threat. But is it not possible that the elaboration of ritual, far from reflecting the puritans' sense of insecurity, was simply symptomatic of their increasing conformity with contemporary English practice?[13]

These examples will suffice to illustrate the lively interest in past attitudes to death which has developed among historians in recent years, and some of their differences of opinion about the nature and causes of significant change. It is time to say something more about the essays which follow. A comprehensive survey of the social history of death in England would be beyond the scope of a collection such as this, and has not been attempted here. Our volume explores a field of research which may be likened to a vast continent whose coasts are disputed by rival bands of colonists while much larger inland tracts remain unexplored. Many of these essays are primarily designed to open up the unknown rather than to engage in existing debates, though at least half of them throw some light on matters in controversy. Very broadly speaking, the questions raised by each contributor are ones suggested by previous work in the field. The most important of these may be listed as follows. To what extent was death viewed as a test of the dying individual? What was expected of him or her? How might the dying be assisted by those around them? What were the most significant elements in funeral rites? In what ways were their shape and content influenced by religious beliefs and social demands? How did grief manifest itself in the past? How effective were the support and consolation which the bereaved derived from their beliefs, from the sympathy of other people, and the operation of ritual and custom?

The major subjects alluded to in our title – Death (above all the death-bed), Ritual, and Bereavement – were the original guideline themes of the conference from which this volume has sprung. The price paid for the thematic unity made possible by the choice of certain clearly bounded areas of investigation is the exclusion of other important topics in the social history of death. As has already been pointed out, changing patterns of mortality and conceptions of the after-life fall into this category. Other topics we have not broached include (to name only a few of the more obvious examples) suicide, accidental deaths, and the impact of war. It will also be clear that the coverage even of its own period and themes achieved by this volume is somewhat patchy: inevitably so, given the fact that so much work has yet to be done.

Within the bounds set by the demands of thematic coherence there has nevertheless been room for a considerable variety of vantage point, social coverage, and materials used. Among the authors dealing with the death-bed, for example, Lucinda Beier assesses the behaviour of the dying in terms of the Christian ideal of the good death, while Roy Porter focuses his attention on the doctors' ministrations. The social groups studied extend from the politically active upper class to the respectable working class. Sources employed range from newspapers and periodicals through private letters and diaries to the oral testimony of aged people. Such variety is a strong and positive characteristic, made possible by the co-operation of scholars working on a number of different projects. But it naturally makes for a certain caution when one attempts to frame broad generalizations about the long-term course of change. Although there is a reassuring degree of compatibility between most of the arguments advanced here, we do not claim to present a new and comprehensive interpretation of the social history of death in England.

The history of the death-bed is the first major theme of this volume. It should perhaps be made clear at the outset that none of the contributors writing on this theme has attempted an assessment of the experience of death from the point of view of the dying individual. Too much of that experience cannot be known to the living. Rather we have been concerned with what might broadly be described as the 'management' of the death-bed by those around it, expectations as to how the dying should behave, and the extent to which these expectations were, or seemed to be, fulfilled.

The achievement of a good end was a major preoccupation of the pious during the centuries immediately before and after the Reformation. A rapidly growing volume of literature devoted to the *ars moriendi* described how the various temptations of the death-bed might be overcome. A good death was the keystone of a life well lived, but it could also (though this was much less likely to happen) cancel the debit sheet of a bad one. Lucinda Beier shows how important this ideal still was in seventeenth-century England, not only to the dying, but also to the survivors whom it helped to come to terms with bereavement. But, she emphasizes, its successful implementation depended upon the nature of the terminal illness and the availability of effective support from those around the death-bed. This is a point which I elaborate, drawing attention to the very great variety of death-bed experience in sixteenth- and seventeenth-century England. I also suggest that the nature of the support given to the dying underwent important changes in that period. The sacramental ministrations of the clergy lost much of their previous importance, and the process of will making escaped their supervision, ultimately to be increasingly separated from the last illness. The tendency for death to become more private was probably under way by 1700.

These changes form the prelude to Roy Porter's picture of eighteenth-century developments. At their heart lay an increasing emphasis on the merciful nature of God and a growing readiness to explain sickness and death in naturalistic rather than providential terms. The role of the doctor became more prominent, even eclipsing that of the minister to whom he had previously been a subordinate partner. Before, it had been his responsibility to give an honest diagnosis which might help his patient prepare to meet his Maker; now he took over the management of the death-bed, diminishing the scope for initiative on the part of both the dying man and his spiritual adviser. The 'good' death came to be seen, not as the supreme trial of Christian fortitude, but rather as a transition made as peaceful and free from pain and fear as possible. To this end, Dr Porter shows, narcotics were being used well before the end of the century on a massive and hitherto unsuspected scale.

To what extent the evangelical revival brought in its train a restoration of the older pattern of a good death is an intriguing question which awaits investigation. It is clear, however, from Diana Dixon's study of the treatment of death in Victorian juvenile magazines that the tradition of exemplary and cautionary accounts of children's deaths which had originated in such seventeenth-century works as James Janeway's *Token for Children* was still very much alive. They showed how good children coped bravely with agonizing ordeals before being delivered by a merciful death, while naughty ones all too often died suddenly or suffered tantalizing vain regrets. But though lingering illness offered the best opportunity for the exercise of the sort of fortitude most prized by the writers of children's religious magazines, it was the death in action which was most frequently described in the radically different tradition of boys' adventure papers.

The English funeral has usually performed both religious and social functions since the Middle Ages. The Reformation brought a major change: the repudiation of purgatory drastically curtailed prayer for the departed among Protestants. But, Clare Gittings has shown, the major social functions, especially the confirmation of the social status of the deceased person and his family, and the convivial expression of solidarity, were remarkably little affected by the religious developments of the period. The reformers not only curbed intercession for the soul but also sought to discourage excessive concern for the mortal remains. Though (as my analysis of will preambles suggests), testators increasingly paid lip service to the new ideal of detachment, a surviving, even growing solicitude for the protection of the corpse seems evident in the spread of coffin burial, so fully documented by Clare Gittings. (And, I suggest, the rise of memorial inscriptions and personal tributes in funeral sermons served to compensate, at least in part, for the abolition of intercessory rites.)

As yet no thorough study of eighteenth-century funeral and burial practices has been published. Clare Gittings believes that from the later seventeenth century onwards the middling ranks of society increasingly spent money on funeral paraphernalia rather than convivial eating and drinking. She attributes this development very largely to the rise of the undertaker. 'In early modern England, respectability would in general come from a large turn-out of voluntary mourners, perhaps partly attracted by generous provision of food and drink. By the Victorian period, respectability was conferred by the quantity of material trappings – sashes, hatbands, gloves, scarves and so on – which could only be purchased from the undertaker for cash.'[14] But the outlines of this development remain hazy, in the absence of the detailed accounts on which her picture of the period up to the 1650s is based, and the part played in it by changing sensibilities needs fuller analysis.

Ruth Richardson argues in this volume that behind the growing desire in the eighteenth and early nineteenth centuries for strong coffins, solid monuments, and secure, sequestered burial places lay fear of the grave robber, that macabre product of the rise of anatomical science during the century of the Enlightenment. Diminished respect for the bodies of the dead, and growing readiness to sacrifice their remains on the altar of knowledge useful to the living, thus stimulated a new elaboration of burial. But the 1832 Anatomy Act, by guaranteeing a steady supply of pauper corpses for dissection, removed the need for grave robbery. As this threat receded, Dr Richardson believes, 'attention and expenditure focused increasingly on funerary display': resources freed by the achievement of security could be diverted into ostentation.

The desire for greater security was an important early motive for the establishment of great new extramural cemeteries from about 1830 onwards, but by no means the only one. The overcrowding of churchyards in rapidly expanding cities threatened the health of the living as well as the repose of the dead. As Jim Morgan points out, hostility towards the Anglican monopoly of burial provision was an important reason for the foundation of new cemeteries first by private companies and later by local authorities. The breach of this monopoly was one of many developments assisting the emergence of a more secular society. And, as Jennifer Leaney reminds us, aesthetic motives were also at work. By removing interment from the hearts of towns, burial reformers made the face of death less visible; in laying out more spacious and beautiful cemeteries, they also sought to make it more acceptable. Not surprisingly, some churchmen viewed the whole movement with profound suspicion.

Jennifer Leaney shows how the advocacy of cremation followed naturally as the next, if more radical, stage in the search for a means of disposal of the dead which would be at once more hygienic and less obtrusive. Throughout the Christian era, cremation had been tainted by association with paganism. (Though English memorial inscriptions influenced by classical models had often referred to 'ashes' as a euphemism for the mortal remains, and urns had figured prominently in funeral art.) Many advocates of its revival saw in cremation a means of removing from death some of the unpleasantness upon which churchmen had often played in their calls to repentance, especially before the Age of Reason. It forestalled the process of putrefaction which, of all the aspects of death, aroused the most intense loathing, and hastened the reunion with nature of the 'etherealised and purified' material elements of the body. Leaney concludes that the origins of the tendency to conceal death supposedly so characteristic of the twentieth century should really be sought far back in the nineteenth.

At the very time when a reaction against the ostentatious 'celebration of death' was beginning to gain support in the upper and middle ranks of society, the funerals of the lower orders were becoming more elaborate.[15] This was perhaps due in large part to the desire to assert status and respectability in an increasingly stratified working class. But, Ruth Richardson claims, much of the impetus was supplied by the determination of all but the very poorest to show that they did not belong to the ranks of paupers buried by the parish, whose corpses might end up on the dissection table or (at best) in 'the flimsy coffin and the unmarked grave'. Nor, Jennifer Leaney argues, did the working classes share the desire to render death less conspicuous. They were used to a relative lack of privacy in all the activities of human existence, inured to the frequent experience of sickness and death when these had become less common in more fortunate social groups. The sort of discretion which would have prevented the staging of a proper send-off by the friends and neighbours of the dead held little attraction for them.

So working class conservatism preserved the 'Victorian' funeral pattern well into the twentieth century. This pattern, as recalled by elderly Lancashire people in oral testimony given in 1971–81, is analysed here by Elizabeth Roberts. Laying out at home, often by expert women who also helped deliver babies into the world; viewing of the body by large numbers of neighbours old and young; neighbourly support in the drawing of curtains, help with the preparation of the family's funeral tea, and the collection of money for flowers; the pomp of the funeral itself and the black of mourning clothes which those who wore them could ill afford: these were the things that stood out in people's memories of the working-class 'way of death' in the Lancashire of their childhood. Death was then still a central fact of life and one of the most important occasions for the expression of familial and neighbourhood solidarity.

Grief is something which historians cannot readily measure,[16] but they can analyse the ways in which each age has described and expressed its grief. The relative dearth of intimate personal documents surviving from medieval times has led some historians to the unconvincing hypothesis that a totally different emotional climate existed then. From Tudor times onwards an enormous wealth of material survives, and Anne Laurence draws on it in her demonstration that grief was powerfully and copiously expressed in the seventeenth century. Furthermore, it was regarded as a potentially fatal affliction. The abundance and vividness of the testimony leaves little ground for arguing that it was experienced less intensely then than it is today. However, Dr Laurence suggests, the people who left the evidence she has analysed did cope with grief in ways which are perhaps less familiar or widespread today. In the first place their expectations of recovery from serious illness were far smaller, so that the processes of grieving and withdrawal were more likely to begin before the actual moment of death. Secondly, religious faith was immensely important in helping individuals to come to terms with the loss of people they loved. Martha Garland's comparison of the ways in which grief was described by late-Victorian liberal Christians and agnostics respectively underlines this point. Christianity offered ritual and social support. The Christian emphasis on expiation and reconciliation provided a more effective means of coping with natural anger, guilt, and despair than any available to the agnostic. But above all Christianity held out some hope of ultimate reunion. Professor Garland characterizes Christianity as a 'denial system'. Some refer to the 'denial' of death in the twentieth century when what they really have in mind is its evasion or concealment.[17] Christianity confronts death and denies its ultimate reality. Christians might suffer doubts, but their religion helped them more effectively than did alternative 'denial systems'. Of these, the most important was spiritualism.[18] It offered a superficially beguiling combination: the possibility of contact with the departed, some appearance of compatibility with the scientific discoveries of the age, and both of these without a theology of sin, punishment, and atonement.

While she too emphasizes the importance of religious consolation, Pat Jalland focuses her main attention on widowed people's practical responses to grief and the ways in which the 'support networks' of friends and family helped them to come to terms with it. Her examples, drawn especially from the correspondence of late-Victorian and Edwardian upper-class families involved in politics, do not substantiate the idea that custom encouraged chronic grief or long-term mourning. The reaction of those young widowers cited by Dr Jalland who threw themselves into hard work and ultimately sought solace in remarriage would not seem out of place today. But, she argues, the support available to the bereaved was more effective. Mourning etiquette shielded them during the periods of greatest grief and readjustment without being found irksome (though of course the upper classes comprised the people least likely to find the material costs burdensome). Letters of condolence, then as now, helped the bereaved to feel that their sorrow was shared. The retention of mementoes of the dead, which might be thought morbid today, helped to assuage grief during the moments of most intense distress. In short, according to their personal testimony, the late Victorian upper classes found mourning rituals supportive, but far from the straitjacket portrayed by some later historians of the period.

After this brief summary of the arguments of the various essays, something should perhaps be said about the approaches we have followed, the methods and sources we have employed, the social context of the phenomena examined, and the most powerful motors of change identified. One concern shared by several contributors has been to explore the relationship between ideas and ideals on the one hand and actual practice and experience on the other. Thus, Lucinda Beier asks how far the notion of the 'good death' influenced the comportment of the dying in the seventeenth century. Anne Laurence shows that it was sometimes difficult for the bereaved to shape their own behaviour according to Christian ideals of restraint and submissive acceptance. Roy Porter demonstrates that the practice of the medical management of the death-bed anticipated by some decades its reasoned advocacy in print. Jennifer Leaney explains how in the later nineteenth century social circumstances allowed the germination of an idea – cremation – put forward several decades earlier. Martha Garland examines contrasting experiences of grief in the light of different beliefs or unbelief. At least half our essays may be described as contributions to the history of ideas.

Ideas, attitudes, and expectations, with which we are so largely concerned, are notoriously difficult to quantify. They cannot be tabulated like tonnages and acreages. In this book, social history does not bristle with statistics – though Jim Morgan's tables illustrate in graphic fashion the burial problem in Leeds and help to explain the strength of feeling it aroused in early-nineteenth-century local politics. In order to understand the mentalities of past epochs, social historians have sometimes drawn on insights offered by other disciplines. The techniques of psychological investigation can offer useful means of getting to grips with the experiences of the dying and the bereaved, though of course the dead (with whom this book is mainly concerned) cannot be interrogated in the same way as the living. Martha Garland's careful analysis of individual examples of Victorian grief has been guided to some extent by the conclusions of modern analysts. Pat Jalland, while well aware of the pitfalls involved, attempts to assess the incidence of chronic grief among her Victorian widows and widowers with the help of indicators comparable with those worked out in more recent clinical practice. Social anthropology has prompted a number of the questions asked by historians of funeral and burial customs – witness, for example, the work of

David Stannard on seventeenth-century New England. The absence of anthropological comparisons from the chapters in the present volume dealing with these subjects is not due to any failure on their authors' part to appreciate the value of such analogies. The explanation lies instead in the fact that these chapters are concerned with specific developments whose causes are best sought in the realms of religious change, demographic growth, and legislative action.

The approaches and methods of analysis pursued by contributors have been influenced by the strengths and limitations of the sources which shed light on the questions posed. Over half these essays have drawn on printed vehicles of ideas and ideals of conduct such as newspapers, journals, novels, and works of Christian counsel (especially the *ars moriendi*). Four of them (those written by Lucinda Beier, Anne Laurence, Martha Garland, and Pat Jalland) have been founded on personal written testimony, especially in the shape of letters, diaries, and autobiographies, and these types of source have also been used to a lesser extent by some other authors. Although the materials in this second category do not readily lend themselves to quantitative analysis, they provide insights into individual feelings and attitudes unobtainable elsewhere, and some indications of the extent to which actual practice was influenced by the ideas and prescriptive models set out in 'literary' sources. Elizabeth Roberts's essay is, in its dependence upon oral testimony, unique in this volume. It illustrates both the special rewards which oral history yields, and, as she readily admits, the problems which it presents. (In this instance the desire to record a wide variety of aspects of a vanishing way of life precluded searching enquiries into the significance of particular customs and rituals, which aged respondents might in any case have found hard to answer.) A few other sources employed in individual contributions may be mentioned more briefly. Jim Morgan's account of the making of policy at national and local levels rests in large part on parliamentary papers and vestry minutes. Much of the evidence cited in my own sketch of changing death-bed formalities comes from wills and the records of litigation about them.

Many of the sources we have used relate to only part of the population; some of them to relatively restricted social categories. Broadly speaking, the 'elite' groups of the nobility, gentry, and eminent professional people are the ones best represented in these pages. Roy Porter, Jennifer Leaney, Martha Garland, and Pat Jalland are all concerned with ideas and practices current among the upper and upper-middle ranks of society – although some of them were later to spread much more widely. Chapters 2–4, dealing with the period up to the early eighteenth century, are all rather broader in their social coverage, taking in, besides the groups already mentioned, representatives of the literate 'middling sort' in town and country, down to small farmers and artisans. Much of the evidence in chapters 3 and 4 comes, however, from the pens of pious Protestants, particularly the clergy, though one of these writers, Henry Walker, took down the testimonies of a number of humble people. The 'working classes' take the centre of the stage only in the essays written by Ruth Richardson and Elizabeth Roberts, though other contributors refer in passing to the experiences of the poor.

At any one time there may have been considerable differences between social groups in the 'management' of death and the customs and rituals which attended it. Lucinda Beier warns us that her evidence tells us little about the deaths of the 'inarticulate majority' of seventeenth-century English people. (For what it is worth, the testimony afforded by the remarks of educated observers or passers-by suggests that the death-beds of the poor and people of little property were less likely to be well attended than those higher up the social scale, and that religious formalities also played a smaller part in them.) Some important social differences in early modern funeral customs have already been illuminated by the work of Clare Gittings. Among intestates' estates, she found that it was the smaller ones from which the largest percentages were paid in funeral expenses. The costs of entertainment were biggest (proportionately speaking) in the funerals of those of slender means, who could not afford the ostentatious trappings of woe favoured by the rich. Ruth Richardson and Jennifer Leaney explore and explain, from very different vantage points, the origin of divergent trends in the funerals of the wealthy and the poor in the late nineteenth century.

Class and social status were far from being the only sources of variation in behaviour and experience at any one time. The rise of Puritanism brought about differences in death-bed practice among Protestants after the Reformation, as I point out in Chapter 2. Roy Porter, Jennifer Leaney, and Martha Garland all have something to say about the complex interplay of Christian belief and new currents of thought, while Martha Garland is concerned with the contrasting psychological and emotional repercussions of belief and unbelief. Diana Dixon underlines the differences between religious and secular approaches to the writing of children's fiction. We say little here about regional and local variations, though it is clear, to take but one example, that the burial problems which did most to bring about such far-reaching changes as the creation of private and municipal cemeteries and the introduction of cremation were due above all to rapid urban growth. In the countryside, traditional practices were far better able to survive without serious modification. The processes of religious, intellectual, and economic change, uneven in their impact, interacted with wealth, status, family situation, and the still only imperfectly understood chemistry of temperament to produce an immense variety in individual attitudes and responses which defies attempts to tie up the experiences of any epoch in neat and consistent bundles.

A number of motors of social change are identified and discussed in the essay which follow. I single out and follow through some of the multifarious consequences of the Reformation and the subsequent weakening of religious unity. The rise of natural science, the emergence of a more secular climate of opinion, and the increasing influence of the medical profession all have their place in Roy Porter's account of trends in eighteenth-century death-bed management. One might add that the increasing use of the drugs which bulk so large in his essay depended upon the creation and improvement of a global commercial network. The forces which can be seen at work in the chapters dealing with the Victorian era included demographic growth, utilitarian reforming ideas (especially in the realm of public health), sectarian loyalties within Christianity and the external challenges which it faced from agnosticism and unbelief.

Some of our essays sketch ambitious explanations of major developments over long periods of time. Others, however, explore enduring customs and attitudes. The chapters by Lucinda Beier, Anne Laurence, Pat Jalland, and Elizabeth Roberts all belong in this category. They provide a valuable counterweight to the essays emphasizing change, a useful reminder of the strength of continuity and the burden of tradition in this area of human experience. Strong and deep-rooted sentiments could, like massive boulders, deflect the stream of change or set up cross-currents within it. Take, for example, the enduring concern for the decent disposal of the individual's mortal remains. I draw attention to the superficially paradoxical fact that coffin burial was spreading at the very time when an increasing number of testators, complying with new standard formulae influenced by Protestant teaching, ceased to specify where they should be buried. Such formal unconcern should not be allowed to obscure the probable character of their true feelings. Ruth Richardson argues that the callous indifference to the corpses of the destitute evinced in the Anatomy Act of 1832 strengthened the determination of all but the poorest of the poor to secure for themselves and their families an adequate seemliness in funeral rites.

Some interpretations of the social history of death advanced by previous explorers in this field have been sketched earlier in this introduction. It is clear that no one comprehensive scheme or theory has succeeded in gaining general acceptance. There is no dominant orthodoxy ripe for rebuttal; nor do the contributors to this volume, among whom there are differences of opinion, method, and standpoint, present a coherent new alternative. Nevertheless, although our primary concerns are far from polemical, several of us contribute to ongoing debates or sound notes of disagreement with arguments advanced elsewhere. My sketch of changes in English death-bed formalities and funeral practices in the sixteenth and seventeenth centuries assigns the chief roles to the Reformation and to subsequent changes in the relationship between church and society, rather than to the advance of individualism. Such an advance is of course the leading theme of Clare Gittings's work on the same period, but its most influential exposition in the context of the history of the family is to be found in Lawrence Stone's work. Among Stone's critics is Anne Laurence, who shows that deep grief was a commoner response to the loss of close relations than he suggested. She agrees that religious doctrines helped believers to come to terms with bereavement, but denies that the process was an easy one. Roy Porter's findings challenge Guy Williams's colourful characterization of the eighteenth century as an 'age of agony', showing that the truth was a great deal more complex, and in particular that opium was being widely used as a painkiller much earlier than has generally been appreciated.

Debate about the social history of death since the early nineteenth century has tended to focus on its 'celebration' during Victoria's reign and its subsequent concealment or 'denial'. Very broadly speaking, participants in the debate have tended to support or oppose the proposition that the 'management' of death used to be better than it now is. Hardly any of the contributors to the present volume have joined the debate as thus defined. Pat Jalland has come closest to doing so. But here she focuses her attention not on those aspects of the subject, especially funerals, which have previously figured most prominently in the controversy, but on individual responses and the ways in which moral support and sympathy were given to the bereaved. In doing so, she dispels some misconceptions about the 'way of death' of the late-Victorian upper classes, and shows that the contrasts between the attitudes of that period and those of the decades since the First World War have to some extent been overdrawn. A similar lesson can be drawn from Jennifer Leaney's essay, which underlines the fact that changing attitudes to the disposal of the body need to be set in a longer perspective than is allowed for in straightforward comparisons between Victorian and mid- to late-twentieth-century practices. Other essays have only an indirect bearing on the debate about the respective merits of Victorian and post-Victorian 'ways of death'. As her title implies, Ruth Richardson sets out to explain, not to commend, the prominence of the rituals of death in the consciousness of the Victorian working classes. Martha Garland compares the bereavement experiences of Victorian believers and agnostics at a moment of transition. The Victorian agnostics she has studied suffered a double deprivation: bereavement coming on top of a loss of faith. Their experience was therefore different from that of the typical agnostic of the later twentieth century, an age of 'calmer, more widely diffused secularism',[19] and arguably more painful.

Despite their authors' different points of departure, these essays provide a consistent picture of some key developments in the social history of death in England since the close of the middle ages. The first of these was the decline of the role of the clergy at the death-bed. This was an uneven process, and for some people their ministrations remained important long after the Reformation: for a minority they remain so today. Dying continued to be widely regarded as a test of virtue, and it was indeed some time after the Reformation that the volume of printed advice on preparation for death reached its peak. The greater part of it was, however, now directed to literate laypeople rather than their clerical advisers. But the ideal of the final trial of fortitude was always unrealistic in the case of many, perhaps the majority of the dying. To make death less of an ordeal, indeed to make it as painless as possible, ultimately became, in the eighteenth century, the avowed aim of many members of an increasingly influential medical profession. To some extent, the doctor replaced the clergyman. The decline of the older idea of the death-bed as a test, and the gradual separation of will-making from dying, made for greater privacy within the protective circle of the family.

The centuries spanned by this book saw two major drives to curtail or simplify funeral rituals. The first formed part of the Protestant Reformation. The reformers speedily transformed the character of the ecclesiastical rites, but the efforts of the more rigorous among them to curb the vain expense of concomitant social observances was much less successful. The tradition of funeral conviviality in particular long survived the Reformation. During the later years of Victoria's reign there began a reaction against the lugubrious ostentation of funerary trappings which was ultimately to have far-reaching effects. But attachment to a measure of funeral pomp, albeit on a comparatively small scale, survived among the working classes. It will be argued in this volume that fear of the shameful consequences of pauperdom was a more powerful cause of this attachment than either straightforward conservatism or social emulation.

The practice of burial in church or churchyard was not affected by the Reformation despite the fact that some of the reformers had misgivings about what they regarded as superstitions connected with it. Nor was the Church's near monopoly of burial provision challenged in principle by emergency recourse to the digging of mass graves in times of plague. But the all too obvious problems of overcrowding caused by massive urban growth in the early nineteenth century, the demands of the sanitary reformers, and nonconformist unwillingness to finance the further extension of

church burial grounds led to the increasing participation of secular agencies – private companies and local authorities – in burial provision. The revulsion aroused by the squalor of many early-nineteenth-century urban churchyards was a powerful element in the movement to create resting places which would be at once more beautiful and less obtrusive. Finally, the acceptance of cremation was helped by the widespread disgust with the process of bodily decomposition.

Mortality rates far higher than today's persisted for nearly the whole of the period covered by this volume. But the deaths of infants made up a substantial proportion of the total, and life expectancy after the early childhood years was sufficiently high to allow a reasonable hope that most family relationships would last a considerable time. There is little evidence that individuals guarded against the possibility of 'premature' bereavement by limiting their emotional involvement with members of their families; much to show that they commonly suffered deep grief in the face of loss. Religion was a powerful source of consolation throughout these centuries. It may also be true that the moral support given to the bereaved by kinsfolk, friends, and neighbours was generally more effective than it is today, when deaths in childhood, youth, or middle age are sufficiently rare to leave many would-be consolers somewhat at a loss what to do or say. But this is one of the questions broached in this book which needs more thorough investigation.

There are some other large gaps in the main lines of development which emerge from the essays collected here. The history of the eighteenth-century funeral has still to be written. We do not yet know when, or how far, the funerals of the lower orders were re-shaped by the diversion of resources from conviviality to the trappings of a sober pomp, in the manner suggested by Clare Gittings. The influence on this development of changing notions of respectability has yet to be assessed. The rise of the undertaker and the commercialization of funerals await detailed investigation. The history of the management of urban churchyards and burial grounds in the century before the major controversies of the 1830s and 1840s would repay closer examination.

We have not carried the history of the death-bed forward through the nineteenth century. Did the Evangelical Revival reinvigorate the ideal of dying well as a test of individual virtue? Was the family's supportive role at the core of the Victorian model

of the good death, as Roy Porter suggests in his remarks on Lucy Warren's last illness? Did the reality of death in the bosom of the family more often resemble the awful loneliness of Mrs Pargiter, so vividly portrayed by Virginia Woolf in the opening pages of *The Years*? Did the medical 'management' of the death-bed continue to develop along the lines sketched by Roy Porter? To what extent did hospitals assume the burden of caring for the dying in the course of the nineteenth century? Some of these questions may never be answered: yet they beckon the historian into the fastnesses of a dark continent.

2

DEATH, CHURCH, AND FAMILY IN ENGLAND BETWEEN THE LATE FIFTEENTH AND THE EARLY EIGHTEENTH CENTURIES

RALPH HOULBROOKE

In the social history of death, there are certain periods whose importance seems clear. Among them are the later Middle Ages and the eighteenth century. The former apparently experienced an increasing concern with death and the after-life, evident in the emergence of the *ars moriendi,* a growing demand for intercessory prayers, and the appearance of artistic themes such as the *danse macabre.* During the latter, horror and pain in death and the hereafter came to seem increasingly hard to reconcile with the compassion of a benevolent Creator, while confidence in the powers of science gave rise to new hopes that the incidence of death might be reduced and life prolonged. But what of the years in between? In Catholic Europe, continuity outweighed change in theology, liturgy, and devotional practice. Despite the influence of the new currents which flowed through the post-Tridentine church, the most vigorous forms of 'Baroque' piety had their roots in the later Middle Ages. It was otherwise in England, where the Protestant Reformation heralded a transformation of the religious landscape. But the Reformation and its consequences have yet to be integrated into the social history of death, in large part because the most influential studies of the subject published up to now have been mainly or wholly concerned with the experience of a Catholic country – France. Clare Gittings's recent work on the development of the English funeral, to which I am heavily indebted, does indeed take the Reformation into account, but sees individualism as the mainspring of change.[1] Professor R. L. Greaves's study of *Religion and Society in Elizabethan England* contains a valuable chapter about the influence of reforming

thought on funerary practices, but, as its title indicates, it is concerned with the first half-century after the Reformation.[2] The scope of this chapter is different in two respects. First, it traces the main effects of religious change over a longer period. Secondly, it is concerned with the death-bed and the last will as well as the funeral, burial, and the means of commemoration. It is in part a survey of what is already known, in part a sketch of developments which need further investigation.

The last rites underwent important changes during the Reformation. Beforehand, the part played by the priest had been crucially important. The Visitation of the Sick, Extreme Unction, the administration of the viaticum and the commendation of the soul *in articulo mortis* comprised an elaborate chain of prayers, exhortations, admonitions, and ritual gestures. The sick man should have been asked whether he believed the main articles of the faith, and enjoined to forgive those who had wronged him and confess his sins. The initiative remained with the priest, whose ministrations provided the proceedings with their essential framework. At the Reformation Extreme Unction disappeared altogether, and though the main outlines of the rest of the last rites survived successive liturgical revisions, they were drastically simplified, and confession of sins became optional. In the classic English Protestant text of the *ars moriendi*, Thomas Becon's *Sicke Manne's Salve* (1561), the sick man received his principal support and encouragement from godly friends. One of them had various attributes of a pastor, yet was not explicitly described as a clergyman. The dying man took the initiative in making a full confession of faith. Exhortations to the members of his family and their last farewells also occupied a prominent place in Becon's dialogue. As Nancy Lee Beaty has pointed out, the removal of the doctrine of purgatory, 'the minimizing of heavenly intervention, and the repudiation of all sacramental help, *in extremis*,' could have placed the doubting sinner under terrible strain.[3] More conservative opinion within the Church of England lacked expression in a work of comparable stature until the publication in 1651 of Jeremy Taylor's *The Rule and Exercises of Holy Dying*, with its emphasis on the comfortable ministry of the 'holy man', and his encouragement of a full confession. Meanwhile the art of dying well had been expounded in a stream of tracts and sermons.

A simpler, looser liturgical framework and the emergence of

differences of emphasis within the Church left the dying and those closest to them more freedom of choice as to the extent and nature of clerical assistance at the death-bed. The eye-witness accounts which survive in vastly increased numbers from the sixteenth century onwards point to a considerable variety of practice. For many people, the Visitation of the Sick and the reception of the last Communion remained important. Others, particularly puritans, while not apparently availing themselves of the set rites of the church, drew considerable comfort from the prayers and counsel of godly ministers.[4] But depositions taken in testamentary cases give the impression that death without priestly help grew more common. The Reformation changes left more initiative in the hands of the dying and enhanced the importance of their role as the leading actors in the culminating drama of their lives; but this role could impose heavy burdens.

The ideal pattern of dying set out in the thanatography of the period was one of patience in the face of trial, arduous but ultimately successful struggle with fleshly pains and spiritual temptations, and final quiet sleep in the Lord. Dr Beier points out in this volume how important prior preparation and a 'cooperative' malady were for the successful practice of the *ars moriendi*. By no means all deaths, even among the godly, conformed in every point to the ideal pattern. Nehemiah Wallington, a London turner, remembered his mother's frequent cries of 'No more, Lord, no more; no more, Lord, no more!', during her long and agonizing decline in 1603.[5] Elisabeth Kübler-Ross has given in her study *On Death and Dying* (1970) a classic description of the different stages, including denial and anger, which commonly precede final acceptance during terminal illness.[6] The resigned yet responsive lassitude which often accompanied the last stage of illness in the course of nature probably enabled many whose earlier 'performance' had in various respects fallen short of the ideal pattern to make what could nevertheless be regarded as a good end. Before his death in 1670, Robert Moore, a distiller, encouraged by the doctor in vain hopes of recovery, apparently postponed spiritual preparations, despite the presence of his brother, a clergyman. At one stage of his illness he complained that his anguish, misery, and pain were worse than Job's and tried unsuccessfully to drown himself. Yet six hours before he died he 'sent forth' in his brother's words, '3 or 4 most Divine short prayers'.[7] Mortal illness, stealing on its victims unexpectedly, often allowed no time for the performance of all the expected duties. Perhaps it was precisely because the third Earl of Huntingdon, who died in 1595, became almost speechless some time before death and never even made a proper will, that his chaplain felt impelled to write a detailed account showing that the end had nevertheless been a good one.[8] Before the pious Margaret Godolphin's death of puerperal fever in 1678 she lapsed rapidly into delirium punctuated only by intervals of extreme languor. Her friend John Evelyn could nevertheless console himself with the reflection that, unlike many people in her state, she had uttered nothing offensive.[9] In the portrayal of the good death much depended on sympathetic presentation.

But very many deaths could not be squeezed into the pattern of the Christian good end. Some died in or near despair, like the Duchess of York in 1671, 'full of un-speakable torture'. Very different, but in its way equally shocking to the pious observer, was the stubborn stoicism of 'Old Duckworth', an impoverished octogenarian who 'having been a prophane swearer, blasphemer, grown poor, begging, dyed miserably May 8, 1681, his toes rotting off, he slighting it, said they never did him good . . .'.[10] Other descriptions, particularly those incorporated in depositions in testamentary cases before the church courts, suggest that many people's last lucid moments were concentrated rather on the settlement of their affairs in this world than on preparation for the next. Such people frequently ended their days full of worries about the difficulties their widows would face or possible family quarrels after their deaths. Other testators seem to have wanted to control or punish members of their families. Instead of encouraging them to loosen their grip on the world, the imminence of death seems rather to have enhanced such people's desire to enjoy power over those around them while they could.

The attendance of supportive family and neighbours at the bedside forms part of our picture of death in 'The World We Have Lost'. Their spiritual role probably became more important among the godly after the Reformation. The prayers of spouses, children and friends, mentioned in many pious accounts of good deaths, replaced to some extent the elaborate liturgical chain of the medieval last rites.[11] Lawrence Stone has written of 'the enormous psychic benefit of diverting attention from fear of death itself to the struggle to put on an impressive show for the spectators'.[12] Some writers of the period thought differently. Jeremy Taylor believed that death was easier without 'the women and the weepers, the swoonings and the shriekings, the nurses and the physicians, the dark room and the ministers, the kindred and the watchers', and he was not alone in expressing this point of view.[13] Some of the dying were clearly troubled by the anguish of those around them. There was too a darker side to the picture of the family at the bedside which is particularly evident in many testamentary depositions. The dying were often pestered by kinsfolk trying to persuade them to change their wills in their favour; the process of uninhibited manipulation sometimes went on well after the power of speech had gone. John Donne was thinking of scenes like this when he referred to the behaviour of those who made the death-bed 'a rack to make them stretch and increase jointures, and portions, and legacies, and sign schedules and codicils, with their hand when his hand, that presents them, is ready to close his eyes, that should sign them.'[14]

The last will is of all documents connected with the final phase of the individual's existence the one which has attracted most attention from social historians, who have used it for a great variety of purposes. Here I am concerned with it above all as a means of gauging the testator's preoccupations as he contemplated the prospect of his own death. My preliminary impressions are based on an analysis of 600 wills selected from those proved in the courts of the archdeaconries of Berkshire and Norwich between the closing years of the fifteenth century and the middle of the eighteenth, made for the most part by members of the middle ranks of society – yeomen, husbandmen, craftsmen, and small traders.[15]

The centuries following the Reformation witnessed a gradual secularization of the English will. In the Middle Ages, will-making was often associated with the last rites. It was the confessor's responsibility to urge the dying man to dispose of his worldly property. The church enjoined the duty of making a will as a vehicle for pious donations for the health of testators' souls and a means of reparation for wrongs done during their lives. On the eve of the Reformation, a high proportion of wills were witnessed by clergy, the most readily available source of scribal expertise. Afterwards, churchmen became less important as scribes, and testators drew on a widening range of writers, including notaries public, local gentry, yeomen, shopkeepers, and even husband-men.[16] This change reflects the spread of literacy and (probably) the diminished importance of the last rites.

Various changes took place in the first part of the will, the one particularly concerned with the health of the individual's soul. The most significant of these were the transformation and decline of pious bequests. Before the Reformation almost all wills contained such provisions. Their variety was great, but church lights, intercessory masses, parish guilds, and church fabric funds were the most important objects of pious generosity in the middling ranks of society. Afterwards, the proportion of testators making pious bequests fell sharply, though some people, especially in the early post-Reformation years, continued to hope that benefactions would help their souls.[17] Gifts to the poor, often for distribution as a dole, already found in the wills of many wealthy testators in the later Middle Ages, became much more popular after the Reformation. Such bequests remained popular till the early-seventeenth century, but then declined sharply, and the typical early-eighteenth-century testator made no pious bequests of any kind. The increasingly efficient and impersonal operation of parochial poor relief was probably one reason for the decline of individual charity. This was foreshadowed as early as 1570 in the reply which the vicar of Kirk Merrington in County Durham received from one parishioner whom he had asked what he would give to the poor man's box. 'I gyve dayly to the poore, as other neighbours doith; and therefore I will nothing to the poore man('s) box.'[18]

The custom of prefacing wills with a bequest of the soul persisted for a long time after the Reformation, though Protestantism, as is well known, brought major changes in the content of the most widely used preambles. Invocations of the Blessed Virgin and all the saints in heaven disappeared, to be replaced by affirmations of trust in Christ's death and passion. Some of the formulae employed are highly distinctive, even idiosyncratic, and they probably reflect the personal opinions of testators.[19] But the majority were always content to follow one of a fairly limited range of stereotypes. Writers sometimes set down preambles without waiting for any directions from the testator, in one case when he was already all but speechless.[20] The most primitive and rudimentary wills, the ones which show fewest signs of professional assistance, are also, in my experience, the ones least likely to contain preliminary clauses concerning the soul. Elements of spontaneity and individuality are increasingly hard to discern in the formulae of the late seventeenth century, and by the 1740s a growing number of testators were omitting them altogether.[21]

Probably connected with the increasingly secular tone of wills was the fact that a growing number of them were being given their final shape quite a long time before testators died. Towards the end of the Middle Ages, most of the wills proved were drawn up shortly before death. Of a sample of fifty wills registered in the archdeaconry of Norwich between 1497 and 1500, about 40 per cent had been made within forty days of probate, nearly 90 per cent within a year. Books of Common Prayer from 1549 enjoined that men were to be 'oft admonished' to settle their temporal affairs while still in health, but this was slow to take effect. 'That which should be the *living* Man's care, is too often the *dying* Man's task', one preacher complained as late as 1684. Jeremy Taylor believed that 'the making of a will (was) a mortal sign' in many people's eyes, so it is not surprising that one Berkshire widow had to be assured, towards the end of Elizabeth's reign, that she would not 'dye any whit the sooner' if she settled her affairs.[22] But though old habits died hard, an increasing proportion of testators nevertheless seem to have been making their wills before their final illnesses as time passed. This trend appears to have been clearly established in the archdeaconry of Norwich by 1600, in that of Berkshire a little later. It accelerated during the eighteenth century, and over half a sample of wills proved in the archdeaconry of Norwich in 1746 had been made over a year before probate, nearly a third over five years beforehand.

Some people seem to have been loath to make wills because they feared that by doing so they would lose effective control of their property or lay themselves open to pressure to change their dispositions. We may better understand such fears if we bear in mind the likelihood that the commonest way of ensuring a will's execution for much of our period was to declare it, or have it read, before witnesses. Two were normally sufficient, but many more were often present. So to make a will was for many testators, perhaps most, to make it known. But if a testator could read his will to himself, and all witnesses had to do was testify to the fact of his approval (e.g. by subscription) without themselves knowing the contents of the will, much greater privacy of disposition was possible.[23] So the spread of literacy after the Reformation may well have made testators more confident of their control over the process of will making and less reliant upon the testimony of witnesses to the substance of their dispositions.

For whatever reason, the hitherto close association between will making and the death-bed was loosened. This development probably affected both the will and the death-bed. Testators were probably less concerned with the hereafter than they would have been when facing the immediate prospect of death. But it also tended to reduce the elements of publicity and formality in the death-bed scene, and, by removing a weighty responsibility from the shoulders of the dying man, helped prepare the way for the changes so vividly described by Dr Porter in Chapter 5.

A series of interrelated developments diminished ecclesiastical influence over the form and contents of the will and enhanced the individual testator's control of its provisions. But at its core we find an enduring pattern of intimate relationships. Throughout the period, provision for wives and children was the dominant material concern of those testators who had them. Most of the identifiable kinsfolk mentioned by testators were related to them within two degrees. There were no obvious changes in the range and types of consanguineal and affinal relatives mentioned. But spiritual kinship seems to have grown weaker in the course of time, and references to godchildren were far rarer by the early eighteenth century than they had been on the eve of the Reformation.[24] The pivotal relationship in the wills of married people was clearly that of husband and wife. Most married men named their wives executrices of their wills throughout the period. A possibly significant change occurred during the seventeenth century. Adjectives expressive of affection or appreciation, such as dear, beloved, most loving, hitherto seldom applied to wives, became much more common and finally customary by the end of the century. The hypothesis that this was due to an improvement in the emotional climate of the family is tempting, but one I am inclined to mistrust. Rather was it part of a larger process in which, as we have seen, the first, 'spiritual' part of the will, once arguably the most important, underwent a gradual atrophy, and the testator felt more free to express his worldly affections in what was an increasingly secular document as well as perhaps a more private one.

Hitherto our attention has been concentrated on the dying or those expecting death. From now on we turn to the survivors and the services they performed for the dead. Much of the fascination which funeral customs have for social historians lies in the multitude of interlocking and overlapping purposes which they fulfilled. They served both religious and social ends. The religious rites comprised the committal of the mortal remains to consecrated ground to await the resurrection and the commendation of the immortal soul to the mercy of Almighty God. (This second element was replaced in 1552 by a bald statement that God had of his great mercy taken the soul of the deceased to himself and a simple affirmation of sure and certain hope in the resurrection.)[25] The service was also intended to instruct and edify the survivors: it reminded them of the inevitability of death, of the need to prepare for it, and of resurrection, judgement, and eternal life. The social purposes of funeral rites and customs have been analysed by anthropologists and sociologists in many different ways. Four of these purposes were perhaps particularly important in late-medieval and early-modern England: the discharge of duties towards the dead, the fulfilment of obligations to kindred and community by his or her representatives, an affirmation of the position held by the dead person in the social hierarchy, and the succession of his heir to that position. Respect for the memory of the dead person and grief at his loss demanded the attendance of relatives, friends, colleagues, fellow parishioners, and members of fraternities, guilds, or corporations, and the wearing of appropriate dress. The deceased's representative dispensed largesse and hospitality on his behalf. Provision for the unfortunate (often already specified in the dead man's will) was made in the form of doles of food or money, and, by those who could afford them, gowns for poor men who would take part in the funeral procession. Kinsfolk, friends, colleagues, and neighbours would be invited to drink and feast. The social position of the deceased was affirmed by such things as the scale of the procession, the range of different categories of people taking part, the numbers of mourning gowns bestowed, and the quantity of black cloth used in the hangings adorning the deceased's house, the church, and even the street in which he had lived. Above all it was demonstrated in the case of the upper classes by the presence of heralds, carrying an array of accoutrements whose permissible range was carefully graded according to rank. Finally, aristocratic funeral rites incorporated special ceremonies which symbolized the transfer of status and responsibility to the heir.

The Protestant Reformation was the most obvious source of the changes which took place in funeral rites and customs during this period. By removing the intercessory elements from the funeral service, the reformers made it first and foremost a vehicle of instruction for the living, not a means of assisting the dead. In particular, the funeral sermon probably achieved greater prominence and importance. The number of services was reduced and the obsequies were concentrated in a shorter period. Beforehand, the major rites had often been spread over two days, with the main procession, the dirge, and relatively light refreshments taking place on the first day, the sermon, mass of requiem, and feast on the second. Then, a month later, had come a further service, the 'month's mind'. The custom of marking the month's mind was continued by some people during Elizabeth's reign, though with diminishing frequency. But in general funeral rites were increasingly restricted to the day of burial.[26]

The reformers regarded various trappings of the medieval funeral with suspicion or hostility because they smacked of superstition or ostentation. The candles borne along with and set around the body were drastically reduced in number or removed altogether. Many puritans were hostile to lavish expenditure, especially on the outward trappings of mourning, because it was wasteful and often seemed hypocritical. Such paraphernalia were inappropriate even if the underlying sorrow was genuine; excessive manifestations of grief were selfish in the case of a good man, pointless in that of a bad one. The influence of such criticisms is hard to assess. Certainly there seems to have been some reduction of expenditure on aristocratic funerals in the second half of Elizabeth's reign, but Professor Stone has attributed this above all to economic rather than religious considerations. In the early seventeenth century, the desire to escape the stranglehold of the heralds, in theory disinterested guardians of order and degree, but increasingly seen as rapacious parasites, encouraged the practice of nocturnal burial, free of the heralds' supervision.[27]

The effects of religious change on the charitable and hospitable aspects of the funeral were complex. At first the Reformation promoted the spread of the dole both by condemning other forms of pious bequest and through its positive teaching in favour of almsgiving. But before long doles were to decline in the face of concern about public order, growing doubts about the equity and efficacy of charitable handouts, and the increasing efficiency of parochial and municipal poor relief. Clare Gittings found that the percentages of accounts submitted by the administrators of intestates' estates mentioning doles fell in the early seventeenth century in all the three counties she studied, though most gradually in Lincolnshire, the furthest from London.[28]

The most substantial item of funeral expenditure on the accounts of middling and humbler people was the cost of the funeral entertainment – feast or drinking. This does not seem to have fallen before the Civil War – indeed the rise in spending on funerals in the previous six decades at least kept pace with inflation. Gittings suggests, however, that in the longer term spending was to be siphoned away from food and drink. Such a development may have been due, at least in its early stages, to puritan influence. Inebriate conviviality was one way of drawing death's sting, but some of the godly deprecated the drowning of sorrow at least as much as sorrow's drowning Christian self restraint. The growing desire of the 'middling sort' for order and decorum was perhaps inimical to excessively lavish entertainment as well as to funeral doles. The convivial aspects of the funeral may also have suffered in the long run from increased spending on other items such as coffins, gloves, scarves, hatbands, rings, funeral sermons, and headstones. Gittings has shown that payments for coffins and sermons were being recorded in larger percentages of administrators' accounts in the first half of the seventeenth century. What happened thereafter is not clear, because the numbers of detailed administrators' accounts declined sharply after 1650. But there are some signs in the ones that *were* drawn up, as well as in other sources, that the practice of giving gloves, scarves, and rings to mourners was on the increase after the Restoration. In part, most clearly in the case of rings, this was due to the desire for commemoration, which will shortly be explored more fully. But the scale and speed of change must not be exaggerated. Generous entertainment, including abundant liquid refreshment, remained an important part of many well documented funerals, especially in the countryside, long after 1700.[29]

The desire of survivors to help their dead is a deep rooted one. Keeping their memory alive, and showing that they are not forgotten, does something to satisfy this desire, even in people who rationally accept that the dead are beyond help. But the beliefs about the hereafter held by many civilizations, including that of medieval Western Europe, have encouraged survivors to assist their dead in a more active fashion. Enormous resources were devoted to intercessory masses and other good works performed on behalf of the souls of the dead. A great range of intercessory provisions was available, from the endowment of masses in perpetuity to the humble parishioner's share in the prayers of his confraternity. The concentration of services was densest during the year following death, when the trental of thirty masses, the month's mind, and the year's mind, helped to keep the dead in memory. A substantial proportion of the endowments made was ordained by those who hoped to benefit from them. But people often made provision for souls other than their own. Joel Rosenthal has pointed out that spouses and parents were by far the most frequently named individual beneficiaries in fourteenth- and fifteenth-century licences to alienate in mortmain, and the same is true of wills dating from the decades preceding the Reformation.[30]

The emotional and psychological consequences of the abolition of the doctrine of purgatory and curtailment of prayers for the dead constituted one of the great unchartable revolutions of English history. Perhaps the disappearance of purgatory made the prospect of suffering in the next world more remote and improbable. Individuals who might have been ready enough to accept that they deserved punishment for their sins may well have been unable to believe that they were bad enough to deserve eternal damnation at the hands of a merciful God.[31] On the surface the abolition of intercessory services was accepted with remarkable alacrity.[32] Some testators continued for a time to hope that charitable benefactions would help their souls, perhaps by securing the prayers of the poor.

The funeral sermon also satisfied in some measure the psychological needs met by prayers for the dead. Such sermons were often preached before the Reformation, and the diary of the

Londoner Henry Machyn shows that they were a fairly common feature of both Protestant and Catholic funerals in the capital during the 1550s. Unfortunately, we know little of their contents. But from Elizabeth's reign onwards they were printed in increasing numbers, usually at the request of relatives or friends of the deceased, which made them enduring memorials. The sermon also became, as Clare Gittings has shown, an increasingly common element in provincial funerals. The main part of the sermon, consisting of the exposition of a biblical text, was designed to give admonition, encouragement, consolation, or a combination of all three. Favourite themes included the transitoriness of human life, the inevitability of death, and the certainty of resurrection and everlasting reward for the elect. But most sermons also included some account of the departed, which commonly took up a quarter, or even a third, of the whole. In this, a description of his death usually occupied a prominent place. For, as one preacher remarked in 1614, 'the end of a man perfectly trieth a man'. Most preachers who gave some sketch of the individual concerned managed to draw comforting conclusions concerning his present state from the quality of his life or the manner of his death. Puritans had serious doubts about funeral eulogies because they were often undeserved, and because of the psychological connection between the present advertisement of the good deeds of the dead and the previous offering of intercessory prayers on their behalf. This connection was most obvious in the case of the series of obit sermons in remembrance of a particular benefactor, which might be coupled with a dole and prayers of thanks to God for the deceased's bounty and liberality. But puritans who overcame their scruples are well represented among the authors of surviving printed sermons. A number justified what they were doing by invoking scriptural or patristic examples or injunctions to keep the example of the good alive.[33]

The Reformation also influenced attitudes to burial and commemoration of the dead by means of funeral monuments. The practice of burial in the churchyard went back to Anglo-Saxon times. A reason for it mentioned by Gregory the Great had been the benefit that the dead might derive from the prayers offered by worshippers reminded of them by passing their graves.[34] Before the Reformation almost all testators wished for burial in a particular church or churchyard. The great majority (in the wills I have examined) specified the latter. Only a few mentioned a more particular location.

In the reformers' writings on burial differences of emphasis are evident, but what may be called a 'mainstream' body of opinion can be discerned. Excessive attachment to the idea of burial in hallowed ground was deprecated as superstitious. God would resurrect the bodies of the dead wherever they lay, however complete their apparent destruction. The prayers of living Christians would do their souls no good. But it was right that the body, as the temple of the immortal soul, should be accorded respect and buried in a decent and Christian manner. It was also convenient that it should be interred in ground specially set aside for the purpose. Nearly all writers on the subject accepted churchyard burial.[35] The clauses in wills relating to the body responded to Protestant teaching, though more gradually than did those concerning the soul. By the mid-seventeenth century, most testators no longer mentioned burial in a particular churchyard but simply requested decent and Christian burial, or burial in the earth wherever God should call them from the world, or even relied upon the discretion of their executors.

Very few gravestones have survived from medieval English churchyards. But graves were probably marked; this at least is what the orderliness of the churchyard in the deserted village of Wharram Percy in Yorkshire seems to indicate. The memory of the individual's resting place might therefore be retained for a generation or two, at least while the pace of burial remained fairly slow.[36] Such a memory is clearly implicit in the requests for burial near relatives which one finds in some wills, mainly in the first half of our period.[37] In towns, where the burial rate was faster, charnels were built to receive 'clean' bones from the churchyard. Underlying this provision was the idea of the safe keeping of remains to which a certain respect should be paid.[38]

Despite the signs of compliance with Protestant teaching in wills, the desire to cherish the mortal remains of the dead would not be thwarted and was indeed probably strengthened by the denial of opportunities to assist the immortal soul. It manifested itself in a variety of ways which tended to delay, if not prevent, the disturbance of the corpse, especially burial in coffins and the erection of more substantial gravestones. The use of wooden coffins goes back to Anglo-Saxon times. But Clare Gittings's analysis of administrators' accounts suggests that it was still a minority practice in the sixteenth century, though spreading very rapidly thereafter. (Deep burial was a further precaution to which some people resorted. The solicitude which was one powerful motive for it emerges clearly from the way in which the Rev. Henry Newcome recorded the interment of his well loved father-in-law: 'I caused him to be laid deeper than ordinary in the chancel there, that I believe his body will scarcely be disturbed if others that come after make use of the grave'.) The provision of more durable gravestones in the churchyard, and grave slabs in the church, seems to have become much more common from the seventeenth century onwards.[39]

Commemoration was a major purpose of funeral monuments. At first restricted to outstanding members of lay and ecclesiastical elites, they gradually spread through larger sections of society. Two major developments assisted this process: the introduction of the memorial brass, and the spread of literacy. The use of brass permitted the presentation of far more detailed information, both pictorial and in writing, than would otherwise have been possible in the same space. The rise of literacy prompted a long-term shift from pictorial representation to the epitaph, which could say more, and say it more eloquently, than all but the very best and most expensive engraving or sculpture. The fact that some puritans perceived dangers of superstition or idolatry in tomb portraiture may have assisted the transition. In 1653, Samuel Fairclough the younger urged the widow of Sir Nathaniel Barnardiston of Kedington (Suffolk) to

> Adde to his memory no pictur'd stone
> Lest whilst within the church my vows I pay
> I to the Image of this Saint should pray.[40]

But the quantity of surviving monuments to members of puritan families suggests that the influence of such misgivings was very uneven at best. More than this, the commonest medieval design – the recumbent or kneeling figure attended by praying children – retained, despite its implicit suggestion of intercession, an enduring popularity, until a variety of new types, notably the portrait bust, superseded it in the course of the seventeenth century. The commonest type of medieval funeral inscription invited prayers for the soul of the deceased. After the Reformation, some inscriptions continued to call for prayers or beseech God's mercy, but these were reduced to a trickle during Elizabeth's reign. The emphasis changed from intercession to commemoration. The development of epitaphs was stimulated by Renaissance humanism and the growing respect for learning among the gentry. They often included not only a list of the offices of honour and trust held by the individual and a description of his family connections, but also a recital of his personal virtues. Domestic virtues were gradually given more prominence: this was of course particularly true of women. Wives were praised for their chastity, fidelity, and affection, mothers for their tenderness and solicitude. Epitaphs upon married couples often emphasized their mutual love, the union of their remains in one grave, and their hope that their souls would be reunited in heaven.

The Reformation set in train a series of changes in the English 'way of death', some of which took immediate effect while others were much more gradual. It is widely agreed that the sixteenth-century reforms reduced the prominence and authority of the clergy in English society. In no area of life was this more evident than in preparation for death. Simpler, shorter last rites and less widespread reliance on sacramental help restricted the scope for clerical influence over the dying. The decline of this influence was reflected in wills. The growth of literacy made a wider choice of scribes available. A movement away from death- bed will writing can be discerned, gradual at first, but accelerating rapidly by the early eighteenth century. The church ceased to be the main focus of pious bequests, and by the eighteenth century the number of people making such bequests had dwindled in dramatic fashion. Among the pious, the death-bed was regarded for much of this period as the supreme test of Christian fortitude. But though this ideal was powerfully reinforced, especially by puritan writing, it is questionable whether it was ever realized by more than a minority. In the case of the majority, the weakening or removal of inherited elements of formality in the death-bed scene probably helped prepare the way for the ultimate triumph of the ideal of the easy death. The reformers' repudiation of intercession for the dead took away what had hitherto been the most important religious purpose of funeral rites. Their denial of the existence of purgatory, which might have been expected to heighten the perceived contrast between salvation and damnation, and enhance the latter's terrors, may in practice have made the prospect of punishment in the hereafter less widely credible.

Variety and continuity must be emphasized as well as change. There was an immense diversity of individual experience of death, shaped by social class, religious belief, the nature of the terminal illness, and the attitudes of close relatives. Continuity is evident in the earthly preoccupations and responsibilities which loomed large in the minds of so many of the dying. The social functions of funeral rites, especially demonstration of proper respect for mortal remains in accordance with the deceased's rank and place in society, and the provision of hospitality for his neighbours and kinsfolk by his surviving representatives, underwent, in contrast with their religious elements, no dramatic change. New notions of respectability and decorum would in the long run divert resources away from funeral conviviality. Yet how far religious sentiment contributed to this development remains unclear. Although the reformers disapproved of anxiety about the place or manner of burial, increasing use of coffins points to an enduring, even growing concern for the protection of the corpse. The century after the Reformation also witnessed a remarkable burgeoning of all the major means of commemoration – especially sermons, sculpture, and epitaphs, to which the rejection of intercession may have given some stimulus.

The styles of funerary sculpture and epitaphs were however among the elements of the culture of death which penetrated confessional barriers. The point is underlined by the readiness of that staunch Protestant Sir Ralph Verney, in 1651, to have a family monument designed in Rome by an artist who enjoyed papal patronage.[41] A preoccupation with the 'craft of dying' was shared by both militant Protestants and fervent supporters of the Counter-Reformation; it was part of their common concern with fuller and more effective Christian living. Yet there were major differences between the experiences of Protestant England and those of the countries of Catholic Europe. More significant in the long run than adherence to rival doctrines (important though these undoubtedly were) was the fact that the English reformers, after pulling down the structure of inherited observances, failed (partly because of their own divisions) to create a generally accepted way of death thoroughly imbued with their spirit. The obstacles were too big, the compromises made too numerous. This facilitated in England the relatively early advance of more secular attitudes.

3

THE GOOD DEATH IN SEVENTEENTH-CENTURY ENGLAND

LUCINDA MCCRAY BEIER

Social historians are concerned primarily with ways of living –
culturally dictated approaches to universal human needs and
events. Death, and ways of dying, provide a stimulating focus for
historical research since, although the experience is universal,
ways of dealing with it vary enormously. Every society possesses
deeply rooted attitudes about death, preferences for some deaths
over others, and ways of approaching this most inevitable of
experiences. This chapter will describe a very small tip of the
cultural iceberg.

Before embarking upon discussion of the good death in
seventeenth-century England, a few general observations about
death in the period are in order. As a medical historian, I am
concerned with dying, rather than death – with death-beds, rather
than funerals. This paper results in part from research I did for a
book on seventeenth-century suffering, which was largely
concerned with the ailments people lived with, rather than with
the ones they died from.[1] I consulted diaries, autobiographies,
collections of correspondence, healers' casebooks, and the published medical and popular literature, to obtain information about
the sufferer's attitudes and experience. One cannot do the same
kind of research about dying. As at least one literary pirate said,
dead men tell no tales. None the less, the pages of seventeenth-
century diaries and autobiographies are peppered with descriptions of the last illnesses and deaths of loved ones, acquaintances,
and strangers. These descriptions, together with the published
advice on how to die well, will form the basis of this essay.

We scarcely need reminding that life in days gone by was a
precarious business indeed. Demographers provide us with an

increasingly accurate picture of mortality rates in seventeenth-century England – a picture mirrored in contemporary observations.[2] Infants, young children, child-bearing women, and the elderly inhabited a kind of no-man's-land between life and death. Indeed, these groups were so at risk that mention of the age group or category itself was sufficient explanation of the cause of death. The London Bills of Mortality cite the deaths of 'infants', 'chrisoms', and the 'aged', as well as deaths in 'childbed', without recognising as necessary further diagnoses or descriptions of symptoms.[3] In addition, any disorder, however minor, could become a killer. Samuel Pepys reported, with only moderate surprise, the deaths of one Mr Newburn from eating cucumbers, 'of which the other day I heard another', and the solicitor, Mr Clerke, from a cold 'after being not above two days ill'.[4]

Equally commonplace is the observation that seventeenth-century healers were relatively powerless against the disorders they treated. Thus, while sufferers sought treatment from a variety of practitioners and dosed themselves intensively, expectations concerning medicine-taking, surgery, and medical authority were different then from what they are today. In seventeenth-century England, whatever their hopes, people did not expect healers and medicines to cure them.

In addition, seventeenth-century medicine-taking, illnesses, births, and deaths were very social, in contrast to the privacy required by twentieth-century conventions. All of these events took place at home, witnessed by crowds of family members, friends, and neighbours, as well as healers. All women were expected to prescribe for, nurse, and lay out relatives, friends, and neighbours. A married woman who had not been invited to the childbirth of someone closely connected to her might justifiably feel slighted.[5] Visiting the sick was a religious and social duty performed by both sexes. Routine responsibility for and witnessing of birth, illness, and death brought people closer to the events of their own mortality than we are today.

To the aid of both healers and sufferers came natural death. This boon to humanity dealt with a multitude of potential problems. It excused the healer's failure to cure, while reassuring survivors that they had done everything possible for the deceased. Along with the promise of heavenly health, it comforted the grief-stricken.

Natural death came in many guises. As indicated above, it was considered natural for infants and the very old to die of almost any illness. It was also natural for people to die of wounds, epidemic diseases, childbirth, and certain chronic disorders, such as cancer. Even death from minor ailments could be regarded as natural if the symptoms were unusually severe.

A natural death, however, was not the same as a good death. Natural death relieved the dying person and survivors of responsibility for an event interpreted as inevitable. Good death encompassed the duties of all present in the death chamber regarding the quality of the event itself. I owe my recognition of the good death to Philippe Ariès's study, *The Hour of our Death*.[6] Ariès describes the 'tame' death in traditional Europe as one in which the dying person was able to put his or her spiritual and temporal house in order before taking leave of earthly life. Worldly goods were distributed, funerals described and provided for. In addition, the dying sufferer made peace with God and set an example for the living by his or her pious behaviour. The following discussion will examine ways of dying in seventeenth-century England.

John Evelyn's mother died of a malignant fever on 29 September, 1635, at the age of thirty-seven. Evelyn was summoned to her death-bed on September third. Since hers epitomises the good death, I will quote her son's description of it at some length.

Therefore, summoning all her Children then living . . . she expressed herself in a manner so heavenly, with instructions so pious, and Christian, as made us strangely sensible of the extraordinary loss then imminent; after which, embracing every one of us in particular, she gave to each a Ring with her blessing, and dismissed us. Then taking my Father by the hand, she recommended us to his care; and because she was extremely zealous for the education of my Younger Bro[ther]: she requested my father that he might be sent with me to Lewes; and so having importuned him that what he designed to bestow on her Funeral, he would rather dispose among the poor . . . . She laboured to compose herself for the blessed change which she now expected. There was not a servant in the house, whom she did not expressly send for, advise, and infinitely affect with her counsell, and thus she continued to employ her intervals, either instructing her relations, or preparing of herself: for though her Physicians ... had given over all hopes of her recovery, and Sir Sanders Duncomb tried his celebrated and famous powder upon her; yet she was many days impairing, and endured the sharpest conflicts of her sickness with admirable patience, and a most Christian resignation, retaining both her intellectual, and ardent affections for her dissolution to the very article of her departure; which happened, as I said, on the 29 of September after she had fallen into a Crisis by a profound sweat (the only change through all her sickness) after which laying her hand upon every one of her children, and (having) taken solemn leave of my father, with elevated heart & eyes, she quietly expired and resigned her soul to God.[7]

All of the elements of the good death are here. The lady, recognising that an active and fruitful life was coming to an end (she had been married for twenty-two years!), summoned her family and servants. In their presence, she uttered a series of pious speeches, making her own peace with God and consciously attempting to inspire piety in her listeners. She then took care of her worldly business, particularly concerning the futures of her children. Even her requests concerning her funeral were conventionally dictated, although her own admission that she had spent a good deal on the 'pomp' of her daughter's recent funeral suggests that her survivors probably disregarded her directions. She died peacefully, having completed both her secular and her religious duties.

Mrs Evelyn acquitted herself well. It could be objected that her affectionate son exaggerated the virtue she displayed on her death-bed. While this is possible, it is also true that adults – particularly women – attended a veritable university course on the proper manner of dying. Women nursed the sick and laid out the dead. In their own deaths they were capable of heroism – a role usually reserved for men. Women also contributed to the *ars moriendi* literature, begun in the early fifteenth century, which was composed of works dealing specifically with the art of dying.[8] Attendance at several death-beds, combined with sermons and manuals devoted to the subject, potentially qualified most people to play their parts adequately. Mrs Evelyn deserved a first class degree.

The ideal death took place at home. It should not be sudden. In addition, the final illness should not be so painful that the person dying became totally distracted from his or her duties. Perhaps not surprisingly, seventeenth-century illnesses frequently cooperated with these requirements. Whether or not it ended in death, illness was often a long drawn-out affair, requiring weeks and months of bed rest.[9]

In addition, lengthy or not, illnesses, both of the self and of loved ones, served as practice fields for the death which must, in any case, come some time. The Reverend Ralph Josselin, for instance, frequently resigned an ailing child to God, counting it as a providence if the child recovered. In addition, when he suffered from a severe ague in February, 1648, and the relatives and friends he had summoned worried that he might die, he 'drew up [his]... thoughts and purposes concerning [his] ... estate in writing.'[10] Such behaviour was only fitting for a good Christian and worthy minister. Indeed, the duty of the priest or minister of instructing believers in how to die was secondary only to instructing them in how to live.

Seventeenth-century contributors to the *ars moriendi* literary tradition followed both their Catholic and their Protestant forebears in advocating stoicism in the face of death and, indeed, in celebrating the glories of the good death. The works directed toward educating laymen in the proper method of dying are too numerous to be adequately detailed or described here, and, in any case, have received expert analysis elsewhere.[11] Books such as Thomas Becon's *The Sick Man's Salve*, first published in 1561 and appearing in at least another eighteen editions by 1632, found a wide readership in their day, and remain well known. And Jeremy Taylor's *The Rule and Exercises of Holy Dying* (1651) is regarded by at least one authority as the work in which 'the religious and literary tradition of teaching man to die well and gladly achieved its apotheosis'.[12]

Writing midway between these more illustrious colleagues, Robert Hill, minister at St Martin's-in-the-Fields during the first decades of the seventeenth century, was a conventional contributor to this genre whose work provides an accurate indication of the instruction the godly received. In his treatise, entitled

A Direction to Die Well, published in 1613, he set out a step-by-step programme by which the most desirable death might be achieved.

Firstly, the believer must think often about death in general, and his or her own death in particular. The reasons for this were, in part, as follows:

> 1. Because it is appointed that all must die . . . Death spares none: and therefore there was never sacrifice offered to her. 2. It is uncertain when, where, or how I may die; and therefore uncertain, that I may ever think of it. 3. Many go merrily to the pit of perdition, for want of this meditation. 4. Death by this will be more welcome unto me; for, dangers foreseen, are less grievous.[13]

After pointing out the benefits of death, and suggesting reasons people may justifiably either desire death or wish to delay it, Hill defined death:

> It is nothing else but the privation of this natural life, or the departure of the soul from the body: or as it were the deposition of an heavy burden of troubles in this life, by which we are eased; especially if we carry not with us such a burden of sins, as may weigh us down to the pit of perdition . . . Death is an eternal sleep, the dissolution of our bodies, the fear of rich men, the desire of poor men, an inevitable event, an uncertain Pilgrimage, a robber of mankind, the mother of sleep, the passage of life, the departure of the living, and a dissolution of all.[14]

Hill sensibly advised people to live well all their lives in preparation for the death which might surprise them at any time. Like the good churchman he was, he felt that the worst death of all was

> The death of sinners: for them we must mourn most, and their death is most miserable. Their birth is bad, their life is worse, their departure is worst of all: their death is without death, their end is without end, and their want is without want. But precious in the sight of the Lord is the death of his Saints.[15]

The godly need have no fear even of sudden death, since a good life was the best preparation for a good death. However, for sinners, 'sudden death is a fearful judgment, for who then can be persuaded of God's favour towards you? and this makes the wicked of all kinds of death, to pray to be delivered from sudden death.'[16]

When illness came and the believer took to his or her bed, care of the soul was of the highest priority. In most cases, the minister should be summoned. If, as in the case of plague visitation, the minister's presence was not possible, the sufferer must do his or her best. In addition, Hill subscribed to the increasing trend of advising the sufferer to summon a reputable physician, since God sanctioned the ministrations of such healers and, in any case, the cure of the soul and the body went hand in hand. (Like reputable medical writers, he frowned on the consultation of unlicensed healers, reminding readers that such practitioners did the devil's work.)

Having first cared for his or her own soul and body, the sufferer must turn to others. Hill asked rhetorically, 'But now when I am sick of any disease, as I must reconcile my self to God, so ought I not to reconcile my self to my neighbour?' The answer was predictable: 'If you have wronged him in his body, by striking; soul, by seducing; person, by imprisoning; goods, by stealing; name, by slandering; or any other way have done him hurt, you must seek to be reconciled unto him'. Ideally, the wronged individual should be summoned to the sufferer's sickbed. However, if this were not possible, 'God accepteth the will for the deed', and 'You must testifie your desire to friends present.'[17] Having dealt with past sins, the sufferer must have a care for his or her own family by making a will, if that task had not been done before the onset of illness. Hill gave advice about how goods should be distributed to bereaved family members, servants, and the poor. He also discussed how executors should be chosen.

Then, after offering lengthy consolation to the believer confronted with the certainty of death, he made a number of suggestions (filling four pages) about what speeches the sufferer should utter if he or she had the capacity 'for speech unto the last gasp', beginning with, 'Lord into thy hands I commend my spirit: for thou hast redeemed me, O Lord God of truth', and finishing with 'Lord I thank thee, that I am a Christian, that I lived in a Christian Church, that I die amongst a Christian people, that I go to a Christian society. Lord Jesu, son of David, have mercy upon me, and receive my soul. Even so, Come Lord Jesu, come quickly. Amen.'[18]

Hill's treatise contributed to the small body of literature which was exclusively devoted to the manner of dying well. As was the case with other theological works, it concentrated upon the spiritual aspects of dying. However, the art of dying was also discussed in secular works which dealt more generally with social conduct. Richard Brathwaite's book, *The English Gentleman. Containing Sundry Excellent rules or Exquisite Observations, tending to Direction of every Gentleman, of selecter ranke and qualities; How to demean or accommodate himself in the manage of public or private affaires*, advised gentlemen not to fear, but, indeed, to embrace death. Brathwaite, also, reminded readers that a virtuous life is the only sure way to prepare for death. After quoting a number of death-bed speeches delivered by such ancient gentlemen as Saint Ambrose and the Venerable Bede, Brathwaite wrote

> These last funeral tears, or dying men's hymns, I have rather renewed to your memory, that they might have the longer impression, being uttered by dying men, at the point of their dissolution. And I know right well (for experience hath informed me sufficiently therein) that the words of dying men are precious even to strangers.[19]

Better known than Brathwaite's volume, and of, at least theoretically, more general application, was William Gouge's *Of Domesticall Duties*. Gouge's concern with dying had little to do with the ultimate destination of the dying person's soul: he concentrated upon the obligations dying people and survivors owed each other. Children owed parents tolerance and support in infirmity, decent burial after death, payment of parental debts, and protection of deceased parents' reputations. Parents' obligations were greater. Gouge described at some length the duties parents had to support their surviving children after their own deaths. Parents were responsible for arranging suitable marriages and callings, providing portions, and appointing 'faithful friends' to supervise the education and care of minor children. Morally greatest of these parental obligations was that of providing a last blessing.

Let parents therefore as they commend their own souls into

God's hand, so commend their children unto God's grace
and blessing. God's providence is a good inheritance: many
children do thereby exceedingly prosper, though they have
but small outward means; whereas others that have great
means used for their good, come to ruin; God's curse
following them. Now no such means can be thought of to
procure God's blessing, or to withhold his curse, as the
faithful prayers of parents for their children; especially when
parents are leaving their children, and going to God.[20]

Hill, Brathwaite and Gouge all emphasized the significance of
what the dying person *said*. Death-bed speeches performed the
dual functions of educating and comforting survivors and
establishing the heroism of the dying individual. For instance,
Holinshed's *Chronicles*, published in 1587, described the death of
Mary Sidney as follows:

During the whole course of her sickness, and specially a little
before it pleased almighty God to call her hence to his mercy,
she used such godly speeches, earnest and effectual
persuasions to all those about her, and unto such others as
came of friendly courtesy to visit her, to exhort them to
repentance and amendment of life, and dehort them from all
sin and lewdness, as wounded the consciences, and inwardly
pierced the hearts of many that heard her.[21]

Speech was more important than any other part of the dying
person's responsibility. Thus, education for death instructed
people in what to say.

It is difficult to assess the importance of literary advice on the
subject of dying. In an age when devotional works composed the
bulk of published literature, it is certain that such advice was read.
It is also certain that the sort of introspective piety advocated by
Robert Hill was fairly common.

At the beginning of the century, Margaret Hoby's spiritual diary
illustrates daily self-examination as an attempt to keep her
relationship with God fresh and immediate.[22] Ralph Josselin's
diary, covering the mid- to late century, reflects a similar concern.
From time to time he suffered from what he described as a
'deadness' in what was normally a more satisfactory relationship
with God. He worried about potential and apparent divine

retribution for lack of spiritual attention and intensity. Josselin apparently felt that his own life and the lives of his family members were virtual hostages dependent upon his piety and virtue, reporting the deaths of local sinners as confirmation of God's disapproval and the ailments and providential escapes from epidemic diseases of his own family as a kind of barometric reading of how well he stood in God's favour. Josselin certainly viewed the good life as a necessary preparation for both the good death and the hereafter.

In addition to minute attention to spiritual relationships, it can also be shown that people were aware of the imminence of death, fearing and preparing for it. An interesting example of obsession with death (justifiable, as it turned out) is provided by Elizabeth Joceline whose book, *The Mother's Legacy to her Unborn Child*, was first published in 1624. Elizabeth had much occupied herself with pious studies, perpetually meditating on death. When she discovered she was pregnant with her first child at the age of twenty-seven, she became convinced that childbirth would kill her. 'Accordingly when she first felt herself quick with child (as then travelling with death itself) she secretly took order for the buying of a new winding sheet.'[23] Worried that she would be unable to perform the primary duty of providing her unborn child with spiritual instruction, she wrote her little book. One might be forgiven for accusing Elizabeth of excessive morbidity; however, she justified her pessimism by dying of fever nine days after her daughter was born. While Elizabeth's preparedness was unusual, her apprehension was not. Other women, among them Alice Thornton and Jane Josselin, feared childbirth and prayed for divine protection at that time.

Of course, men as well as women feared death and prepared themselves in advance for that universal experience. The ideal seventeenth-century death was deliberate, incorporating regard both for the next world and the world left behind. It was a skill which could be learned by the academic pursuits of reading and listening to sermons or in the more practical forum of a succession of death-chambers. It could be the crowning triumph of a virtuous life.

It should be pointed out here that, although the good death was very much the business of the church, society gave the final verdict. Regardless of the church's official line, a good death could be achieved more or less without its help. In his *Brief Lives,* John Aubrey described the death of Edward, Lord Herbert of Cherbury, as follows:

> Usher, Lord Primate of Ireland, was sent for by him, when in his death-bed, and he would have received the sacrament. He said indifferently of it that 'if there was good in anything, 'twas in that', or 'if it did no good 'twould do no hurt'. The primate refused it, for which many blamed him. He died at his house in Queen Street, very serenely; asked what was a clock, answer so: 'then', said he, 'an hour hence I shall depart'. He then turned his head to the other side and expired. In his will he gave special order to have his white stone-horse (which he loved) to be well fed and carefully looked after as long as he lived. He had two libraries, one at London, the other at Montgomery; one whereof he gave to Jesus College, Oxon. . . . Mr Fludd tells me he had constantly prayers twice a day in his house, and Sundays would have his chaplain read one of Smyth's sermons.[24]

While the manner of his death was not completely orthodox, Lord Herbert clearly conformed to most of the requirements for the good death. His life had been reasonably virtuous. He had obviously prepared for death by drawing up a detailed will which cared for both human and animal survivors. Furthermore, his apparent clairvoyance about the timing of his death is something Ariès recognizes as being a frequent feature of traditional deaths.[25] Again, the primary benefit of this clairvoyance was that it gave the dying person time to complete all of his or her business on earth.

The dying did not, of course, have to be clairvoyant to recognize the fact that death was near. As it does today, occupational medicine often provided its own clues regarding a patient's condition. When Christopher Wandesford lay dying of a fever in 1640, his physicians were loath to tell him and his wife how ill he was. None the less, he became suspicious when the physicians applied pigeons to his feet – a treatment commonly recognized as the 'last remedy'.[26] Last remedies, by definition, were applied only as long as there was hope of recovery. Illness, not death, was the healer's province; healers generally withdrew when death seemed inevitable. The management of dying was left to ministers, family, friends, and the sufferer.

Thus far, our discussion has concentrated upon the deaths of adults. However, children also achieved good deaths. In 1652, Frank Kelly, a nine-year-old Irish boy living in the household of Alice Wandesford, died of smallpox. His foster-sister, later Alice Thornton, described his death in her autobiography. She wrote,

> All the time of this boy's sickness he was so full of sweet expressions and heavenly minded, with much acts of religion, that it was a great comfort to my mother, and all about him, with abundance of patience and gratitude to God and my mother for all they had done for him. . . . This poor boy . . . still prayed for me; when he heard I was in danger of death [from the same illness], desired with tears that God would be pleased to spare my life, and to bless me, that I might live to do much good to others, as to him, and that he might rather be taken away and I spared.[27]

The duties of dying children were wholly moral and spiritual, since they had no estates to dispose of. Many children, like Frank, died well. Tom Gyles, the adolescent cousin and servant of Robert Hooke, died very quickly of smallpox in 1677. However, despite the short duration of his final illness (three days), Tom achieved a good death. Hooke wrote of his last morning,

> Tom spake very piously, began to grow cold, to want covering, to have little convulsive motions, and after falling into a slumber seemed a little refresht and spake very sensibly and heartily, but composing himself again for a slumber he rattled in the throat and presently died.[28]

When eight-year-old Mary Josselin lay dying of worms in May, 1650, her father wrote, 'My little Mary, very weak, we feared she was drawing on, fear came on my heart very much, but she is not mine, but the Lord's . . . she was tender of her mother, thankfull, mindfull of God.' On the day of her death, Ralph Josselin wrote:

> it was a precious child, a bundle of myrrhe, a bundle of sweetness, she was a child of ten thousand, full of wisdom, woman-like gravity, knowledge, sweet expre[*ssions of god, apt in her learning,*] tender hearted and loving, an [*obed*]ient child [*to us*]. It was free from [*the rudeness of*] little children, it was to us

as a box of sweet ointment, which now its broken smells more deliciously than it did before, Lord I rejoice I had such a present for thee, it was patient in the sickness, thankfull to admiracion; it lived desired and dyed lamented, thy memory is and will bee sweete unto mee.[29]

Mary could hardly have had a better tutor in the approved method of dying than her father. Josselin's account is obviously coloured by his love and grief for his daughter. But this observation helps rather than hinders us in our understanding of the good death in seventeenth-century society. Reports of good deaths, whether of children or adults, gave the dear departed the status of household saints in the memories of those who survived them. The demeanour of the dying could cleanse from the minds of the bereaved the horror of the final illness and the stark reminder that, not only must we all die, but that most of us die in pain and filth. Frank Kelly and Tom Gyles were disfigured by smallpox. Mary Josselin's worms made her bowel movements the focus of household attention during the month before her death. Yet their behaviour created a sort of justification for the awful fact of their young deaths. God could not help but smile upon such angels as these. And adult observers could bring themselves to believe that such children were indeed happier in death, having escaped the repetitive miseries of a long life.

An important part of the learning process involved in the good death was attendance at many deaths, both good and bad. Death by execution, death in the home, death in the streets and fields, provided repeated examples of the ways its many guises could be handled. Presence at a death-bed, like visiting the sick, was a religious and social duty from which no one was exempt. Indeed, although imminent death increased the number of people in the sufferer's chamber, it would be a distortion to view visits to the dying as something apart from visits to the ailing. The death-bed was, in most cases, the sickbed renamed.

Whether minor or serious, acute or chronic, most disorders entitled the sufferer to visits from friends, relatives, clergymen, and acquaintances. Even when physic-taking confined an individual to his or her chamber, and no illness existed, visitors were welcomed. Modern conventions regarding privacy simply did not exist. Apparently, no one ever wanted to be left alone. As far as

I have been able to determine, only infectious diseases, like plague and to a lesser extent smallpox, deprived sufferers of visitors.

Visits served a number of purposes. Both clerical and lay visitors prayed with the sick. Indeed, conventionally the minister took the place of the healer when death approached, and he was welcomed as the physician's equal or superior in the sick-room. Ralph Josselin was summoned in his dual role as vicar and friend to pray with ailing parishioners on many occasions. Roger Lowe, a mercer's apprentice, prayed with fellow Presbyterians.[30]

Practical services were also performed during visits. Any educated person might be asked to draw up a will for someone in danger of death. Roger Lowe frequently performed this service. In addition, visitors undertook nursing care and household tasks. Mothers routinely travelled to be with daughters when the daughters gave birth. They also frequently visited adult children in times of illness. In return, adult children hurried to the bedsides of ailing parents. The Josselin daughters returned to Earls Colne to visit and nurse their parents during serious illnesses. John Evelyn spent nearly four weeks at his mother's death-bed. And he spent from June to October, 1640, travelling between Oxford and his father's house when the elder Evelyn was suffering from the illness which finally killed him.[31]

Visits undeniably helped the sufferer. However, the visitor also benefited. Visits cemented relationships between people. Supplying services and comfort allowed visitors to feel that they were helping. Proximity prevented the mystification of illness and death and the alienation of sufferers and the dying which are so apparent today. Visitors were both comforted by the assurance that they also would have social support during their own crises and taught behaviour which they might themselves employ. Pious responses to suffering and the spiritual satisfaction of a good death fulfilled the needs of both sufferers and visitors.

Conventions governing visiting the ill and dying suggest why certain ailments and certain deaths were so feared. Plague terrified not only with its killing power but with the alienation it produced. Sufferers and their households were deprived by the imposed quarantine of friends, medical attention, and clerical supervision. Robert Hill undertook discussion of this problem, but his answers must have provided small comfort to readers. Concerning the lack of visitors, he wrote, 'O, but God will never forsake you'. He was even less encouraging about the probability that clergymen would not visit a person suffering from the pestilence, writing:

> If you labour to get comfort by the word and sacraments in your health, you will not so much desire his presence in this sickness: and this is the just judgement of God, upon many at their death, that as they regarded not the public means of comfort in their health; so he will not vouchsafe it unto them being sick.[32]

He went on to enumerate the reasons ministers could not visit plague sufferers, saying that if they did they could not preach in public, return home to their own families, or visit any other ailing Christian. Furthermore, by making such visits they might become responsible for the deaths of themselves or family members through the contagion. Even Hill, with his indomitable confidence in the spiritual abilities of the committed Christian, obviously did not view death from plague as a good death.

Another death, viewed with horror for other reasons, was death from syphilis. In his *Natural and Political Observations Made upon the Bills of Mortality*, published in 1662, John Graunt expressed his surprise that although it appeared to him that 'a great part of men have, at one time or other, had some species of this disease', very few were reported to have died of it:

> upon inquiry I found that those who died of it out of the hospitals . . . were returned of ulcers and sores. And in brief I found, that all mentioned to die of the French Pox were returned by the clerks of Saint Giles's, and Saint Martin's in the Fields only; in which place I understood that most of the vilest, and most miserable houses of uncleanness were: from whence I concluded, that only *hated* persons, and such, whose very noses were eaten off, were reported by the Searchers to have died of this too frequent malady.

Graunt observed that most who died of syphilis died 'emaciated and lean'. Thus, the searchers, 'after the mist of a cup of ale and the bribe of a two-groat fee', were nearly justified in reporting as the cause of death consumption, hectic-fever, atrophy, or infection of the spermatic parts.[33]

Graunt's general observations are borne out by the specific

example of the death of Samuel Pepys's brother Tom. Upon being summoned to his brother's sickbed, the diarist was told, to his

> great astonishment, that my brother was deadly ill and that their chief business of coming was to tell me so; and which is worse, that his disease is the pox, which he hath heretofore got and hath not been cured, but is come to this; and that this is certain, though a secret.

Tom was too ill to question, being delirious and barely able to recognize his brother. Samuel was annoyed by the fact that Tom's friend, Mrs Turner, was 'full now of the disease which my brother is troubled with, and talks of it mightily' in front of the assembled company, which consisted of an unspecified number of Mrs Turner's friends, Mrs Croxton, Mrs Holding, and Samuel's wife, Elizabeth. He was also worried about the state of Tom's finances, writing 'if he lives, he will not be able to show his head. Which will be a very great shame to me.' At some point, Tom became temporarily lucid, thus able to deny that he had syphilis. Encouraged, Pepys demanded a second medical opinion. He and Dr Powell 'searched my brother again at his privities; where he was as clear as ever he was born, and in the Doctor's opinion had been ever so'. Then Pepys summoned Dr Wiverley, who had given the unpleasant diagnosis, whereupon Dr Powell 'fully confuted and left the fellow, only saying that he should cease to report any such thing.' Pepys himself 'threatened him that I would have satisfaction if I heard any more such discourse.' Poor Tom did not die particularly well, continuing to 'talk idle, and his lips working even to his last'. None the less, he managed to avoid the stigma of a syphilitic death; Samuel left his wife to see Tom laid out, palpably relieved that the worst had been avoided.[34]

The example of Tom Pepys demonstrates that not all unsatisfactory deaths happened in solitude. Indeed, it was the very public quality of Tom's potential shame which disturbed his brother. As in Tom's case, illness itself often deprived the dying of the ability to die well. Thomas Crosfield reported on Christmas day, 1631, that Mr Coperthwait, like himself a Fellow at Queen's College, Oxford, was 'so exceedingly distempered with sickness that he could scarce be kept in bed'. The sufferer was outraged by slanderous remarks which had been made about him, threatening to leave his bed in order to 'clear himself before Mr. Provost'.

Crosfield 'laboured to persuade him to patience, that he would suffer these injuries done him according to Christ's precept, and to rejoice rather in his saviour, to meditate on him who was born this day, to think upon an all seeing God, that knew his innocency, etc.' Coperthwait died fourteen days later, some suspecting 'that the infirmity was in his head, but being opened by the surgeon, his lungs were found to have been perished'.[35]

Ralph Josselin, convinced of the providential quality of events, recorded details of numerous bad deaths among his neighbours as reminders of God's omniscience and justice. Typical of such entries was that of 17 March, 1657:

> One John Chrismas a miller in our town whose parents were
> godly, and one in a way of doing well, but his heart leading
> him to tipple and game, and his wife being sharp to him, he
> got what he could together and left her, his brother brought
> him home, but about a week after he was sick of the pox and
> died, a warning not to go out of god's way.[36]

Chrismas's death conformed to the stereotype of the bad death. He had been a flagrant sinner, who had died of a disreputable illness quickly, without either spiritual or temporal preparation.

As indicated above, preparation for death was of paramount importance. Even the godly feared unprepared death. Josselin reported an occasion where he was 'Alarmed as if Goodman Mathew were dying suddenly. I hasted and found it a fainting fit, he was troubled his estate was not disposed so that his wife should enjoy it, but that we did the next day to his content.'[37] Goodman Mathew had presumably kept himself in spiritual readiness for death. Not so the Ghost of Prince Hamlet's father, who complained that by murder, that most sudden of deaths, he had been

> Cut off even in the blossoms of my sin
> Unhousel'd, disappointed, unaneled;
> No reckoning made, but sent to my account
> With all my imperfections on my head:
> O, horrible! O, horrible! most horrible![38]

Hamlet's father had died unprepared. Hamlet, desiring above all things to avenge his murder, decided that he could not wreak appropriate vengeance when he found King Claudius at prayer, having just confessed his crimes. He deliberated as follows:

> Now might I do it pat, now he is praying;
> And now I'll do't: – and so he goes to heaven;
> And so am I reveng'd: – that would be scanned:
> A villain kills my father; and, for that,
> I, his sole son, do this same villain send
> To heaven.
> O, this is hire and salary, not revenge . . . .
> Up, sword; and know thou a more horrid hent:
> When he is drunk asleep, or in his rage;
> Or in th' incestuous pleasure of his bed;
> At gaming, swearing; or about some act
> That has no relish of salvation in't.[39]

Hamlet desired a bad death for Claudius and refused to give him a good one. Shakespeare, as always dealing in the currency of conventional beliefs and attitudes, mirrored in drama the message of the *ars moriendi* writers.

The impression left by a bad death could, to some extent, be mitigated by a good funeral – an event which is beyond the scope of this discussion.[40] It could also be diminished by the memory of an exemplary life. As Robert Hill said, although sudden death was indeed to be feared by sinners, for the godly such a death might be the best of all. Certainly, death in battle was traditionally regarded as good death. One recalls the eighteenth-century ballad concerning the death of Brave Wolfe on the Plains of Abraham: in the final verse, 'He raised up his head where the guns did rattle. And to his aide he said, "How goes the battle?" "The field is all our own, they can't prevent it." He said without a groan, "I die contented".'

Equally, a good death could dim public recollection of crimes committed in life. The execution of the Earl of Essex for treason on 25 February 1601 provided popular memory with an exemplary death. Upon the scaffold, Essex confessed and asked forgiveness for his rebellion, exchanged pardons with his executioner, and offered a number of prayers. Then,

> Lying flat along one of the boards, his hands stretched out, he said, 'Lord, have mercy upon me, thy prostrate servant', and

therewithal fitting his head to the block, he was willed by one of the doctors to say the beginning of the 51st Psalm, . . . whereof when he had said two verses, the executioner being prepared, he uttered these words, 'Executioner, strike home. Come, Lord Jesus, come Lord Jesus, and receive my soul; O Lord into thy hands I commend my spirit'. In the midst of which sentence his head was severed by the axe from the corpse at three blows, but the first deadly, and depriving absolutely all sense and motion.[41]

The above discussion clearly indicates that a consensus of opinion concerning desirable and undesirable deaths existed in seventeenth-century England. Good death was pious and pre-pared. Bad death was unregenerate and, with the possible exception of suicide, unprepared. While most of the examples chosen illustrate the deaths of relatively privileged people, some information here and more elsewhere suggests that the good death was not an exclusively upper-class phenomenon in the period.[42] That the good death existed as both an ideal and a reality in seventeenth-century England there can be no doubt.

4

GODLY GRIEF: INDIVIDUAL RESPONSES TO DEATH IN SEVENTEENTH-CENTURY BRITAIN

ANNE LAURENCE

It is questionable whether grief is properly a subject for investigation by historians or whether, instead, it falls into the realm of timeless emotions unaltered by period or place. Since, however, there has been much discussion recently about affective relationships and the family in early modern England, and the experience of grief seems to distil individuals' feelings about one another, it is a subject worthy of consideration in an historical context.

Lawrence Stone's remarks on the topic of family relationships have been the subject of much criticism. He says that 'high mortality rates made deep relationships very imprudent', that 'evidence of close bonding between parents and children is hard, but not impossible, to document', and that 'evidence of close affection between husband and wife is both ambiguous and rare.' He also argues that 'belief in the immortality of the soul and the prospect of salvation was a powerful factor in damping down such grief as might be aroused by the loss of a child, spouse or parent.'[1] He sums up by saying that he believes that the society of England in the sixteenth and early seventeenth centuries was one in which 'a majority of the individuals who composed it found it very difficult to establish close emotional ties to any person', and he contrasts this with the eighteenth century which was, he argues, one of 'ease and warmth' in personal relationships.[2] Stone's view is shared by Michael Mitterauer and Reinhard Sieder who say that 'Changes in membership took place so frequently in a peasant household of the eighteenth or nineteenth century that there could be no comparable sense of loss throughout the group.'[3] At a superficial level these observations might seem to be true and there is evidence to bear them out. On the other hand it is possible to argue that family relationships were such an important element of life in seventeenth-century England that people took it for granted that these bonds were more important than any others. It is only with the popularization of Freudian ideas about relationships within the family and their supposed breakdown during the twentieth century that an enormous literature about family relationships has appeared.

This chapter examines some of the evidence which would seem to contradict Stone's assertions about family relationships in seventeenth-century England, in an English congregation in Dublin, and in some Scottish ministers' families. Much evidence of the responses of individuals to deaths of members of their families is to be found in diaries, spiritual autobiographies, and religious testimonies. The largest quantity of material was produced by ministers and their families and bereavement was an important subject, partly because it occurred frequently, and partly because it was a spiritual trial and the purpose of such writing was usually that of spiritual self-examination. Although the evidence is limited, it is not, however, confined to the literate. The religious testimonies delivered in two Independent churches as a condition of membership and taken down by the minister are an important source. The members of John Rogers's Dublin congregation and of Henry Walker's London congregation were by no means exclusively middle class and literate, especially those of Walker's church, but they were distinguished by having a Puritan consciousness of themselves in some relation to both God and the society in which they lived. They were probably representative of urban artisans rather than the very poorest peripatetic labourers. Such was the strength of the grief manifested in this kind of material that it is difficult to sustain Stone's assertions about the relationships between spouses and between parents and children. This discussion is inevitably based upon the anecdotal rather than the statistical, but it is one in which it is worth engaging if we are to try to understand seventeenth-century mentalities.

THE EXPERIENCE OF BEREAVEMENT

In the twentieth century it is usual to see death primarily as a personal rather than a material tragedy. In seventeenth-century England the death of a husband or father could mean a radical change in a family's material circumstances. A widow in the 1650s said of her plight, 'I had lost a good estate, had no body to looke after my businesse, had many injured mee, and had lost (above the rest) a precious husband, whom I intirely loved'.[4] Recent work by Barbara J. Todd and Mary Prior has tended to suggest that widowhood offered a rare opportunity for women to operate independently in economic life.[5] Death could also mean release from an unsatisfactory marriage which could not be ended in any other way, but these are by-products, sometimes recognized after the event as benefits. The death of a husband and father was an economic catastrophe in most households. The death of a wife and mother was a catastrophe of a different kind, evidenced by the high rate of remarriage. One of Lawrence Stone's most interesting statistics is that the average duration of a marriage in early modern England was 17-19 years compared with 31 years in the US in 1955, and Michael Anderson claims that the figures for the dissolution of marriages in England and Wales in 1980 are similar to those for the termination of marriages by death in the 1820s.[6]

In this context it is worth saying something about the composition of the early modern family. The idea that everyone lived in extended families with large numbers of relations nearby who acted as a mutual support network has been largely exploded.[7] Most families consisted primarily of parents and children and, in better-off establishments, one or more domestics. These domestics rarely stayed for more than a couple of years in the fairly modest households of clergymen. Both Ralph Josselin and Giles Moore refer to frequent changes in their domestic staff; Josselin had one woman living in and Moore had a man and a woman.[8] City life might have come closer to the idea of the extended family for Nehemiah Wallington, a London artisan, took in his wife's nephew as an apprentice and seems to have regarded such members of his household as his family.[9]

There has been a good deal of discussion about how far the family extended beyond parents and children and there was almost certainly much variation between classes and regions.[10] The evidence of the diaries used for this paper would suggest that, especially in more geographically mobile families like those of the clergy, adults kept contact, but not very closely, with their brothers and sisters, occasionally with aunts and uncles, and that they knew who their cousins were and, if a matter of patronage was involved, would invoke the relationship, but that these were not relatives with whom most adults had close emotional ties, unless, like Nehemiah Wallington, they were brought together by geographical proximity. Today grandparents are naturally the focus for connections between aunts, uncles, and cousins but in the seventeenth-century it was probably unusual for families to contain more than two generations. The short interval between deaths and funerals often made attendance at either difficult for relations who lived at any distance. The relationships which had a significance from the point of view of rites of passage were those of the household rather than a wider kin group.[11]

The incidence of death inevitably affects the experience of death and thus of grief. There was a difference between urban and rural mortality and the economic fluctuations of the period combined with epidemics did make the experience of death more catastrophic in some areas than others.[12] Writing in 1657, Henry Newcome said that in the country he had rarely performed more than one burial a month, whilst in Manchester he visited 3 or 4 sick persons a day and performed several burials in a week. At first he was much chastened by this, 'yet, in time, this grew familiar, and but too common with me'.[13]

Rom Harré suggests that 'situations make emotions intelligibly present', and that 'What distinguishes grief from remorse and disappointment from shame is not a determinate inner feeling but responses, actions, appraisals and situations in the social world.'[14] Modern psychological writing inclines towards the belief that the core experience of grief is very similar across societies and the stages through which the bereaved person passes are also the same: shock, anxiety, rage, acceptance, but that expressions of mourning differ markedly between one culture and another.[15] To some extent this is likely to be the result of the circumstances in which people die. In seventeenth-century England they usually died at home, often leaving young dependants. Many people, especially children, died of short, acute illnesses; protracted illnesses were probably more common amongst the old. Members of the household and neighbours frequently had a clear apprehension that death was imminent and started to prepare themselves for it, something which is now recognized in modern writings which observe that the process of mourning often begins during the fatal illness. Few of those who wrote about the deaths of their relations interpreted them in anything other than religious terms, though this is not unrelated to the reasons for which people wrote: the spiritual testimony is an important source of autobiographical writing. Since the deceased was necessarily going to better things it was believed to be wrong to protract the mourning process. It may be that recently deceased children and spouses feature little in this kind of autobiographical writing because of the conviction that any expression of missing them was to desire something that now properly belonged to God.

CHILDREN AND PARENTS

We tend to hear more of the deaths of children than of those of parents partly because people have only two parents yet they commonly lost more than two children. Mrs Elizabeth Walker blessed the Lord for the survival of two of her eleven children.[16] There does seem to have been some difference in the attitude of parents to their dependent children living at home and their adult children who had established independent households. Anderson suggests that a quarter of all children had lost one or both parents by the age of sixteen.[17] But few of those who lost parents when they were children wrote about their deaths subsequently and adult children were commonly separated from their parents at the time of their deaths.

Dependent children

Only recently has it been recognized that there is an acute need for parents of miscarried or stillborn children to grieve. It is easy to believe therefore that children in the seventeenth-century who were stillborn or who survived only a few days were just forgotten, but this is almost certainly a mistake. They would have had proper funerals and, if the birth was not attended by a midwife, an investigation was supposed to be carried out to see whether there was any possibility of infanticide, though in the case of births to married women who already had one or more children this was probably pretty cursory.

Childbirth was of course fraught with difficulties and perinatal mortality was extremely high. Caesarian sections were not yet successful so that a difficult delivery was likely to cause the death of either mother or baby. Henry Newcome wrote of Lady Fytton, who had been in 'lingering labour', 'We begged life for mother and child very earnestly at first; after, we begged either, which God pleased. After that we were brought to beg the life of the soul; for all hopes were over.'[18]

Ralph Josselin's experience shows how dangerous the first days of life could be. His fourth child was so ill six days after his birth that the physician was sent for. He wrote, 'my wife perswaded her selfe that it would die it was a very sicke child indeed: I tooke my leave of it at night, not much expecting to see it alive, but god continued it to morning' and the following day the baby was baptized. Josselin himself was resigned to the death, though not without some hope for the child's recovery, and wrote, 'Lord thy will be done . . . it becommeth mee to submitt to his will.' When the boy died a few days later Josselin was concerned that he was not facing his son's death with a sufficient degree of submission, writing 'the Lord . . . teach mee how to walke more closely with him: I bless god for any measure of patience, and submission to his will.' Both he and his wife obviously felt terrible grief

> Thes 2 dayes were such as I never knewe before; the former
> for the death, and this for the burial of my deare sonne . . .
> (who) was buried with the teares and sorrows not onely of the
> parents and Mrs Mary Church, but with the teares and
> sorrowe of many of my neighbours.

During the following days Josselin rehearsed his faults, especially desiring 'god to discover and hint to my soule, what is the aime of the god of heaven in this correction of his upon mee'. He allowed himself not to preach on the fast day which followed the funeral because when Aaron's sons died he forebore to offer a sacrifice. And for some weeks afterwards there are references to troubles, though with someone of the pessimistic temperament of Josselin, it is hard to say for certain that these are signs of grief alone.[19]

It is perhaps unfair to rely too heavily upon Josselin, but there are other similar cases. Mrs Elizabeth Walker 'fell into a Melancholy . . . and was very ill' after the delivery of a stillborn child.[20] It is possible to argue that this was perhaps some form of post-natal depression, but it seems probable that grief made an important contribution. Women were likely to refer in rather different terms to the deaths of newborn children than their husbands, for many of whom there was the agonizing wait to see whether either mother or child would survive. The Lancashire squire Nicholas Assheton wrote of how his wife's delivery 'was with such violence, as the child dyed within half an hour, and but for God's wonderful mercie, more than human reason could expect, shee had dyed; but hee spared her a while longer to mee, and took the child to his mercie'.[21]

One of the worst aspects of children's deaths was that they were sometimes the result of epidemics in which more than one child died. Josselin described the deaths of his daughter and son within a week, though he claimed that his daughter's disease was not infectious.[22] Sir John Oglander lost two grandchildren within a week and Katharine Ross lost two children within a month, which she saw as the price exacted by God for sparing a minister who had been particularly helpful to her.[23] Henry Newcome tried to resign himself, but wrote, 'I . . . thought it must be which child the Lord pleaseth. I thought when I feared Daniel that I should then have lost my finest boy; and now Harry is sick, I think I should lose my best child.'[24] Mrs Elizabeth Avery lost three children close together 'at which I was left in an horror, as if I were in hell, none could comfort me, nothing could satisfie me, no Friends, nothing'.[25]

Individual responses varied. Josselin wrote a fortnight after his daughter's death 'I am sometimes ready to be overwhelmed in remembrance of my dear Mary', and a month later, 'many times I find the memory of my deare babes bitter as death'.[26] Mrs Alice Thornton had her thoughts distracted by her own ill-health from the not infrequent deaths of her children, though she did write on the occasion of the death of her son Willy that she 'had many sad thoughts of God's afflicting hand on me, and one day was weeping much about it', and on that of her daughter Joyce 'I shall not repine at this chastisement of the Lord'.[27]

Parents of children old enough to be considered responsible for their actions were concerned that such children should be spiritually prepared for death. A Scottish minister's wife wrote of her dying child

I was somewhat taken up about her eternall condition . . .

being three years old and a half, and so guilty of actuall sin, att least in words, and being very capable to discern between good and evill, the Lord did wonderfully condescend to me, and made her speak to admiration.[28]

An anonymous Scottish woman whose child was struck with fever reported that 'it was concluded That he was dying, which threw me into great distress, nor could I possibly get him resigned', and of another child she wrote that 'When death came within his view (he) seemed to be very much concerned about his Lost State by Nature and how to be saved'.[29] Mrs Veitch, wife of a Covenanting minister, was comforted when her daughter 'died with as much composedness as if she had been going to see a Friend and without any pain'.[30]

Parents seem to have felt that a particular lesson was intended when God took their children from them. It seems possible that this was related to the responsibility for their children's spiritual welfare which they felt devolved upon them as parents. The woman whose son was concerned about his lost state seems to have felt a very immediate need to act, 'his Indisposition increasing he turned insensible, which was very grievous to me; And I was made to wrestle earnestly for his salvation'.[31] An anonymous woman, in a testimony, interpreted the death of her child 'which was a very great trouble to mee to part with', as part of God's aim to convince her more fully of sin 'so that I could seldome have any other thought but of desperation'.[32] And Katherine Sutton's child died 'which was to my casting down, and for some time I was under a cloud, and questioned whither I were a child of God? and whither my child was saved?'[33] Some parents were more composed about the lesson. The death of the Reverend Edmund Trench's son from a convulsion fit led him to write, 'May we more practically believe we must also die, and not cease preparing for it, till we come to desire it, and live in the constant joyful expectation of Eternity.'[34]

Children who were more than a few days old were still regarded as innocents but parents felt a responsibility for their immortal souls greater than that for the newborn. They also expressed very clearly their ideas about the lessons to be learned from children's deaths, though these lessons were not easy to bear and Nehemiah Wallington's wife admonished him for grieving too much for the loss of their first child.[35] It would seem that though lessons were to be learned from all deaths, those of children were believed to be particularly salutary.

Independent children

Few parents lived long enough to see their children survive into middle age, their adult children who predeceased them were often only in their twenties, and their daughters commonly died in childbed. Mrs Elizabeth Walker wrote of Satan renewing his assaults on her, 'taking advantage of my Melancholy disposition' after the death of her married daughter.[36] Parents were less liable to see the deaths of their adult children as punishments upon themselves, though Mrs Veitch believed that her eldest son's death was the result of her having 'been too peremptory with God in desireing to have all my Sons Ministers'.[37] Their grief was also less tempered with feelings of personal responsibility for the fate of their adult children's souls unless, like Henry Newcome's wayward son Daniel, the children had not led good Christian lives. 'I have desired the world for him . . . and have not been so concerned for his eternal state as I should have been; and how sad it may be with me if he die in a sad uncertainty for his soul'. Daniel was ill for some weeks, but Newcome was comforted by hopes of his repentance. A week after Daniel's death he wrote, 'I am sad by fits on this loss of mine in my poor child', and two days later, 'Things are discomposed and difficult about Daniel. It will be hard to preserve any credit of honour to those that have sinned and dishonoured God.' When, two months later, Daniel's widow gave birth to a son, he wrote, 'It was sorrowful to me to reflect on the loss of my son.' He later expressed satisfaction that his eldest son lived at some distance 'lest I should over enjoy him.'[38]

Many parents, like Sir John Oglander, were completely prostrated. When told of his twenty-two-year-old son's death in France he wrote 'what a case I was in and how deeply stricken, insomuch as I had much ado to get home. With my tears instead of ink I write these last lines.' His meditations on his son's death dwelt upon the young man's unfulfilled promise, 'his poor parents that expected his return with joy and comfort and to reap the fruits of their charge and care in his education, hoping not to lose him but to gain an improvement by his travel? But this is our comfort. The Lord that gave him would have him for Himself.'[39] Josselin showed more resignation in describing the death of his twenty-year-old daughter, writing of her following her brother 'to lie in his grave, loving in their lives and in their deaths they were not divided.'[40] It seems that the deaths of adult children were seen as occasions for mourning the passing of another adult; parents did not feel less grief but they felt less immediate responsibility than for the deaths of their dependent children however much they mourned their unfulfilled promise.

Parents

There are few accounts of people's feelings at the deaths of their parents, either because they were too young at the time or because they lived at too great a distance from their parents to be involved in their deaths and funerals. An unusual account of the grief of a young family is given by Henry Newcome who recorded that at the funeral of a dyer, whose wife had died shortly before, leaving nine children, 'The cries of the children at the funeral, moved most that were present.'[41]

There seems to be more writing about grief at the loss of a father than at the loss of a mother, though there are many accounts of mothers' deathbeds and pious descriptions of their lives and good qualities. Sir Simonds D'Ewes was exceptional in writing after his mother's death of 'the wants and miseries I tasted of many years together, after I had lost her', and Alice Thornton's grief was increased by the 'exceeding torment' which her mother endured 'which made me more willingly submitt to part with her'.[42] Lady Twysden wrote of her father's death at the age of eighty-seven after three or four days' illness, 'I to my grefe was in Kent so could not know of his illnes, to be with him'.[43] Nehemiah Wallington, who was forty when his father died, seems to have felt a certain amount of relief, 'I lost an earthly Father and found a heavenly Father, that is, I did find after my Father's death more joy and comfort in my poor soul from God than ever I did before.'[44] Ralph Verney, writing of his father, the King's standard-bearer who was killed at the battle of Edgehill, said of his death that it was 'the saddest and deepest affliction that ever befell any poore distressed man; I will not add to your greife by relating my own deplorable condition, neither can my pen expresse the meseries I am in'. Verney's death had an important element of martyrdom which the more prosaic circumstances of the other parents' deaths lacked.[45]

The most reasonable conclusion to draw from this is that though parents and dependent children led closely emotionally involved lives, these ties often diminished in adulthood, partly because of the effect of distance and the problems of maintaining contact. This is not to say that the relations between parents and children became more distant as the children reached adulthood, rather that they were less immediate.

HUSBANDS AND WIVES

It goes almost without saying that relationships between husbands and wives are very difficult to chart and the evidence is hard to interpret. However, virtually all marriages were ended by the death of one of the partners and a high proportion within a short space of time. We are rightly warned against overestimating the frequency of early spousal bereavement; nevertheless loss of a partner in youth or middle age was a common experience of marriage in seventeenth-century England.[46]

Bereaved husbands turned to God. John Shaw, minister in Hull in the 1650s, wrote of how, after twenty-five years' marriage, 'my mirth was turned into mourning' when his wife died. 'Then did my harp hang on the willoughs; yet the assurance of her happyness did something mitigate my griefe; to divert which, and to make some improvement of that sad stroke, for my own and my six dau'ters' benefit, I printed a book called 'Mrs Shawe's Tomb-stone'.[47] Richard Baxter, who wrote 'God called my sin to remembrance by his heavy hand on my dear wife', also took up his pen in her memory. 'In depth of grief I truly wrote her life . . . In the same passion I published some poetical fragments written partly in gratitude for myself formerly, and partly in grief for her in former sickness and affliction'.[48] John Hervey, first Earl of Bristol, writing to his father on the death of his wife, a cousin, combined praise of her qualities, 'wise & vertuous, kind & pious', with a more secular description of grief, 'my rackt heart having oft suggested to me that, if its pains are capable of any relaxation or remission, it could only be procured by giving of its grief some vent'. He praised God for the blessing of such a wife, but he did not look for God's hand in her death; his soreness is undisguised, referring to the 'bitterness . . . of my present soul', he likened himself to 'wretched Job'.[49] Sir Ralph Verney was distraught at the death of his wife and aware of the practical problems which now beset him, 'The great & sad afflictions now uppon me, make me utterly unable to think how I had best dispose of myselfe & children'.[50] Sir John Oglander, always given to the histrionic gesture, wrote in blood, 'Thy death hath made me most miserable. Indeed greater grief and sorrow could not have befallen any man. No man can conceive the loss but he that hath had a good and careful loving wife.'[51]

These accounts by husbands suggest much love and some appreciation of practical problems, but for women the practical problems attendant upon a husband's death could be very acute, as there were frequently financial difficulties. The largest number of accounts is by ministers' wives and it is quite likely that the idea of companionate marriage was better developed in such households. An anonymous Scottish minister's wife, writing in the later years of the century, described the death of her husband, 'my greatest earthly comfort'. On the fifth day after the start of his fever, 'my hope of recovery quite failed', and on the sixth day 'I was in such a Case, as it was not possible to express my grief, nor could I come at the least Degree of submission to a final parting with him'. She sought comfort from prayer and consultation with a minister, as a result of which, when he finally died, 'I was perfectly composed'.[52] Henry Newcome's mother, seeing the lawyer come to her husband for him to make his will, left the room 'in extremity of grief'. Despite the fact that she was not told of his death, she called herself a widow and wished him not to be buried till she might be buried with him, 'and so the Thursday after she was ready to go to the grave with him, dying the night before.'[53]

For many women the loss of their husbands was a serious test of faith. Authors of diaries and autobiographies naturally stressed this aspect of bereavement because they set out to describe spiritual trials which they had overcome. Nevertheless, these accounts were concerned with the cataclysms of the believer's life. Mrs Hannah Allen, much of whose married life was spent apart from her first husband, wrote that when she heard of his death, some months after the event as he died overseas, 'I began to fall into a deep Melancholy, and no sooner did this black humour begin to darken my Soul, but the Devil set on with his former Temptations'.[54] Only her second marriage seems to have lifted her out of this melancholy. Mrs Alice Thornton wrote of the period following her husband's death as 'this vaile of tears and shaddow of death'. She added, 'My sorrowes and laments cannot be weighed for him which parted with the great and sole delight and comfort I esteemed of my life.'[55] Some women believed that their husbands were taken from them because they loved them too much. One testified that 'all this was to weane me from my sinnes, and too much doting upon an Husband, and other worldly injoyments', and another that 'The Lord discovered to me, that I had loved my Husband in a fleshly love, making an idoll of him'.[56] There is a striking familiarity in these accounts of the numbness, confusion, and despair of grief. These are not people whose feelings for one another are in any doubt.

CONCLUSION

One of the most important features of life in the seventeenth-century was the way in which people prepared themselves for death, both their own and the deaths of those nearest to them. It is in this area that Lawrence Stone's conclusions are most dubious. He deduces from the fact that people began to distance themselves emotionally from their dying relations that these relationships were less close than they are in the modern family. Childbirth and infection killed many people before they had a chance to develop protracted illnesses, and relatives seem to have begun the process of grieving during the short illnesses from which so many people died. These who were spared felt that they were the recipients of God's mercy.

Although many seventeenth-century expressions of grief seem rather abrupt and centred upon religious concerns, they are not indicative of any less affection, rather they are indicative of a more conscious process of withdrawal by the living person from the dying or the dead. It was this withdrawal which promoted the resignation which it was essential to cultivate in an age when medical intervention was likely to precipitate rather than prevent fatalities. The frequent repetition of fears that the dying person would not last the night or the next few hours, the mental leave-taking were all part of the preparations made by the living in the face not just of the likelihood, but of the probability that the sick person would not recover.

Writers of diaries and religious testimonies tended to shun prolonged expressions of grief as being something which intruded upon God's workings; God had decided to take one of his people who would be better off in the hereafter than in this troubled world, hence protracted grief seemed to be challenging God's will. Bitterness at the loss of someone was an even more reprehensible emotion. On the other hand, much of the evidence used here had the declared intention of spiritual self-examination, so it was natural for writers to describe their feelings in terms of God's working on the human world and to say more about their relationship with God than about that with the deceased.

So far, grief has been considered as an aspect of people's emotional and spiritual lives, but in seventeenth-century England it was also regarded as a potentially fatal affliction. We have seen how Henry Newcome's mother died within a few days of her husband and John Evelyn was convinced that the deaths of his sister and her baby contributed to his mother's death.[57] John Graunt's late-seventeenth-century study of the London bills of mortality shows that grief was recognized as a cause of death; in the City of Westminster in 1632 eleven deaths from grief were listed, compared with 628 from old age. In his analysis of the figures for the whole of London, Graunt distinguishes between diseases and casualties and numbers amongst the casualties 279 cases of grief.[58] Unfortunately we know nothing more about these cases, though it is probable that they were people who had recently lost a spouse or close relation.

The physician Richard Napier often included grief in the lists of symptoms of his patients, sometimes for the death of a relation months or even years previously. Alec Chapman consulted Napier in 1607, and his case notes for her record 'A greife taken some 3 yeare agoe about her frende, short winded, payne in the brest and back ill by fitts noe child this 10 yeare, her sicknes not above a day, but only a showe, urine white and thine'.[59] Even where he did not include grief, he often mentioned bereavement, as in the case of Mrs Mary Rider, 50 years a widow, whose husband died 3 weeks after Michaelmas and 'she payned in her head'.[60] Michael Macdonald says 134 of Napier's patients became mentally disturbed after the death of someone they loved and that nearly a third of the episodes of illness, despair, and madness in bereaved patients were attributable to the death of a spouse.[61] John

Symcotts, a Bedfordshire physician, attributed an attack of mother-fits in one of his female patients to 'taking much grief for the death of her daughter'.[62]

It was widely believed that grief could send people mad. Some examples have already been given and there are plenty more. Sarah Savage wrote on the death of her baby 'I could not keep my passion in bounds.'[63] John Sym, in his important work on suicide, stated that 'a man may indirectly murder himselfe, by way of omission; if out of sullennesse, griefe, or nigardize', though he argued that certain people were not guilty of self-murder because they were not responsible for their own actions.[64] It is, however, not always easy to distinguish between grief and melancholy; even Robert Burton does not do so, and both were associated with moist humours.

In conclusion, then, it seems probable that people in the seventeenth-century did not grieve less than they do now, their relationships were not less intense, but, because death was a much more everyday occurrence, they were better prepared for it. They knew better how to invoke the resignation which is an important part of accepting death. This can be seen most clearly in the spiritual preparations which people made for other people's deaths. Spiritual preparation for death is usually thought of as being something that one does for one's own death, but it is a very necessary part of grieving for someone else. It is this which appears so strongly in diaries and spiritual autobiographies of the seventeenth-century and can mislead us into thinking that the relationships which people were preparing to sever were in some way not as close as those which exist today.

5

DEATH AND THE DOCTORS IN GEORGIAN ENGLAND

ROY PORTER

Et plurima mortis imago – the face of death is everywhere – reads the caption in Hogarth's engraving, *The Company of Undertakers,* starring a cabal of the most notorious quacks of mid-Georgian England lording it over the august heads of the College of Physicians.[1] Hogarth was not alone, of course, in hinting that the medical profession, far from being death's enemy, was in reality its closest ally. Witticisms and proverbs alike reiterated the theme: 'a young doctor fattens the churchyard', 'a physician is more dangerous than the disease', or 'one doctor makes work for another'[2] – and it is a view much bruited in countless letters and diaries. 'About 4 o'clock yester Evening', the Revd William Jones of Broxbourne recorded in his diary, 'a putrid Fever, seconded by a blunderer in physic, carried off the poor Major'.[3] The widespread suspicion that medicine and mortality were in cahoots was pithily summed up in David Hume's advice to a friend:[4]

> I entreat you, if you tender your own Health or give any Attention to the Entreaties of those that love you, to pay no regard to Physicians . . . You cannot pay a moderate regard to them: your only safety is in neglecting them altogether.

– a sentiment summed up in Matthew Prior's mock epitaph:

> Cured yesterday of my disease
> I died last night of my physician.

Robert Burns for his part gave the theme a slightly different twist, seeing the relation between Death and the Doctors as one of rivalry to seize their victim. He conjured up a mock complaint by the former against the physician:[5]

77

Thus goes he on from day to day
Thus does he poison, kill an' slay
    An's weel paid for't!
Yet stops me o' my lawfu' prey
Wi' his damn'd dirt.

The suspicion that the medical profession positively revelled in the slaughter of the innocents was exacerbated, long before Burke and Hare, by public clamour against the surgeons' practice of *post mortem* dissections, and by the associated scandals of grave robbing and the resurrection men.[6] James Boswell for one, ever terrified of death, delighted in recording the supposed callousness of the profession, noting this tavern conversation while on an early visit to London:[7]

1 CITIZEN. Why, here is the bill of mortality. Is it right, doctor?

PHYSICIAN. Why, I don't know.

1 CITIZEN. I'm sure it is not. Sixteen only died of cholic. I dare say you have killed as many yourself.

Historians have echoed these charges, and statements abound in the recent literature implying that the most life-threatening thing a sick person could do in the Georgian age was consult a doctor. One highly influential interpretation has termed eighteenth-century hospitals 'gateways to death', and an American feminist has called the contemporary emergence of man-midwifery positively 'gynecidal'.[8]

This view of the Georgian medical profession as playing Jack Ketch to Death, physicking people to death, is of course bizarrely implausible: if doctors truly represented such an appalling health threat, why were people patronizing them in ever larger numbers, enabling the practice of medicine, as Geoffrey Holmes and Irvine Loudon above all have insisted, to become one of the eighteenth century's substantial growth sectors?[9] In any case, the facts, when scrutinized carefully, do not bear out the charge. But it would be no less dubious to fly to the contrary, eupeptic claim, as advanced by Peter Gay, that the eighteenth century witnessed a 'medical revolution' which made a substantial contribution to demographic growth.[10] The only disease which medicine made great strides towards conquering during the age of Enlightenment was smallpox, thanks first to inoculation, and then, at the very close of the century, to vaccination.[11] Smallpox aside, waves of typhus, typhoid, scarlatina, diphtheria, and half a dozen other lethal epidemic fevers – continued, intermittent, remittent, and eruptive – continued to decimate a population essentially unprotected by medicine's best efforts.

Man's vulnerability seemingly knew no bounds, and the slightest cause could have the most fatal effects.[12] As the Verney letters dolefully record, in 1699 the Queen of Portugal 'dyed with only making a holl in her yeare for to wear pendants' (fatal gangrene set in).[13] Dwelling upon the empire, the ubiquity, the omnipresence, of Death was not just a trope of Hellfire-preachers and lugubrious poets, but formed an integral part of the collective mind. Looking around his parish of Broxbourne at the close of the eighteenth century, the Revd William Jones reflected:[14]

> I have been *reading* the parish & hamlet; & cannot remark any one house tenanted by the same mortals with whom I conversed thirty-six years ago. Most of the houses have frequently changed their tenants. The houses, gardens, grounds & have been, to their utmost 'capability', improved & beautified: – & then Death has, without ceremony, or much previous notice, ejected the occupiers.

Overall, however, to hope to answer the question of how doctors and death related to each other in the eighteenth century by examining the Bills of Mortality, in order to gauge the aggregate demographic effect of medicine, is to tackle the problem in a misleading way.[15] Doctors certainly did change what Hogarth called 'the face of death', but they did so, not by substantially reducing its ravages or by increasing longevity, but by playing their part in a shift in common attitudes towards death and in forging new ways of coping with it.

As recent scholarship examining the early modern period has emphasized, Christianity represented – indeed, personified – Death as the Terror of Terrors.[16] The Black Death had, of course, cast a long, dark shadow, and its aftermath was the culture of the Dance of Death, the *Danse Macabre*, the worm-corrupted cadaver, the skull and crossbones, and the charnel house. This morbid brood was reinforced by a theology which saw death as the wages of sin, and stressed that for untold millions dying literally meant plunging into the infinite, endless torments of Hellfire. For its part, Protestantism severely repudiated the comforts of Roman Catholic doctrines of efficacious death-bed repentance and of salvation through sacraments or, in the long run, through purgatory.[17] Indeed, Protestant voluntarism stressed how the providential hand of God smote man with sudden death. Death would strike, out of the blue, at any instant. Hence the pious Christian must needs compose himself for death every day.[18] As Cotton Mather put it, 'A prudent man will *Dy Daily*'; Robert Horne recorded in similar vein 'I know not when I shall die, and therefore, every day shall be as my dying day',[19] and Bishop Ken's hymn advised Christians to 'Live ev'ry day as if 'twere thy last'. Indeed, latter-day handbooks of the *ars moriendi*, such as Jeremy Taylor's *Holy Living* and *Holy Dying*, emphasized how one's entire life should be preparatory for death. It 'must be the business of our whole Lives to prepare for Death', proclaimed William Sherlock in his influential *A Practical Discourse Concerning Death* (1690).[20]

For the divine arrow could strike at any moment: certainly providential, probably punitive and retributive. Death held a double terror, because it truncated this mortal life, while opening out a new unknown.[21] To men poised on the brink of eternity, the confrontation with death was bound to be awesome and overwhelming: 'death's a fearful thing', judges Claudio in *Measure for Measure* ('to die and go we know not where'), calling to mind similar chilling passages from *Hamlet*.

Thus all the pieces of the cultural jigsaw puzzle – from the macabre icons of Stuart funeral tablets, with their grinning deaths' heads, to the testimony of Puritan diaries, typified perhaps by Oliver Heywood, who kept meticulous memorials of every death that came to his attention[22] – interlock to confirm that within societies torn apart by the psychomachies of the Reformation and Counter-Reformation, death was the uniquely traumatic event. A man's unavoidable duty – his interest too – was positively to confront Death, and fill his mind and life with it. It was the ultimate test of a Christian. Above all, Death had to be faced head-on and vanquished. An eighteenth-century medical self-help manual, *Every Patient His Own Doctor*, significantly subtitled itself: *The Sick Man's Triumph Over Death and the Grave*.[23]

Death was the Terror. But it would be silly to assume that this perception of Death's Sting, understood within a faith vibrant with providentialism and eschatology, produced mass hysteria (though, as Michael MacDonald has demonstrated, the fear of death, damnation and perdition led many to despair and even suicide in Jacobean England).[24] Panic was obviated, above all, because religious practices and cultural resources helped people gird themselves against the Arch-foe, Death. Family prayers, fasting, repentance, devotions, Bible-reading, and so forth, both before and at the death-bed, fortified the faithful as they came to die the good death. For what the business of dying predominantly meant amongst the articulate élite in Stuart England was a religious rite, the liberation of the soul from its carnal prison, and its escape, hopefully, into the company of the blissful. The death-bed of the Puritan, Philip Henry, offers a good exemplar of the charged drama of this rite of passage. Sensing death coming over him, Henry took elaborate farewells of his family, bestowing upon them religious blessings and warnings, and uttering repeated pious ejaculations, mixed with prayers and Scripture texts. His biographer concludes:[25]

> His Understanding and Speech continued almost to the last Breath, and he was still in his dying Agonies calling upon God, and committing himself to him. One of the last words he said, when he found himself just ready to depart, was *O Death, where is thy* —— with that his speech falter'd and he quickly expired.

Within such religious protocols, specifically medical procedures for treating serious, prospectively fatal, illness, typically remained in the shadows, secondary, almost irrelevant. Both medical theory and medical practice traditionally respected the fact that life and death lay in the hands of Nature, as the best Classical medicine stipulated, or those of Providence. The art of physic as handed down from the Hippocratics was the business more of diagnosis and prognosis than of cure, and certainly not of 'miracle cure'.[26] Doctors and laymen accepted that death was inexorable, implacable. As the late-seventeenth-century children's rhyme 'Tom Thumb, his life and death' put it,[27]

> Where lying on his bed sore sicke
> King Arthur's doctor came

With cunning skill by physick's art,
To ease and care the same.

His body being so slender small,
This cunning doctor tooke
A fine perspective glasse with which
He did in secret look

Into his sickened body downe
And therein saw that Death
Stood ready in his wasted guts
To sease his vitall breath.

Hence, except in special cases, such as the lives of sovereigns, doctors did not attempt heroic intervention to delay or defy death. Indeed, the protracted and excruciatingly painful death-bed of Charles II – who of course civilly apologized to his physicians for being an unconscionable time a-dying – perhaps indicates why the faculty was wise to steer clear of futile heroics.[28]

What then did doctors do? Stuart physicians seem to have believed their role was to give an accurate and honest prognosis. It was their duty unambiguously to inform the dying of their imminent fate, to provide them good opportunity to put their affairs in order. Some, like Dr John Radcliffe, did so with extraordinary bluntness; on one notorious occasion, Radcliffe forecast William III only a short time to live, telling him, 'I would not have your Majesty's two legs for your three kingdoms', and on a later occasion he actually declined to attend the death-bed of Queen Anne.[29] Many physicians practised upon themselves what they preached. At the turn of the eighteenth century, Dr Samuel Garth, for example, suspecting his own end to be not far off, summoned fellow physicians to himself, commanding them to give an honest and explicit prognosis.[30]

Traditional medical etiquette thus required that the patient be fully informed of his likely fate. Then, their active part in the proceedings complete, physicians would withdraw, leaving the dying man to compose his mind and his will, and to make peace with God and his family. Case-notes show that Stuart practitioners such as Thomas Willis seemingly quit their patients after 'giving them over' ('he groaned horribly like a dying man . . . then judging the issue to be settled I bade farewell to him and his friends. At evening he died',[31] conclude Willis's notes on one of his patients). Here we should not attribute the doctor's departure to callous indifference, but rather to a sense of place, proper resignation, and dignity. Physic was for the living. Death was hardly integral to the agenda of medicine at all. Comb such huge medical compilations as Dr Robert James's *Medicinal Dictionary*, and you will find not even an entry for it.[32]

There was no sudden change of mind or practice with the coming of the eighteenth-century. Death's blow remained fell, mysterious, fatal. If certain eighteenth-century developments – such as the emergence of actuarial tables and life assurance[33] – betoken more secular attitudes, it remains beyond dispute that even in the polished obituary columns of the *Gentleman's Magazine*, death was still seen as aweful, arbitrary, absolute, striking out of the blue, bang in the midst of life, the divine reminder to man of his puny mortality:[34]

> Suddenly, the Rev. Mr M'kill, pastor of Bankend, of Duresdeen in Scotland. The manner of his death was very remarkable, and has made an impression upon the minds of his parishioners . . . He mounted the pulpit in good health, lectured as usual, and it being the last sabbath of the year, chose for his text these words: 'we spend our years as a tale that is told'. He was representing, in a very pathetic manner, the fleeting nature of human life, and of all earthly things, when, on a sudden, he dropped down in the pulpit and expired instantly.

Occasionally the dying man himself even spared the *Gentleman's Magazine's* obituarist the need to point the moral. One entry reads:[35]

> Suddenly, at Oswestry, Mr Harrison, supervisor of excise in that town. Just before he fell, he exclaimed, 'O Lord! how suddenly I am struck! All medical skill and assistance are useless!'

Protestant Dissenters above all continued to regard the act of dying as the ultimate duty of meeting one's Maker face-to-face. But the notion of Death as the supreme ordeal was not exclusive to them. Samuel Johnson's lifelong dread of death and his vision of it as a judgement were not unusual amongst Anglicans, especially those schooled, like Johnson, upon William Law.[36] Boswell shared Johnson's death fears, which perturbed him to the quick, and he himself emphasized in his journalism that it was foolish to regard Death in any other light than as a fearsome 'evil'.[37]

In 1712, Nathaniel Spinckes, a clergyman of the Church of England, penned a 500-page book, *The Sick Man Visited,* for the benefit of those undergoing what he programmatically called their 'last conflict with Death'. Spinckes said hardly a word about routine medicine, but elaborated at vast length about 'spiritual physic', spelling out protracted exercises in penitence and humiliation which the dying person ought to undergo, Joblike, under the 'correction' of disease and the 'usefulness' of sickness, all to gain a final glorious 'victory over Death'.[38] And a generation later, a pious physician, James Stonhouse, wrote a handbook for the gravely sick, *Friendly Advice to a Patient,* in which cleansing the conscience took absolute priority over any last-ditch measures the physician might try. The 'smarting rod' and the 'afflicting hand of God' should rightly render the patient 'chastened', since they were the 'effects of sin', albeit designed to prepare man for Death's 'awful sight'.[39]

Nevertheless, amongst the politer parts of the community, attitudes towards death did modulate with the spring-tide of the Enlightenment, or at least with the cooling of the fever-heat religiosity of the age of the Saints. In his recent analysis of responses to bubonic plague, Paul Slack has shown that the providentialism perhaps predominant in 1600 had largely given way by the 1720s to outlooks setting greater store by the practical efficacy of medical and civil measures in combating plague.[40] Other studies have shown how widely Georgian Anglicans, even Anglican clergymen, came to interpret sickness in naturalistic rather than providentialist terms: there is a profound gulf between Ralph Josselin and Parson Woodforde when confronted with sickness and death.[41]

Amongst the élite, rationalist, philosophical, and Stoic attitudes towards dying grew more conspicuous. The providence-challenging concept of 'natural death' became more widely-accepted.[42] A few *esprits forts* such as David Hume openly questioned the afterlife, accepted oblivion, and met their ends calmly, fired with neither hope nor fear. Hume notoriously bantered with Adam Smith on his death-bed as to how he lacked any good excuse for delaying embarkation upon Charon's boat across the Styx:[43]

> I thought I might say to him, 'Good Charon, I have been correcting my works for a new edition. Allow me a little time that I may see how the public receives the alterations'. But Charon would answer, 'When you have seen the effect of these, you will be for making other alterations. There will be no end of such.'

Attitudes such as Hume's positively scandalized Boswell and Johnson, terrified of damnation, oblivion or Hell. Hume, however, remained one of a tiny minority, though many more, while not denying the Christian message, distanced themselves from its regular liturgical forms. Thus essentially pagan burials became not uncommon, as in the funeral of John Underwood of Whittlesea, reported in the *Gentleman's Magazine* in 1733, in which the requiem involved the singing of the 31st Ode of Horace, and the mourners were instructed specifically to forget the memory of the dead man.[44] And paralleling this, new attitudes towards suicide gained ground, dispelling the traditional canon law characterization of it as a vice, sin, and crime, and increasingly looking upon it with pity, sympathy, and tolerance.[45]

Indeed, Ariès, Illich, and others have rightly perceived a fundamental transformation coming over the protocols of dying during the age of the Enlightenment.[46] It would be a misleading exaggeration to depict it as a dramatic switch of priorities from the expectation of the world to come to the parting from this one – though such a reorientation can be perceived. Rather, and especially in view of the collapse of literal belief in eternal hellfire,[47] much greater confidence came to be expressed in the assurance of a blissful future. Death ceased thus to be the ultimate enemy, requiring heroic acts of will, faith, purgation, and penitence. Instead dying came to be widely treated as an easy transition to a more blessed state, a natural metamorphosis to be accepted, even welcomed. Perhaps to twit the Dissenters, the dying Joseph Addison grasped his son's hand and declared, 'See in what peace a Christian can die'.[48] Death became a gentle friend. As the surgeon John Hunter reported on his death-bed, 'If I had a pen in my hand now, and were able to write, I could tell how easy and pleasant a thing it is to die'.[49]

Of course, such an approach was repulsive, even perverse, to many. James Boswell himself, brought up on Scottish Calvinism, continued to personify Death as the final foe. But in polished circles, the macabre associations of death became minimized – or sometimes displaced onto the vicarious, radical chic of the Gothick novel – and dying could be imagined as easy, as attractive as sleeping. Angels replaced traditional death-heads on tombs, funeral tablets increasingly trumpeted earthly virtues in place of divine justice, and the Gothick paraphernalia of yew trees and screech owls – the ambience of Gray's *Elegy* [50] – transformed death from transcendental trauma into an essentially human morality drama which taught that the paths of glory lead but to the grave. Thus for many, the act of dying ceased to be a joust with death, or a trial before a hanging judge, or even a leap in the dark. The idea of natural death came into vogue; and conversely, undue terror when contemplating that quintessentially natural process became stigmatized as itself a morbid disease: the dreaded hypochondria.[51]

As the eighteenth-century wore on, this reorientation of dying led to one particular development which mirrored so many other changes in life style: the family began to assume absolute centrality in the procedures of dying.[52] Our records of Georgian death-beds, taken from all ranks of society, do not suggest that they typically constituted great public scenes, with clergymen prominent and with doors flung open to the world, as in the traditional Catholic pattern analysed by Ariès and McManners.[53] Rather they reveal a sombre sadness, involving an intense concentrated quiet emotion, expressed largely through private person-to-person contact, within narrow circles of kith and kin. Even the clergy may hardly have been welcome around the sickbed. Attempting to visit ailing Dame Peake, Parson Jones was rebuffed by her nurse: 'She is not bad enough for *you*, Sir'.[54]

The keynotes were intimacy, sweetness, and peace. Lucy Warren, a seventeen-year-old clergyman's daughter from Edmonton early in the nineteenth-century, was fading away. The family physician diagnosed nervous rheumatism. He played a supportive role in her last weeks, and the family desired that 'no relief which medicine could afford might be neglected'. But what above all buoyed up the dying girl were the ministrations of her close family, as is evident from the elaborate journal they kept of her last days as she slipped into oblivion. It is easy to find such scenes mawkish or morbid even – Victorianism before the Victorians – and certainly their governing assumptions are through and through *Christian*. But what principally transpired on that death-bed was an intensified epitome of regular family relations; a dutiful daughter, who above all 'wished to avoid giving trouble', sustained with 'patience and submission', obeying doting parents who nursed, fed, and watched over her. By then, and in that family, there was no question of wrestling with death. Indeed, death itself had become unmentionable (her mother wrote of Lucy, 'she never mentioned the subject in express terms'). But death was now exemplarily embraced 'with serenity and calmness' as a sweet release, whose ready acceptance was meritorious.[55]

What then was the role of the doctor in this new model of dying? Did the profession play any part in establishing it in the first place? And within it, did they have a leading part? The answer is 'yes', but that role is not quite as depicted by recent historians. Illich in particular has argued that, puffed up by Enlightenment hubris, doctors began to nurse the illusion that they could actually conquer ageing and even eradicate death – could produce, at last, a medical conquest of death. Medicine became fired with the Baconian ambition of the prolongation of life. Indeed, perhaps wilfully blind to the irony of Swift's presentation of the wretchedly immortal Struldbrugs in *Gulliver's Travels*, Godwin, Condorcet, and other philosophers began to entertain conjecture of a this-worldly immortality, grounded upon new laws of health.[56] There is some truth in Illich's interpretation of death-denying doctors, for in hospital foundations, in smallpox inoculation, in the rise of a public health conscience, medicine undeniably went onto the offensive against disease. Certain developments – above all the much trumpeted Humane Movement, designed to resuscitate those apparently drowned – clearly mark a medical campaign to snatch people back from the jaws of death itself.[57]

But it would be wrong to infer from this, as Illich does, that the death-bed became a new battle-ground, witnessing a fight – to the death! – to keep patients alive at all costs, with the physician as the generalissimo – a fight for medical pride, a fight distantly responsible for the evils of today's life-support machine medicine, enslaved to self-imposed technological imperatives.[58]

The evidence we have, both of what doctors recommended, and of what they actually did at death-beds, directly contradicts the suggestion just raised, that the Georgian doctor saw it as his duty and his glory to preserve and prolong life at all costs. Dr John Ferriar insisted, at the dawn of the nineteenth-century, 'the physician will not torment his patient with unavailing attempts to stimulate the dissolving system, from the idle vanity of prolonging the flutter of the pulse for a few more vibrations'.[59] And, taking a broader perspective, the public involvement of doctors in the whole business of death remained fairly marginal: for example, well into the nineteenth-century, no medical competence was required of coroners; in England, though less so in Scotland, forensic and legal medicine, with their key roles in establishing the causes of death, remained backward disciplines.[60]

We can, however, perceive a certain medicalization of death emerging, though in different ways, a medicalization no less important (some might say 'sinister'), no less pregnant for the future. That is the development of the medical management of death at the bedside. Looking back from the late eighteenth-century, physicians often remarked with surprise upon the absence of their predecessors from the death-bed. Sir William Temple had explained it thus: 'an honest physician is excused for leaving his patient, when he finds the disease growing desperate, and can, by his attendance, expect only to receive his fees, without any hopes or appearance of deserving them'. Countering this view, Thomas Percival, in his pioneering volume of *Medical Ethics*, published in 1803, argued that there was much that the conscientious physician ought to be doing around the death-bed, 'by obviating despair, by alleviating pain, and by soothing mental anguish'. The old 'fanciful delicacy' over accepting fees ought to yield to this higher 'moral duty'.[61] John Ferriar agreed: 'When all hopes of revival are lost, it is still the duty of the physician to soothe the last moments of existence'. The doctor should be the one to decide: 'it belongs to his province, to determine when officiousness becomes torture'.[62] For Ferriar, the physician's continued presence in the position of authority was vital, not least to curb the excesses of nurses and servants, paid to keep watch, with the violent and often cruel folkloric techniques for trying to revitalize the dying.[63]

Possibly paralleling the role that new professional undertakers were assuming in stage-managing funerals,[64] physicians increasingly argued that they possessed unique experience in piloting the therapeutically and emotionally optimum course of managing the last weeks, days, hours, of the dying. Thus, to some degree, the dying person himself ceased to be in charge of his own death, which instead became orchestrated by the physician, with the agreement of the family.

This argument might *prima facie* sound wildly anachronistic; for it so closely resembles the accusation made against today's medicine – the medicine of the terminal ward, the life-support system, and of pious lies and euphemisms. But not so; for the charge was quite explicitly levelled by contemporaries. As Thomas Sheridan contended in the 1760s, people were no longer allowed their own deaths; for, in the name of sympathy and avoiding distress, their families and doctors were allowing them to slip away oblivious to their fate: 'very few now die. Physicians take care to conceal people's danger from them. So that they are carried off, properly speaking, without dying; that is to say, without being sensible of it'.[65]

Evasion on that scale may have been unusual. But as the eighteenth-century wore on, and as fashionable physicians raised their aspirations to become trusted family advisers and intimates, they undeniably adopted a more managerial approach to the death-bed. The most spectacularly successful practice of this medicalization of dying comes from the early nineteenth-century, in the career of Sir Henry Halford, who became physician on an unparalleled scale to royalty and the aristocracy, not least because of his diplomacy in helping to reinforce, at every stage, what had become the widespread desire for easy death.[66] With patients he recognized to be dying, it was Halford's policy long to withhold the truth, and instead to give prevarications or cheerful prognostications. Optimism was therapeutically valuable. The second stage lay in preparing the sufferers and divulging the truth, at the appropriate moment, in time for the sufferer to set his house in order.

By no means, however, did that signal the end of the physician's role. Indeed, the most difficult, but valuable, part of his services was just beginning. For, third, the doctor must manage the actual process of ceasing to be. Here, Halford – a man, we are told, who had an 'innate shrinking from bodily pain' – stressed that the true priority must be to 'smooth the bed of death',[67] or in other words, to undertake the management of pain, thereby overcoming fear and restoring tranquillity, orchestrating an end which would be serene and blissful. In this Halford made it his 'rule in all cases of ministering to them such aid as medicines could supply', often using his own individual preparations.[68] The tactful Halford became the most sought-after physician of his age precisely because his patients had confidence that through generous medication he would not let them die in agony. Rumour had it that:[69]

> A lady of the highest rank is reported to have declared she would rather die under Sir Henry Halford's care than recover under any other physician.

In turn, Halford's own dying was 'only partially relieved by full doses of opium',[70] lamented his biographer, Dr William Munk, who himself went on to write *Euthanasia, or Medical Treatment in Aid of an Easy Death* (1887).[71]

What Halford encoded was already becoming common practice long before. During the course of the eighteenth-century, physicians seem increasingly to have shrunk from telling patients outright of their impending quietus. Dr William Buchan for example repudiated the custom of 'prognosticating . . . the patient's fate, or foretelling the issue of the disease', on the grounds that 'we do not see what right any man has to announce the death of another, especially if such a declaration has a chance to kill him'. Instead of this 'vanity', Buchan recommended something altogether more tactful: 'a doubtful answer . . . or one that may tend rather to encourage the hopes of the sick, is surely the most safe'.[72] Therapeutic management came to the fore. In this, Matthew Baillie's approach was exemplary. He was called in to treat the failing Mrs Wynne. Her daughter records in her diary:[73]

> Dr Baillie saw Mama – he says he cannot cure her, but hopes to relieve her and to prevent her illness from getting worse with a prospect of getting better.

Above all, it seems that in the management of desperate and terminal cases, medical policy came to prescribe optimism, as the most effective psychotherapy. Parson William Jones recorded about the doctors around the death-bed of his friend Mills:[74]

> Mr Worthington, who attended poor Mills at first, and Mr Harold who succeeded him, . . . endeavoured to buoy him &

Mrs Mills up with hopes of his recovery, whereas I
pronounced him, from the first, to all but himself, a
condemned man & his case a lost one.

Symptomatically here, in this new age of supercharged sensibility,
even the parson declined to inform the dying man of his fate.
Above all, doctors devised strategies in which divulgence of truth
to their patients became measured according to their own
yardsticks of therapeutic appropriateness, the physician's view of
the patient's interests. As Benjamin Rush put it,[75]

Physicians are sometimes called upon to mention the deaths
of relations to their patients. This should never be done at
once. They should be first told that they were sick, and in
great danger, and the news of their death should not be
communicated until after a second or third visit.

Death without fear, thought Dr John Ferriar, should resemble
'falling asleep'.[76] Indispensable to that strategy were effective
sedative drugs. It was widely accepted that Halford drew liberally
upon a range of soporific draughts, doubtless mainly opium-based,
to slide his patients towards oblivion. We sometimes assume that
our own generation is the first in which our going out of the world
typically involves being medicated up to the eyeballs. That would
be a great mistake. For the first golden age of the stupefying drugs
was the eighteenth-century. I noted above that Enlightenment
medicine was able to do very little to prolong life. That is correct.
But if it could not delay death, it could make it much less
agonizing. We see sickness and medicine before the coming, say,
of anaesthetics, as being excruciatingly painful: indeed, Guy
Williams has called his popular book about eighteenth-century
medicine *The Age of Agony*.[77] There is much truth in this. But
relative to earlier times, the eighteenth-century was an anaesthe-
tized age, precisely because of the startling surge in the use of
powerful narcotics, drawing above all upon alcohol and opium
and its derivatives, laudanum and paregoric; a habit sanctioned by
regular doctors, and encouraged amongst the people at large by a
free market in the sale of drugs.

Fixated upon the symbolic importance of Coleridge, De
Quincey, and the Romantic imagination, our standard histories of
opium use essentially open their stories near the dawn of the

nineteenth century;[78] understandably perhaps, for we lack in-depth research on the economic and therapeutic history of the whole battery of medicaments as prescribed by eighteenth-century physicians and as bought over-the-counter by that highly self-dosing culture. Abundant evidence, however, points to increasingly heavy consumption of opium before the nineteenth-century, used as an analgesic, a sedative, a febrifuge, and as a specific against gastro-intestinal problems. Opiates were widely recommended, almost as a panacea, as medical magic, by eminent physicians of the second half of the eighteenth century. Terry Parsinnen has claimed that 'it was not until the 1830s and 1840s that opium assumed a crucial therapeutic role in English medicine',[79] but this is certainly wrong, maybe by as much as a century. As early as the 1670s Dr Thomas Sydenham had been praising opium to the skies ('medicine would be a cripple without it'). Sydenham's championship echoed down the eighteenth century in treatises such as Dr John Jones's *Mysteries of Opium Reveal'd* (1700),[80] George Young's *Treatise on Opium* (1753)[81] and Dr Samuel Crumpe's *Inquiry into the Nature and Properties of Opium* (1793),[82] all notably sanguine about the absence of serious risk attending the medicinal use of the drug. Dosing with opium was also programmatic to the therapeutic system – Brunonianism – adumbrated by John Brown in Edinburgh and mirrored by Benjamin Rush in Philadelphia, in which it was used both to calm but, above all, to stimulate. Rush prescribed opium as a universal sedative.[83] In cases of grief and depression, for instance, he wrote, 'the first remedy ... indicated ... is opium. It should be given in liberal doses'.[84]

A glance at Erasmus Darwin's large Midlands practice from the 1760s shows he was prescribing opium to his patients in massive quantities. Darwin advised opium for many complaints (for instance, for sleepwalking, 'Opium in large doses'), and recommended to select patients half a grain of opium a day 'as a habit'. His generous prescriptions of the narcotic may well have been responsible for the addiction of his friend and patient, Tom Wedgwood.[85] Moreover, with the emergence of a flourishing trade in potent patent and proprietary medicines, opiates got to the people in the form of nostrums such as The Solid Panacea, Dr Bate's Pacific Pill, Starkey's Pill, Matthews' Pill, and, most popular of all, Dover's Powders (a mixture of opium and ipecacuanha) and

Godfrey's Cordial.[86] A Nottingham chemist reported in 1808 that 'upwards of 200 lbs of opium and above 600 pints of Godfrey's Cordial are retailed to the poorer class in the year'.[87]

Writing from Jamaica, the Revd William Jones noted that 'opium is greatly used in this Island, & in high esteem among the sons of sorrow to remove their Melancholy & solace their cares. Heard a person mentioned who always spent three quarters of his patrimony on *crude Opium*'.[88] He might almost have been writing about England. Many eighteenth-century figures became almost as reliant upon opiates as did Coleridge or De Quincey a little later. Under these circumstances, it is hardly surprising that many individuals, on their own initiative, swallowed heavy doses of such narcotics in their dying weeks or months: Sir Joshua Reynolds is a well-known case in point. And many physicians themselves prescribed liberal dosages in order to smooth the path to death.[89] Rather like heroic criminals on the way to Tyburn, given Dutch courage with brandy to make a good end, people increasingly died insensible, stupefied with drugs, often medically prescribed, and thus conformed to the new model of the art of dying well. As Benjamin Rush put it, 'OPIUM has a wonderful effect in lessening the fear of death. I have seen patients cheerful in their last moments, from the operation of this medicine upon the body and mind'.[90] The notable late-eighteenth-century clinician, William Heberden, was of a similar mind. Arguing that when physicians could not vanquish death, they should 'try to disarm death of some of its terrors', he prescribed opium liberally so that life might 'be taken away in the most merciful manner'.[91]

Indeed, as with overdoses nowadays, it is sometimes hard to tell with eighteenth-century deaths whether the pharmaceutical fix was intended to calm, stimulate, or to kill, as when Horace Walpole reported the end of Lord Crawford who 'died, as it supposed, by taking a large quantity of laudanum'.[92] It is highly significant that as soon as he knew he was near his end, Samuel Johnson quite deliberately left off his medically-prescribed opiates, so that he could pass over in full possession of his faculties: 'I will take no more physic, not even my opiates; for I have prayed that I may render up my soul to God unclouded'.[93] Was Johnson by then in a minority? The increasing occurrence of 'insensible death' may well help explain late-eighteenth-century fears about premature burial.[94]

In 1800 no less than in 1650, dying the 'good death' was critically important. Back in the seventeenth-century, dying well meant total vigilance, being at every instant prepared to meet your Maker. Death was fearful, courage was essential, and Victory was the prize. Increasingly, such a vision of Death's torments seemed incompatible with a loving and even with a just God, and with humanity towards the dying themselves. Under a benevolent Deity, surely death was not to be feared; it was, after all, only like a sleep. And if like a sleep, surely it could be encountered with all of sleep's serenity. If then dying were no great trauma, its management by the medical profession seemed merely a logical extension of the routine care they offered. Death's sting had indeed been drawn.

6

THE BURIAL QUESTION IN LEEDS IN THE EIGHTEENTH AND NINETEENTH CENTURIES

JIM MORGAN

Earth burial of the dead in churchyards probably began in the Anglo-Saxon period and in the next thousand years they accommodated thousands of bodies. While the population remained small and located in villages the yards could, allowing for the natural processes of decay, cope with these numbers. In towns overcrowding of bodies did occur and this was dealt with by building charnel houses to receive the bones found when ground was reused before decay was complete. The rise of population in the eighteenth and nineteenth centuries and its concentration in towns greatly increased the pressures on burial space in urban communities. The measures taken by sextons to manage their graveyards so as to cope with the demand led to practices which were seen as a threat to public health and decency. The burial question was therefore a special instance of the wider sanitary issues posed by the urban growth of the period. While these wider issues have been thoroughly researched by historians the specifics of the burial question have been relatively neglected. The purpose of this chapter is to establish a conceptual and chronological framework within which the Burial Question may be more widely considered by examining the problem in the expanding town of Leeds during the eighteenth and nineteenth centuries against the background of a brief discussion of national developments.

In 1700 the churchyard of Anglican parish churches provided, by law, a place of burial for all but the unbaptized and the suicide, and usually for those as well in an unconsecrated portion of the yard. Alternative provision by Nonconformist chapels was small and unimportant. In Leeds in the 1730s some 96 per cent of the township's dead were buried in its Anglican churchyards with 79 per cent interred at the parish church itself. Only two dissenting chapels had small graveyards.[1] Burial provision may therefore be viewed as a facet of the universalist claims of the Established Church to cater for the spiritual needs of all English people and the marginalization of the rival claims of the Nonconformists in the early eighteenth century.[2] In its virtual monopoly of burial ground provision in Leeds the Church came close to universality in practice.

In public health terms this meant that financial and administrative arrangements for the continuing sanitary disposal of the dead existed. If more burial space were required the parochial authorities could purchase land for a churchyard by levying a church rate at a vestry meeting. Thus it was easier to respond to a need for additional burial ground in an expanding town than to other sanitary problems like sewage disposal for which only inadequate, if any, authorities existed. For example, the population of Leeds township expanded from about 6,000 in 1700 to 48,603 in 1821 and had the burial space remained unchanged during that period then by 1821 the parish churchyard would have been receiving more than four times the number of bodies with which it could decently cope.[3] In fact the Vestry three times, in 1776, 1800 and 1814, enlarged the parish churchyard and trebled its size at a cost of over £2,300.[4] This maintained a constant balance between the number of burials and the size of the parish churchyard throughout the period. Nor did the Anglican near-monopoly of burial provision change significantly with 93 per cent of burials in its churchyards between 1811 and 1820, a reduction of only 4 per cent on the position in the 1730s. The parish churchyard's contribution had fallen to 70 per cent but this is probably an underestimate caused by defective registration there. Six Nonconformist chapels now had graveyards but only one was used to any great extent.[5] Until 1820, therefore, the traditional parochial arrangements for the burial of the dead proved able in Leeds to cope with the pressures exerted by the huge increase in the town's population.

The period 1820–40 saw these traditional arrangements come under increasing pressure both in Leeds and elsewhere. This was due both to the continued urban population growth and consequent deterioration in public health conditions and to a rising Nonconformist challenge to the universalist claims of the Church of England. The pressures on burial ground were experienced most acutely in London's small churchyards. In 1814 the Westminster Improvement Commissioners reported to the House of Commons that the churchyard of St Margaret's, Westminster could not be used much longer.[6] Later the activities of the 'resurrectionists' in the 1820s led to the first public campaign on the burial ground question led by a London barrister, George Carden, who was instrumental in creating the first major addition to the solution of London's burial space in the nineteenth century.[7] Already, by the 1820s, the inability or disinclination of the small London parishes to provide more burial ground had provided an opportunity for private speculators to step in to meet the demand. They usually provided vaults under chapels which were quickly over-filled and became notorious in the reformers' literature of the 1840s.[8] Carden initiated the discussions that led to the formation by statute in 1833 of the first private cemetery company at Kensal Green.[9] Six more cemetery companies were formed in London by 1841 and they set important precedents and standards. The cemeteries were carefully landscaped and situated on the outskirts of the city, forming a model for the public cemeteries of the 1850s and beyond.[10] They represented a market solution to the burial problem and proved profitable to their investors but their high burial fees and distance from the main centres of population meant they made only a limited contribution to the solution of London's burial ground problem.[11]

The most significant innovation by the companies was the division of their cemeteries into consecrated and unconsecrated portions. This met one of the main Nonconformist objections to the Anglican monopoly of burial provision, that only Anglican clergy could officiate in consecrated ground. However, when Leeds acquired a private cemetery company in 1833 the whole of the cemetery was left unconsecrated so that it was as much a Nonconformist monopoly as the churchyard was an Anglican monopoly, and it was intended as such. The managing committee included many of the most prominent Nonconformists in the town and they were making a political statement of their voluntarist opinions.[12] This brings us to the second, and much more profound, challenge to the traditional parochial arrangements for the burial of the dead.

As we have already seen these enabled new burial ground to be provided by additions to the parish churchyard financed by a church rate. These rates were also levied on property owners to finance Anglican church building and maintenance and increasingly after 1820 Nonconformists were opposed to such rates. Their reason was a fundamental objection to funding the Established Church by a rate levied on everyone regardless of their denomination or belief. On the contrary the Church should be financed by the voluntary contributions of its members in the same way as the Nonconformist chapels. A rate for a burial ground was no different. All paid and yet the burials in the churchyard could be conducted only by Anglican clergy according to Anglican rites.[13] When, therefore, a further enlargement of the parish churchyard of Leeds was proposed in 1825 it was opposed in a vigorous campaign by the local Nonconformists.[14] The local press gave the antagonists the platform for their clash of principles:

> The church, established by law, is the church in which all of his Majesty's subjects may celebrate the worship of Almighty God; and the law which governs that church, admits all his Majesty's subjects to a participation in the benefits of that worship, and excludes none from its ordinances, but on the contrary admits everyone on the same terms. The necessary consequence of which is, that everyone should be rated in respect of the property they possess, to the maintenance of the Establishment which provides for the worship of Almighty God.[15]

> A Church burial ground, though purchased by a rate levied indiscriminately on all classes, immediately becomes the exclusive freehold of the Church. Sextons and curates qualify to vote for Tories in elections on it . . . Dissenters and their ministers who wish to perform the last sad services over their remains are excluded from it; the servants of the established church pocket all the emoluments derived from it; it is part of the closed corporation system and the public should set their faces decidedly against it.[16]

Opinion in the Leeds Vestry changed radically between 1814, when the third enlargement of the churchyard was sanctioned, and 1825 when a further extension was refused. In 1814 the vestry was still controlled by a Tory-Anglican élite of woollen merchants who had dominated the economy of the town throughout the eighteenth century. However, since the 1780s changes in the production and marketing of woollen cloth had been undermining this dominance. At the same time a rival economic élite was emerging, composed of successful entrepreneurs in the expanding textile, engineering, tanning and coal industries. Also the growth of population and wealth gave a new prominence and independence to the professional and retailing sectors of the local economy. This new élite tended to hold Liberal-Nonconformist beliefs. Finally, while the workers of the town did not support their employers uncritically on political issues they were hostile to the established élite and could be relied upon to provide mass support at Vestry meetings. This was important because the Vestry was an open meeting, in theory of ratepayers, at which decisions were normally taken by a show of hands in which non-ratepayers could in fact participate. The Vestry therefore was the institution at which the Tory-Anglican élite's political dominance could be challenged by its Liberal-Nonconformist rival.[17] The challenge was led by Edward Baines, Senior, editor of the *Leeds Mercury* whose ownership Baines had secured with the help of some prominent Nonconformists.[18]

Baines's campaign focused on the issue of church rates and their use to purchase additional burial ground because of a specific controversy that began in 1825. The proposed churchyard extension was attached to one of the three 'New Churches' built in Leeds using the funds provided by the Church Building Act of 1818. Although built with public funds the upkeep of these churches fell on the parish which meant that the Leeds Nonconformists now had three more Anglican churches to pay for.[19] This they refused to do and at stormy Vestry meetings, attended by thousands, in 1825 and 1827 a church rate for the maintenance of these churches and for establishing burial ground attached to one of them was refused. Why should, demanded Baines in 1827, 'the dissenters . . . the methodists, or any person who attends any other place of worship than the new churches . . . be called upon to support those churches?'[20] Baines and his allies were, however, in a difficult tactical position. He recognized the need for more burial ground and that a church rate was the only practicable way of obtaining it but did not wish to concede the principle of financing the new churches out of the rates. His dilemma had to be faced squarely in 1828 when the Tory churchwardens were replaced in the annual Vestry elections by Liberal Anglicans who were opposed to church rates but were not prepared to break the law. As it was now their legal responsibility to levy a church rate they did so to pay, not only for the upkeep of the new churches, but also for the new burial ground.[21] Ironically the rate was the highest of the century but the Liberals had the last word. Strict economy was then enforced so that the rate demands fell and then ceased altogether in 1835; effectively church rates ended in Leeds some thirty-three years before they were abolished by parliament in 1868.[22] Thus the parochial administration in Leeds continued to be the means of providing burial ground but clearly the system was now under severe strain. Also the Anglican monopoly of burial was under greater challenge. Between 1831 and 1840 the Anglican churchyards' share of the township's interments fell to 85 per cent, with the parish church contributing 67 per cent towards that figure. In the final five years of the decade the proportion fell still more to 80 per cent with the cemetery company contributing over 15 per cent to the non-Anglican total.[23]

The final collapse of the system of parochial burial provision occurred between 1840 and 1860. At the national level concern and debate over the state of burial grounds as a threat both to public health and public decency coincided with the wider debate on the sanitary problem. In 1839 a London doctor, G. A. Walker, published his 'Gatherings from Graveyards' which was a passionate exposure of the horrors to be found in London's overcrowded burial grounds.[24] W. A. Mackinnon took up the issue in parliament and chaired a Select Committee on Interment in 1842.[25] The prevailing miasmatist theory of disease transmission suggested that the 'exhalation of the gases and the emanations of the dead into the air' posed a serious threat to public health.[26] Even more serious was the threat to public morality created by the treatment of human remains. Giving evidence to Mackinnon's committee, Robert Baker, the foremost sanitary reformer in Leeds, described the following incident in the parish churchyard there:

> I was in the ground last Wednesday collecting information
> and the sexton took me to a grave which they were digging for
> the interment of a female; two feet below the surface they
> took out the body of an illegitimate child, and it had been

buried for five years; below that and two feet six inches below the surface were two coffins side by side, the bones were in a state of freshness; the matter had putrified off the bones, but they were perfectly fresh; they were thrown on the surface and at that time the person came in who was going to do the interment; he spoke to me about it and made use of the expression, 'Look! these are the skulls of my father and brother and the bones of my relations – is not this a bad business?'[27]

Both these issues aroused the interest of Chadwick and in 1843 he produced an *Interment Report* as a supplement to his *Sanitary Report* of 1842.[28] Chadwick was no friend of what he regarded as corrupt and inefficient parochial authorities and proposed an alternative non-ecclesiastical administration of burial provision.[29] When, as a member of the General Board of Health, he had the opportunity to deal with London's burial problem he obtained in 1850 statutory powers to nationalize both the burial provision and the funeral trade of the capital. One national cemetery was created by the purchase of the Brompton Cemetery Company but when the implications of his schemes for government borrowing and the threat to private funeral interests became clear they were stopped.[30] Nevertheless it was evident to the government that more burial ground was required in the large towns and especially London; it was also evident that the parochial authorities could no longer act in large towns because of Nonconformist opposition to church rates. The Burial Acts of 1852 and 1853 instead empowered localities to elect Burial Boards which could levy a rate with which to establish public burial grounds. This was a non-sectarian provision in that the grounds were normally divided into consecrated and non-consecrated portions so that all sects and denominations could use them.[31]

This was the solution adopted in Leeds ten years earlier. The burial question here reappeared in 1841 when a scandal at the most recent extension of the churchyard revealed that it was nearly full only eleven years after it had been purchased.[32] The Leeds Liberals still controlled the Vestry meeting and therefore the parochial administration but since 1836 Nonconformists, not Anglicans, had been elected to it. Also no church rate had been levied since 1835.[33] Some Liberals, such as Edward Baines, Junior (the son and successor of Baines Senior), were prepared to support a rate for the purchase of a burial ground 'for the *common* benefit of the inhabitants and especially of the poor'.[34]

Most were not and the son of the former leader of opposition to church rates in Leeds was shouted down at the Vestry meeting which discussed the issue.[35] For most Nonconformists it was an issue of principle: 'all compulsory payments, which directly or indirectly, go towards sanctioning the connexion between the State and any one religious sect are wrong.'[36] In 1841 the Vestry decisively rejected a church rate to purchase additional burial ground in contrast to the decision of 1829.[37]

Nevertheless, as Baines wrote, 'the case seems to be one of absolute necessity.... The dead cannot remain unburied, the parochial burial ground will, in four months...be full'.[38] A solution was found by linking the burial ground problem with the wider issue of sanitation. The need for sanitary measures in Leeds had been identified in a report of 1839 and after much debate it was decided to seek a local statute to grant wide sanitary powers to the borough council. In 1842 this was proceeding through parliament and permission was granted to add a separate Burial Grounds Act; both became law in the summer of that year.[39]

This act was the first of its kind and established the first local authority burial ground in the country. It was non-sectarian in that it was administered by a committee of the council and that the ground was divided with separate Anglican and Nonconformist chapels.[40] The ground was opened in 1845 but an acrimonious dispute about compensation to the Vicar of Leeds for his loss of burial fees when the parish churchyard was closed meant that the ground was not fully in use until 1848.[41] The Home Secretary finally closed the churchyard in 1854 and the Anglican domination of burial provision in Leeds finally ended.[42]

The last phase of the Burial Question saw debate shift from the large cities to the smaller towns and villages. The issue too had changed. Many smaller communities had no need for more burial space and so the churchyard continued in use. The difficulty was that Nonconformists could not conduct a service there and from 1860 a campaign began to open Anglican churchyards to the clergy of all denominations.[43] Eventually the Liberal Party leadership adopted the campaign and access rights were gained in 1880 even for those wishing to conduct a non-religious ceremony.[44] Thus Anglican exclusivity was ended. Ironically, during the closing years of the nineteenth century the Church even found itself positively excluded from the burial grounds of some towns. The Burial Acts of the 1850s had insisted on a divided ground but a Cemeteries Act of 1879 provided local authorities with powers to create undivided grounds. Some Nonconformist-dominated authorities did this, ostensibly on the grounds of economy because only one chapel had to be built. The effect was to exclude Anglican clergy because they could not legally officiate on unconsecrated ground. They were therefore now in the same position as the Nonconformist clergy had been at the beginning of the century. These disputes were finally settled by further legislation in 1900 when the Burial Question was finally laid to rest.[45]

Sectarian quarrels were thus inextricably bound up with the sanitary issue of the disposal of the dead. Viewed as a facet of the history of public health in the nineteenth century the Burial Question followed a parallel path in that significant public debate and state action began in the early 1840s. However the barrier to action was not, as with sanitation, a lack of competent authorities with the power to act but the inability of perfectly competent authorities to act because of sectarian dispute, which in Leeds was the vehicle for the assertion of the ideological and political aspirations of new economic and social groups.

These disputes ensured that the Burial Question continued as a public issue long after debate on public health had ceased. The Burial Question may therefore be more properly seen as part of a transition during which the monopolistic claims of the established church were undermined by sectarian challenges, leading to a voluntarist and then ultimately secular society. Thus the Anglican monopoly of burial provision was replaced from the 1840s by cemeteries in which all denominations could officiate; at the same time the cemeteries were administered by secular local authorities. Later in the century the introduction of cremation in the 1880s signalled the beginning of a rational and secular solution to the disposal of the dead very different from the age old practice of earth burial in the churchyard.[46]

One last point may be touched on in conclusion. The new dignified and landscaped cemeteries served many purposes: providing a setting in which the grief of the bereaved could be expressed and assuaged in monument and verse; a setting also in which the wealthy could assert through prominently sited and imposing monuments the influence they exerted in life; and finally as a source of 'rational recreation'. Cemeteries were often the nearest open space in large towns and fountains and public seats were frequently erected in them. Thousands attended some funerals in Leeds and it was hoped by the middle-class reformers who campaigned for the cemeteries that they would create a 'solemn and religious impression on the minds' of the workers who visited them.[47] One may doubt whether the 'socialist' funeral conducted by Robert Owen at the private cemetery in Leeds in 1840 was what the reformers had intended; but they were true to their voluntarist principles in allowing the ceremony to proceed despite the outraged protests of the local curate.[48]

7

WHY WAS DEATH SO BIG IN VICTORIAN BRITAIN?

RUTH RICHARDSON

The historical roots and causes of phenomena as complex as the Victorian celebration of death are rarely simple or easily discerned. Like the well-known historical difficulty about finding the root cause of the Industrial Revolution, there may be manifold answers to the question posed in my title: and the argument I propose in this chapter goes only *part* of the way towards providing one. Nevertheless, I think I have something of importance to contribute which I have not seen raised before.[1] I refer to the influence upon eighteenth- and nineteenth-century death culture of the history of medicine, and more particularly, of the history of anatomical endeavour.

In this chapter, I seek to point out one important influence hitherto missed by historians of death. I argue that both the professionalization of undertaking and the development of the extramural cemeteries received strong impetus from public fear of grave-robbery for dissection. I go on to suggest that one of the sources for the extraordinary energy directed towards the celebration of death in the Victorian era may have derived from the Georgian horror of bodysnatching. Lastly I argue that the means by which the bodysnatchers were rendered redundant itself promoted the development of the nineteenth-century under-taking business and hence the Victorian celebration of death, particularly in lower social strata.

Modern perceptions of the Victorian celebration of death are probably broadly correct. Readers may have a mental picture of the Victorian funeral, with its glass hearses led by undertakers with hats festooned in black, their black horses attired in black velvet and nodding black plumes. Our image of Victorian widows wil' probably be of women seemingly buried under heavy mourning clothes for months, years and even for life. Many readers will be aware of how pervasive were the paraphernalia of death which reached right down to the domestic particularity of mourning teapots, handkerchiefs, jewellery and parasols, window blinds and doorknockers swathed in crape. Even the width of the black edges on stationery was graded by funerary etiquette. And of course there are all those famous cemeteries full of Victorian monuments.

We recognize, perhaps with some disquiet, that the Victorian celebration of death was largely about show – about the conspicuous consumption of what we now view as a dubious good. Death provided the Victorians an opportunity for making public statements about social worth which were, more often than not, in fact largely about monetary value.

Despite the embarrassment and insecurity concerning it in our own era, death has always been the locus for important rites of passage. Funerary display is the focus of much attention in many societies, so it should not be unexpected that this was also the case in one grappling with the social upheaval and flux of an industrializing and colonial power. Such a culture, at such a time, could almost be expected to provide a hospitable growth medium for the commercial exploitation and development of indigenous funerary custom and belief. The Victorian era was one with an obsessive interest in the gradations of social placing; and death served as a prime means of expressing, and of defining, social place.

Nevertheless it should be stressed that a great deal of what is generally assumed a Victorian phenomenon was fairly well formed before Victoria ever took the throne. A study of undertakers' records shows that what we take for the Victorian funeral was already well-established among higher income groups in the Georgian era. Take a glance at the books of a fashionable London undertaker in 1824, the same year Lord Byron died at Missolonghi. The funeral account of an aristocratic lady lists copious details, over two-and-a-half ledger pages, of funerary minutiae, among which appear the following:

> A strong coffin with white padded satin lining and pillow,
> mattress, sheet and a padded satin-lined lid; a very strong
> outside oak case, covered with superfine black cloth, best

silvered nails, and rich ornaments also silvered; a rich plume
of black ostrich feathers, and a man to carry ditto; silk scarves,
hatbands and gloves for attendants; gifts of ditto for
mourners; feather-pages and wands; mutes on horseback; silk
dressings for poles; best black velvet pall and saddlecloths for
horses; more ostrich feathers; cloaks; pages with truncheons
and staves, hatbands and gloves; crape, attendants; rooms on
the road; coachmen; feathermen; and turnpike fees to the
family seat in Herefordshire – costing total of £803.11.0.[2]

Although a mid-Victorian funeral for a person of the same
social status would possibly have been yet more ostentatious, the
paraphernalia of funerary celebration evident in these details
(from a longer list) build up to a picture of a fairly ostentatious
celebration of death enacted for, and funded by, a generation
already adult before Victoria's accession. Yet the undertaker's
provisions are listed and described in such a straightforward and
businesslike way it is clear enough that such a funeral was not a
rarity for a person of high social status in the Georgian era.

Equally significantly, the earliest and most important of the
huge urban cemeteries were planned or already in existence
before Victoria's reign began. The ex-Regent, George IV, was still
on the throne when Liverpool Necropolis was created, and both
Kensal Green Cemetery and Glasgow Necropolis were opened
during the reign of Victoria's predecessor, William IV. When
Highgate Cemetery was opened in 1839 Victoria was just twenty
years of age, and had been Queen only two years. Planning for
each of these enterprises had taken several years to reach fruition.
The shareholders investing in them as well as the customers who
queued to buy burial plots in them represented a constituency of
financially solvent adults whose opinions and attitudes to death
had been formed prior to Victoria's reign. The first great
extramural cemeteries were in fact the product of *Georgian*, not
Victorian, sensibility.

The chronology these evidences present to us suggests that
elements of the Victorian celebration of death may represent
earlier influences working their way through British death culture,
and down the social scale, over the course of the nineteenth
century. If this is so, what could these earlier influences have been?

During the entire period from about 1700 and reaching a peak in the early nineteenth century – in parallel with the growth of private anatomy tuition – bodysnatching was both widespread and lucrative.[3] The only legal source of corpses for dissection during the entire period was the gallows, which provided a pitifully inadequate supply for the expanding and profitable business of medical teaching. Demand promoted supply. A class of entrepreneurs arose whom we know as the bodysnatchers; at the time they were also referred to as 'grave-robbers' and 'resurrectionists'. The period from about 1750 until the passage of the Anatomy Act in 1832 was the bodysnatchers' heyday.

The fear of bodysnatching was extremely pervasive, most noticeably in metropolitan and urban areas, but also in suburban and rural districts. A strong and deeply held antipathy to the violation of the grave was evident at all levels of society. Many expedients were devised to prevent, thwart, or at the very least to hinder the bodysnatchers. There were furious and often physically violent attacks upon grave-robbers when they or their handiwork were revealed. On some occasions the violence was so ferocious as to result in death.[4] More restrained riots are recorded which occasioned the demolition of entire anatomy schools.[5]

Although rioters might have been described by their more educated contemporaries as ignorant, superstitious and inebriate, public sympathy in such events was generally with them, rather than with the bodysnatchers or anatomists. While the customary noises about public order also surfaced in the press, reporting was largely sympathetic. Very few rioters actually reached court, and those that did were treated comparatively leniently. Bodysnatchers on the other hand, unless they were under the 'protection' of an eminent surgeon, could be dealt with less kindly, imprisoned for varying periods, or even transported.[6]

The coexistence of medical, commercial and traditional attitudes towards the corpse was the cause of considerable friction over the course of the eighteenth and early nineteenth centuries. Clinical detachment from the corpse was crucially necessary to the acquisition of anatomical and surgical knowledge. It both encouraged, and itself promoted, the brutality of surgery during this pre-anaesthetic/pre-antiseptic era, when very strong stomachs were needed to cut into the conscious/screaming/writhing patient on the slab, and when even expert surgery could commonly result in death from infection.

The inadequate numbers of gallows corpses available for dissection meant that the acquisition of clinical detachment was gained primarily on dead bodies purchased direct from bodysnatchers. Prices were arrived at by a rough and ready computation of market forces and the anatomical desirability of an individual corpse. Particularly valuable corpses – of physical freaks for instance – could raise hundreds of pounds from collectors. More ordinary adult corpses could fetch between eight and sixteen guineas, although profits would be lower if a corpse had already undergone a *post-mortem* examination. Teeth were a valuable sideline, and dismembered parts of bodies also found a ready market. Children's bodies were sold by the inch.

Most of the corpses the resurrectionists supplied to anatomists were stolen from graves, and it was here in the graveyard that the major conflict arose. Popular death culture in this era reflected a mixed and varied amalgam of sentiments, influenced by the currency of very old notions. Vic Gammon's important work on the English funeral hymn bears witness to the persistence of resurrection and judgement imagery and the currency of belief in physical resurrection in the popular death songs of this era. The mediaeval iconography of the dance of death and *Ars Moriendi* appeared on the broadsheets and street ballads of the Reform era.[7] Death customs like laying out, washing and dressing the dead – and in lower social strata watching and waking – were observed very widely. The dead were ritually viewed and touched, they were buried with grave-goods, often with graves oriented towards the east, to await the last trumpet.

Difficulty in defining and facing death perhaps underlay both uncertainty concerning the possibility of a tie between body and soul after death, and the body's ambiguous spiritual status. However, latent dread of the corpse was balanced in popular death culture by a widespread understanding that customary care of the body would somehow safeguard both the dead and the living: both the future repose of the soul and the comfort of the mourners could thus be assured.

Bodysnatching and dissection threatened the entire conceptual framework of popular death culture. The corpse was at its freshest, and therefore both at its most desirable to the anatomists and its most lucrative to the bodysnatchers – at precisely the same time when mourners were experiencing the first pangs of raw grief.[8]

A great deal of evidence survives of the immense hostility and anxiety bodysnatching provoked in all social classes up and down the country, of which the terrible violence shown to bodysnatchers is an important expression. Equally important are the lengths to which people went to prevent bodysnatching. Of course, the poor were the most vulnerable to grave-robbery, since their cheap coffins were flimsy and their overcrowded common graves and pit burials provided no security at all against grave-robbery. But although the richer you were, the safer you might consider yourself to be, money did not necessarily safeguard wealthy and illustrious corpses. Every body was vulnerable. Sir Astley Cooper, one of the most eminent anatomists of his time, said in evidence to the Select Committee which was eventually appointed to investigate the problem: 'There is no-one, let his situation in life be what it may, whom, if I were disposed to dissect, I could not obtain'. Other commentators – including Thomas Wakley, founder of the *Lancet* – were certainly aware that the bodysnatchers were no respecters of class.[9]

And, society-wide, this knowledge promoted the widespread investment of thought, ingenuity and considerable amounts of money in the enterprise to thwart the grave-robbers. Graves were dug deep and railed in. Patents were taken out for special iron coffins with secure locks, and assorted devices – such as patented coffin screws which could not be loosened after fastening, and permanent bands and straps to secure corpses in their coffins – were devised in the hope of a ready market. Huge cages known as 'mortsafes' were erected over graves, and in some places coffins were stored in stone 'dead houses' until putrefaction rendered their contents useless to the resurrectionists. Elsewhere, massive stones which could only be lifted with a block and tackle were laid over graves for a similar period. Some parishes provided such expedients communally, while others erected watch-houses, and staffed them with men equipped with lanterns, rattles and guns – the parallel with poaching was never far away. Self-help organisations to protect the dead sprang up among the poor in villages and towns across the country to provide shifts of grave-watchers for members and their families. As a last ditch attempt to choke the snatchers' shovels the poor mixed straw with the earth returned to the grave.

The anxiety these expedients articulate also served to make

undertaking a profitable business. During the same period in which the bodysnatcher flourished, so also did the undertaker. The desire for security in the grave went hand in hand with the growth in the commercial provision of funerary services. During the course of the eighteenth and early nineteenth centuries, the same period in which bodysnatching became a separate profession, undertakers had begun to set up shop in urban areas and to purvey their services in the creation of funerals to suit the pockets and aspirations of the growing middle classes. In their hands, the funeral came to possess flexible potential in the assertion of social status: various levels of expenditure would purchase equally various permutations of coffin strength and durability, grave or vault size, security, commemoration, and funerary display.[10]

The early appeal of the funeral industry was fuelled by the endeavour to preserve the body's identity and integrity, and benefited from the close relationship of these to the commercial- ized – and conspicuously 'respectable' – funeral. The funeral came to be the rite of passage par excellence in which to assert financial and social position – a sort of secular last judgement. While it is certainly true that the celebration of death in this period served as an exhibition of worldly respectability, something else was also occurring. The other world continued to exert its influence. For although many of the constituent elements of the Georgian bourgeois funeral were derived from those of the nobility, others related to the ideal of undisturbed repose in the grave. Those who could afford to do so purchased double or triple coffins – one of which would often be lead, a metal known as a corpse-preserver. Coffins were invariably described as 'stout' or 'strong', and rows of coffin nails were a status symbol for a considerable period. The Georgian undertaker provided his more fortunate clients with the prospect of rotting safely in secure coffins, sealed tight against the soil and the dust of less eminent corpses: and above all, safe from the bodysnatchers. Deep graves, secure vaults and the many other expedients available to the financially fortunate were purchased in the hope of acquiring what Lord Radnor admitted in Parliament that he himself desired for his own body – a tomb more secure than his own home.[11]

The relationship between the bodysnatcher and the undertaker in this era thus offers a similar form of symbiosis to that observed in the relationship of criminal and policeman. During roughly the same era in which the human corpse became an article of commerce, so also did the 'respectable' funeral. One celebrated case will perhaps serve to illustrate the symbiosis in process. In 1783 an extremely tall Irishman, who had earned a good living by exhibiting himself to the curious, died. The 'Irish Giant' had warning of his own death, and was fearfully aware that the anatomists coveted his body for their museums. To prevent this possibility he made careful preparations, at considerable expense, for a fine funeral culminating in his burial at sea in a lead coffin. An undertaker received a payment of £500 on the understanding that the Giant's wishes would be carried out to the letter. However, when he finally died, a further £500 ensured that the body was actually delivered to the anatomist John Hunter's dissection room. The skeleton is now a prize exhibit in the Hunterian Museum at the Royal College of Surgeons, London, where standing full height in a glass case the Irish Giant greets visitors as they enter. The undertaker's profit – received from both parties – was considerable.[12]

Probably the finest illustration of the coexistence of the views of the human corpse discussed above – clinical detachment, commercialization, and traditional attitudes – is that of their simultaneous existence in the same person. Sir Astley Cooper, a pupil of Hunter's whose evidence to the Select Committee on Anatomy of 1828 was quoted above, left a fortune amassed from his private surgical practice and from fees charged for the private tuition of dissection and surgery.[13] Attendance at his classes had been greatly sought after by aspiring medical students. His manual dexterity in surgery – gained by daily dissections on the dead – had been rewarded with a baronetcy after a successful operation on George IV. As well as a brilliant dissector and surgeon, Cooper had also been an astute businessman: he had dealt artfully with the bodysnatchers both on an individual and a political level. Somehow, price negotiations invariably worked in his favour – his usual prices, according to Cooper's evidence, were the lowest among the London anatomists. Yet Astley Cooper's robust stone sarcophagus – embedded securely in the vaults of Guy's Hospital chapel – contains at least two, possibly three, inner coffins.

Like Sir Astley, persons of status did their best – often at considerable cost – to avoid burial in urban graveyards. As Jim Morgan's chapter in this volume shows, the dreadful state of urban churchyards and burial grounds in this period hardly provided the ideal setting for polite or safe post-mortem decay. Those who could ensure it were buried elsewhere: if possible, out of town.

The picturesque landscaping of death in the nineteenth century was a reaction to the horrors of the appalling state of urban graveyards. Speculative development of extramural cemeteries from the 1820s onwards rendered the rural ideal attainable to a much wider market, and allowed room for the erection of impressive monuments, as well as for clearer stratification along class lines. But alongside these displays of social status went the appeal of security. John Claudius Loudon, the great promoter and theorist of cemetery landscapes, believed the grave should rightfully remain inviolate. To this end he devised mechanical means, very much on the lines of the dead houses mentioned above, whereby the new cemetery companies could assure the safety of clients' bodies until decomposition rendered them unfit for dissection.[14]

The new cemeteries were to be as unlike the old graveyards as possible: landscaped, picturesque, and secure. Perimeter walls, solid gates and lodge-keeper's houses were crucial design elements in these enterprises, representing a strong commercial appeal to clients' hopes for security of tenure in the grave. Kensal Green and Highgate cemeteries still have extremely high boundary walls and gates, whilst Glasgow Necropolis is approached by a causeway over a wide moat.

Let's have another look at that great list of funerary goods purveyed by the Georgian undertaker, and analyse what all that funerary expenditure articulates in the light of what I've just been saying: the pillow and mattress in padded white satin and the satin sheet provided imaginative comfort for the corpse – softly cushioned as in bed, replete with images of sleep and repose in the grave – and the imaginative potential of a luxurious future waking. The whiteness and smoothness of the satin served to deny the ugly realities of decomposition. All those ostrich feathers, the crape, black silk and so on, and the attendants' cloaks, scarves and gloves – these would have signified sorrow in customary black, and also served to provide pomp and circumstance – the display of social status. And the 'strong coffin', the 'very strong' second coffin, and the silvered nails? – these were in part to do with custom and status, but equally surely to do with security. The funeral made a progress on its long journey for burial out of London – a journey which was probably taken as much for reasons of grave-security as sentiment. London Society a generation later could choose to follow the Princess Sophia, the Dukes of Cambridge and Sussex and the London literati to Kensal Green or Highgate, rather than take the long journey to the country seat.

I have argued that the commercial development and economic viability both of the undertaker and of the private cemetery company in Britain during the early nineteenth century may in fact have been more closely related to the commercial success of the bodysnatcher than has hitherto been recognized. Following on from these suggestions, I propose the further thesis that as the threat posed by grave-robbery diminished, attention and expenditure focussed increasingly on funerary display. First though, I shall explain how bodysnatching came to recede.

The 1832 Anatomy Act effectively rendered the bodysnatchers redundant. It was the result of recommendations from a parliamentary Select Committee which had been set up as a result of a series of successful prosecutions in the late 1820s of doctors involved in receiving stolen bodies. The Act passed in 1832, neck and neck with the Great Reform Bill. It proposed to meet the anatomists' need for dissection material by providing a new, cheap source of corpses. It directed that instead of being given the bodies of hanged murderers fresh from the gallows, the anatomists would henceforth receive the more numerous corpses of people dying in need of parish burial. It thus transferred a centuries-old feared and hated punishment for the crime of murder, to that of poverty.

The Act became law in 1832, and despite difficulties in implementation and bitter popular opposition, it proved a qualified success. By the middle years of the 1830s it had become generally clear that the dead poor could satisfy the anatomists' demand for corpses, and with the growth of this understanding, public fears of bodysnatching began to subside.[15]

The respectable funeral before 1832 had served to signify that the body of the deceased was as safe as money could make it. Raised public awareness of the existing social gradient in coffin strength and burial plot security and the relative degrees of safety these offered from depredation had enhanced death's potential to serve as a locus for the expression of social status and aspiration. The Georgian era had witnessed the emergence of a double metaphor by which even the afterlife figuratively became a marketable commodity, accessible to all but those lacking adequate means. Safe burial had become identified with respectable burial.

By the mid-1830s, the Anatomy Act's success meant that the security value of double and triple coffins, the rows of coffin nails and the patent coffins began to diminish. What for at least two generations had been a legitimate and culturally understood focus of expenditure and personal concern, in a comparatively short period became rationally, but not emotionally, redundant. Funerary expenditure didn't halt. The desire for undisturbed repose in perpetuity – which had underlain the unpopularity of Georgian resurrectionists and anatomists – continued into Victoria's era unabated. Nineteenth-century funerary monuments abound with references to sleep, rest, resurrection and the hope (or assurance) of future meetings.

It's my view that following the demise of bodysnatching, both the anxiety associated with protecting the dead, and the emotional/financial investment in a grave safe from the bodysnatchers, transmuted into and fed the desire to display respectability in death. With increasing concern with social placing, this served to boost the appeal of the commercial 'respectable' funeral. From serving to signal the achievement of respectable *and* safe burial, the respectable funeral became an end in itself.

The Victorian celebration of death represented a society-wide desire to honour the dead, and a large measure of agreement upon what forms that honour could, and indeed should, take. There existed a generally agreed norm of funerary behaviour, a consensus which at times became a social imperative. Respectable funerary display was a powerful social statement, an articulation of social aspiration and attainment, a celebration of the financial ability to honour the dead in an acceptable way.

The funeral of the Duke of Wellington in 1852 is a fine example of the Victorian exhibition of funerary display taken to extremes of redundancy. The Duke had four coffins, and his funeral carriage was so heavy that its twelve horses required the assistance of the Metropolitan Police to pull its wheels out of the mud on Pall Mall.[16] Although this Victorian funeral was indeed unique – one recent historian of death has devoted an entire chapter to it[17] –

huge numbers of less eminent personages also enjoyed fairly spectacular funerary displays. People lower down the social scale could enjoy impressive funerals in special circumstances; take for example the case of Mr James Braidwood, Superintendent of the London Fire Brigade, who died in 1861 when a burning warehouse collapsed into the street where he was doling out brandy to his men. His funeral brought London to a standstill, with a procession over a mile long.[18]

Trades unionists, temperance campaigners and cooperators may have disagreed on a definition of respectability, but the need for a decent funeral was acknowledged across the board. There were agreed, not necessarily commercialized, ways of showing respect: strength in numbers; displays of figurative grief and respect in banners and wreaths; public processional. The much derided showy funerals of the lower classes were invariably the preserve of the lower middle class, especially tradesmen: small shopkeepers, costers and the like. Individual working-class funerals of any pretension didn't really appear until the turn of the twentieth century, by which time the lower-class love of a fine funeral had long been an object of derision and incomprehension among their betters, and flamboyant funerals were already falling from favour in high society.[19]

There were, however, different reasons why a decent funeral was imperative for the financially *un*-fortunate after 1832. The poor were no different from other social classes in wanting to honour their dead, and in knowing how to go about it. The constraints upon their pockets however were much greater, and they had other imperatives besides funerary etiquette and what was and wasn't done in polite society. What served as an imperative for the poor was the perpetual threat of disposal as a pauper. The attraction of social emulation had less effect on funerary expenditure among the poor than repulsion from what would befall them at the other social pole. Their modest funerals certainly marked social status, but what they marked primarily was distance from the workhouse.[20]

The *decent* funeral can really only be fully understood if we can appreciate the *indecent* alternative. The pauper funeral[21] had been an object of popular dislike before 1832, and the provision of dignified burial an important feature in the early appeal of working-class organizations. But abhorrence does not seem to have become *desperation* until the Anatomy Act's crucial exacerbation of the new rite. Burial naked or in a paper shroud in a cheap unplaned coffin stacked in a pit with twenty or more others, and a generous dose of quicklime, was a bad enough prospect. But dissection added a penumbra of fear to this negative image of the respectable funeral, casting fundamental doubt upon the likelihood that any poor person would reach even the flimsy coffin and the unmarked grave. Over the course of the first century of the Anatomy Act's application, 57,000 poor people's bodies were requisitioned for dissection in the London Anatomy schools alone.[22] To die 'on the parish' was the ultimate of failures. The pervasive fear of it helps explain the Victorian working-class custom of keeping dead bodies for long periods. Fear of death on the parish promoted the purchase of death insurance on a mass scale, and helps explain both the mushroom growth of friendly and burial societies from the 1830s on, and the high expenditure on death among the very poor to within living memory.[23]

So, briefly, the theses I propose are as follows: *first,* that bodysnatching was an important factor in the growth and appeal of the respectable funeral: society-wide fear of grave-robbery stimulated both a rapid early growth of the undertaking business and the promotion of the great nineteenth-century cemeteries; *second,* that as the threat posed by grave-robbery receded, attention and expenditure focussed increasingly on funerary display; *third,* that legislative change was calculated to make death in poverty disgraceful, so that people lived in fear of a pauper's burial. The vast majority of those whose lives were passed in the shadow of the workhouse – by which I mean those who never felt fully sure of their distance from it – were infected and afflicted with a pervasive and often desperate fear of death on the parish. The Victorian poor were prodded into expenditure on death insurance and funerals by the intensely painful knowledge that the misfortune of death in poverty could qualify them for at best a bed of quicklime, and at worst dismemberment. The Anatomy Act promoted 'prudence', and hence, the Victorian undertaker.

8

ASHES TO ASHES: CREMATION AND THE CELEBRATION OF DEATH IN NINETEENTH-CENTURY BRITAIN

JENNIFER LEANEY

The Victorian era has been described as the 'golden age of grief'. During the mid decades of the nineteenth century funerary and mourning rituals reached heights of extravagance matched in few other societies or eras. As this orgy of materialist and sentimental indulgence reached its apogee in the 1870s, a reforming movement emerged which challenged accepted practices and attitudes, confronting as it did so some of the central economic, aesthetic, and sentimental preoccupations of Victorian society. The advocates of cremation sought, unlike earlier burial and funeral reformers, not merely to improve sanitary practices, or to simplify funerary rituals, but rather, by manipulating the physical remains of the dead, to alter fundamentally attitudes towards death itself. In this chapter I will examine some of the ways in which advocacy of cremation as a method of disposing of the dead reflected changing attitudes towards death and the human corpse during the Victorian era.

Cremation, that is, the destruction of the human corpse through burning, had not been practised in Europe since the early Christian era, when, owing to its popularity amongst the Romans, it had acquired the seemingly ineradicable taint of paganism. Since this time, cremation had been practised only in exceptional circumstances: in times of pestilence, and as a form of execution. Until the nineteenth century, burial was the almost universal mode of disposal in Christian countries.

Centuries of religious practice and local custom condemned cremation as a method of disposing of the human corpse when, in the 1770s, its reintroduction was first suggested by Italian scientists. Motivated primarily by scientific curiosity, these men produced, in the century following 1774, a huge body of literature dealing with the economic, sanitary, and religious aspects of the question.[1] They were also responsible for the development of the first modern incinerary apparatus using irradiated heat rather than the naked flame. Interest in the issue, however, was restricted to the fairly limited readership of scientific and medical journals in Italy, and in France, where discussion arose in the context of the burial reform movement initiated in the mid eighteenth century by the removal of the cemetery at Les Innocents from Paris.[2]

Little serious consideration was given to the practical reintroduction of cremation as a means of disposing of the dead until the early nineteenth century, when the problem of burial in the crowded European capitals became so acute that alternate methods of disposal were, of necessity, examined. In Britain, discussion was initiated in response to the failure of reformist burial legislation to remedy the problems of cemetery overcrowding and mismanagement. These problems were largely the result of inadequate burial space in areas where population growth was rapid. By the early decades of the nineteenth century, traditional burial grounds were no longer able to accommodate the annual increase in corpses. Various methods of so-called 'cemetery management' were thus unofficially employed to deal with the excess. Graves, for example, were frequently reopened and further coffins added, often with up to twenty lying in a single grave. Graveyards were also trenched every few years, and the contents of graves consigned to bone houses and burning grounds.[3] Under cover of darkness, bodies were regularly exhumed and burnt, and their coffins broken up and used for firewood. Second-hand 'coffin furniture' was readily available for sale, and marine stores did a brisk traffic in coffin handles, name plates, and nails.[4] By using management methods such as these, gravediggers and sextons were able to prolong indefinitely the 'life', and thus the income of the graveyard.

Graveyard overcrowding constituted a major public health problem in metropolitan areas. Drinking water was polluted by cemetery run-off, the soil was saturated with decaying organic matter, and the air, according to contemporary theories of disease causation, was filled with dangerous miasmas.[5] The systematic violation of graves revealed in public and private enquiries made, moreover, a mockery of the aura of sanctity surrounding places of interment. 'What', asked one writer, 'becomes of sentiment or sacred regard for the relics of the dead?'[6]

Several solutions to the problem were suggested at the time. Most obvious was the prohibition of intramural interment, and the establishment of large, publicly owned and operated extramural cemeteries. Legislation to this effect was introduced in 1855. Other proposals, however, were concerned less with the organizational reform of burial places, than with the physical disposition of the corpse itself. The introduction of quicklime into the grave, for example, was suggested as a method of accelerating decomposition.[7] The 'earth to earth' system of burial was another proposal which gained some support.[8] More outlandish solutions included desiccation of the corpse, burial at sea or in concrete, and cremation.

Although a few attempts had been made early in the nineteenth century to introduce cremation for limited purposes,[9] the practice was not seriously considered as a large scale alternative to burial until the 1870s, when a highly publicized article dealing with cremation appeared in the *Contemporary Review* of January 1874. This article, written by Sir Henry Thompson, and entitled 'The Treatment of the Body after Death' was quickly translated into all of the major European languages. Its cogent argument provoked both discussion and controversy, thus bringing the subject of cremation to popular attention.

Sir Henry Thompson, a famed urologist and member of the Royal College of Surgeons, had been converted to the cremationist cause by a visit to the Great Exhibition at Vienna in 1873.[10] Here he had viewed the latest developments in incinerary apparatus, and been impressed with the possibilities offered for sanitary reform. Having the claims of hygiene and utility uppermost in his mind, Sir Henry adopted a clinical, matter-of-fact approach to the question. 'Given a dead body', he wrote, the problem was 'to resolve it into carbolic acid, water and ammonia, and the mineral elements, rapidly, safely, and not unpleasantly.'[11] His prose purged of euphemism and sentimentality, Sir Henry attributed the burial problem to that element of 'unreasoning sentiment' which demanded the delay of burial, and the prolonging of putrefaction in airtight coffins and vaults.[12] The conditions of modern life, he believed, demanded that sentiment be superseded by utility.

Distinguishing between the 'barbarism' and 'superstition' inherent in the practice of burial, and the 'progress' and 'civilization' inherent in that of cremation, Sir Henry stressed those elements of utility, efficiency, and economy which distinguished the process. He described, for example, the disposal of the dead as being of paramount importance to the 'economic system of a crowded country.'[13] Using the metaphors of interest and return, he depicted Nature's capital (i.e. human remains) as being

> intended to bear good interest and to yield quick returns . . .
> shall her riches be hid in earth to corrupt and bear no
> present fruit; or be utilized, without loss of time, value and
> interest, for the benefit of starving survivors.[14]

Thompson gave further emphasis to the economic objections to burial by lamenting the wastage of a precious and valuable commodity in the form of bone and earth, worth in excess of half a million pounds per annum.[15] Not surprisingly, the suggestion that the mortal remains of one's nearest and dearest be used as commercial fertilizer was received with mixed horror and disbelief, as was the unfortunate proposal that the products of organic combustion be used to manufacture illuminating gas for general purposes.[16] The *Medical Times and Gazette* regretted this tactical error on Sir Henry's part:

> Now, the poet may draw some consolation from the thought
> that the body of his friend, who was to him more than a
> brother, is laid in English earth and that
> 'From his ashes may be made
> The violet of his native land,'
> but that is altogether a different thing from deliberately
> manuring the soil with the ashes of the human body. And it
> appears to us that to mix up a suggestion for this utilizing the
> body with a recommendation of cremation is a sure way of
> making the idea of the latter repulsive and abhorrent to the
> public.[17]

The *Medical Press and Circular* was similarly condemnatory;

> Sir Henry Thompson has – in contributing largely to the
> conversion of public prejudice – done something to make the

proposal distasteful and ridiculous by his suggestions for the economical uses of the products of incremation.[18]

Sir Henry's confident application of hallowed economic principles to the rituals surrounding death reflected a serious misunderstanding of the equivocality of his society's attitude towards the dead. Although the rhetoric of economic analysis had clearly been intended by Sir Henry to appeal to the new bourgeoisie of industrial England, the gulf separating the economic sphere from that of religion and sentiment was wide, and was bridged successfully only when appeals to the individual's feelings of reverence for the mortal remains of the dead became part of cremationist language. Recognizing the inappropriateness of arguments involving cost and economy, subsequent cremationist works stressed the propriety, beauty, and reverence inherent in this method of disposal. Attempts were made to invest the process of cremation with a halo of poetic sentiment. Cremation was, according to one writer, 'not only the healthiest and the cleanest, but the most poetical way of disposing of the dead'.[19] A deep vein of rural nostalgia runs through cremationist language recalling in many ways the enthusiasms of the rural cemetery movement earlier in the century.[20] The cremationist's Garden of Remembrance

is beautiful and is bereft of those dismal depressing emblems of death and decay. It is a place suggestive of continued life and happiness, a spot where the ashes of those who have passed over repose unfettered, kissed by the sun, among the birds, the flowers and the trees. It provides a retreat where the living, in peace and quietness may pause to think, an abiding cenotaph, renewed by nature's hand.[21]

Although the more utilitarian recommendations for cremation were downplayed, the concept of progress itself was of central importance to the cremationist argument. In symbolic terms, cremation was described as representing the forces of progress and civilization. Burial, by contrast, represented barbarism and the Middle Ages.[22] The adoption of cremation as a means of disposing of the dead would thus, as Lord Beaconsfield commented in September 1882, 'mark a stage in the march of civilization',[23] for, 'What is called God's acre is really not adapted to the country which we inhabit, the times in which we live, and the spirit of the age.'[24] In advocating cremation, cremationists promoted not merely a necessary sanitary reform, but, more significantly, the claims of the future against those of the past. 'Our task' wrote Professor Gorini, the Italian pioneer of modern cremation,

> is not confined to the mere burning of the dead, but extends to burning and destroying superstition as well, purifying the religion of the urns from the prejudices in which it has been wrapped.[25]

The terms 'science' and 'progress' were used interchangeably by cremationists; the former somewhat ambiguously. The word 'science' as used by cremationists embraced such concepts as hygiene, efficiency, and utility. At the same time, however, sentimental images of 'mother earth', of 'pilgrimages', of 'reintegration with nature' were given currency as aspects of 'natural science'. The sentimentalization of science found its practical expression in the concealment of utilitarian functions and processes, and in the fabrication of romantic associations with the classical and medieval past. Crematoriums of a classical or gothic design were thus placed in rural settings where trees or buildings concealed their practical functions.[26] Furnaces were on no account to look like furnaces, and chimneys were not to rise above the surrounding foliage.

The conflicting concepts of progress and nostalgia, and of science and sentiment, which infuse cremationist argument appear, however, to have been those which motivated nineteenth-century British society as a whole.[27] It is perhaps, therefore, unreasonable to judge the inconsistencies of cremationist thought in isolation from their wider social context.

Response to Sir Henry Thompson's original article was generally favourable. The counter-attack, however, was swiftly launched by those opposing cremation on religious, sentimental, and legal grounds. P. Holland, the Medical Inspector of Burials, struck the first blow in a hurriedly written article for the February 1874 edition of the *Contemporary Review*. Holland affirmed the basic soundness of the burial system, representing the problem as one that could be resolved through modification, rather than abandonment, of current practices. Subsequent writers expressed religious objections to cremation, forcing cremationists into theological controversies for which they had neither the learning nor the patience. In the course of controversy, cremationists were stigmatized as modernists, as irreligious men, imbued with the material spirit of the age, and seduced by the fancied progress of material science.[28] Cremation itself was condemned as a practice which, being of pagan origin, was incompatible with the Christian faith.[29]

Although the issue of cremation and Christian tradition was an extremely contentious one, the teaching of the Synagogue and the Church, together with the example of the Patriarchs and the Saints, were seen to favour earth sepulture. Earth burial formed 'part of the unwritten code in which so many of the divine ordinances are implied rather than expressed.'[30] Cremation, moreover, was seen as militating against a belief in the resurrection.[31] The pro-cremationist Bishop Fraser was quick to respond to these allegations:

> Could they suppose that it would be more impossible for God to raise up a body at the resurrection, if needs be, out of elementary particles which had been liberated by the burning, than it would be to raise-up a body from dust, and from the bodies which had passed into the structure of worms?[32]

The same response was put in a more succinct form by the Earl of Shaftesbury. 'What' he asked, 'would in such a case become of the blessed martyrs?'[33]

Some opponents of cremation, however, saw the doctrine of the resurrection as possessing more than simply religious significance. It was believed rather to underpin a whole philosophy of social and political conservatism. Any attempt to undermine the faith of mankind in the doctrine was interpreted not only as an attack on the Christian religion, but also on existing forms of political organization. Theologians of the Church of England, and of the Catholic Church, traced the modern agitation for cremation to a decree of the French republic, 25th Brumaire 1797, giving cremation a permissive sanction,[34] and saw in this movement an attempt to introduce naturalism among the population which would 'inevitably destroy, little by little, the necessary conditions of moral order and even the security of States.'[35] Licentiousness and immorality would be the inevitable outcome of this 'disastrous social revolution.'[36] The opinions of dissenting clergy on the subject are less well documented.

On the Continent, advocacy of cremation had long been equated (often justifiably), with the assumption of 'progressive', socialistic ideas. In Germany, for example, the cremation movement was ideologically connected with political liberalism. Liberals opposed those theological dogmas and prejudices which had prevented the cremation of men like Frederick the Great, who had expressed a wish that their bodies be so disposed.[37] In Italy also a link was drawn between cremation and political liberalism. Most burial grounds at the time were controlled by religious orders, and since the liberals supporting the movement for Italian independence were forbidden the use of these grounds, many advocated the practice of cremation. An element of anti-clericalism was thus mixed up with the sanitary and political motives of cremationists, accounting, perhaps, for the vociferousness of reformers in Italy.[38]

The political allegiances of English cremationists were believed to be similarly radical. Mrs Basil Holmes, in her work entitled *The London Burial Grounds*, noted that

It has to a certain extent happened hitherto that those who have been cremated have been more or less associated with the advanced school . . . those that consider themselves 'enlightened', Radicals or Socialists, or persons of little or no professed religious views.[39]

Religious objections to cremation were not in Britain, however, particularly potent. This may relate first, to the absence of a dominant Catholic establishment, and second, to the division of opinion which existed among clerics themselves concerning the practice. The *Sanitary Record* of 1874 noted that

The bench of Bishops are divided on the subject of cremation. The Bishop of Lincoln is very much opposed to it, and thinks that it will undermine the belief in a resurrection, while the Bishop of Manchester and other prelates (as well as their wives) are warmly predisposed in its favour . . . . The clergy generally appear to take a very favourable view of cremation; a considerable number of well-known clerical names appear subscribed to the declaration in favour of cremation. . . [40]

There appears to have been no real basis, either theological, geographical, or social, for this division of opinion. Personal preference seems to have been the deciding factor. The tendency even of clerics to view the issue of cremation in sanitary rather than religious terms reflects both the increasing secularization of English society in the nineteenth century[41] and the declining influence of materialistic or corporeal interpretations of Christian teaching during the period.[42]

Of greater importance to contemporaries, were the medico-legal objections to cremation. It was argued, for example, that cremation would destroy the evidence of poisoning, and thereby not only conceal, but act as a positive incentive to crime. The link between cremation and crime was forged by F. S. Haden, indefatigable promoter of the 'earth to earth' system of burial,[43] in a lengthy series of pamphlets and lectures. He argued that persons skilled in the use of poisons 'would more frequently resort to them if it were not for the knowledge that their operations were liable to be handicapped by exhumation.'[44]

Conscious of the strength of these objections to a society obsessed with murder and illicit poisoning, cremationists devoted a great deal of time and effort to their refutation. One proposal developed to counter objections was for the implementation of an improved system of medical certification along French lines. This system required the examination of the corpse by at least two medical practitioners, one of whom was to have had no previous contact with the deceased.[45] The benefits of this system were twofold; not only would it act as a safeguard against crime, it would also provide accurate statistical records of cause of death.[46] In 1893, a Select Committee of the House of Commons was appointed to investigate the issue, but no legislative action was taken.[47]

The prominence given to medico-legal objections to cremation by both opponents of, and adherents to the system, reflects a certain orientation of contemporary thought. Murder, and particularly the slow and secret murder by poisoning, appears to have had an extraordinary hold on the imagination of the period. Although the actual incidence of violent crime during the Victorian era is difficult to ascertain, owing to the inadequacy of criminal statistics, contemporaries appeared convinced of its prevalence.[48]

The obsessive fascination with murder reflected in the persistence of medico-legal objections to cremation was complemented by the equally strange fear of premature burial. Although a less distinctively contemporary phenomenon, the fear of premature burial was very potent in the nineteenth century, and numerous individuals made explicit provisions in their wills to obviate the possibility of being buried alive.[49] Cremationists argued that implementation of the process of incineration would effectively remove the horror of premature burial, since the intense heat to which the body would be subjected in the furnace would extinguish life instantaneously.[50] Hardly surprisingly, this argument did little to advance the cause of cremation; the prospect of being burnt alive was no less fearsome than that of being buried alive.

Opposition to cremation was aimed specifically at the group which actively advocated the practice: the Cremation Society of England. This society had been formed soon after the publication of Sir Henry Thompson's article in January 1874, and numbered amongst its patrons such prominent individuals as the Dukes of Westminster and Bedford, the Lords Bramwell and Playfair, and Sir T. Spencer Wells. Rank and file membership was almost equally exalted, consisting of the scientific and literary elite of Victorian England.[51] The middle- and upper-class basis of society membership remained strong well into the twentieth century. In 1908, the *British Medical Journal* commented that

> Cremation in this country is almost wholly confined to
> persons of some intellectual distinction. The average citizen is
> still held in the bondage of custom, in which sentiment has
> taken root so deeply as to make it hard to eradicate.[52]

The situation was similar in the United States, where a correspondent with the *New York Evening Post* of 17 January 1914 regretted that although the practice of cremation could have valuable social benefits if widely adopted, 'It doesn't take with the *poor*, only among the professional, intellectual, and well-to-do people.'[53]

The first step taken by the newly formed society was to obtain the opinions of eminent counsel concerning the state of the law on the subject. Learning that there was nothing in English law forbidding cremation, the Society acquired in 1878 a site for a

crematorium in the grounds of Woking Cemetery. The crematorium was not put to use until 1885, however, owing to the
opposition raised to the practice by the then Home Secretary, Sir
Richard Cross.[54] The issue might well have lain dormant beyond
1885 but for a strange chain of circumstances initiated in January
1884 by a Dr Price, of Llantrissant, Glamorganshire.

Dr Price, an eccentric Welsh physician who claimed to be the
nineteenth-century representative of the ancient Druids, had
retired to a hilltop one night in January to dispose of the remains
of his infant son. This he did in the fashion practised by the
Druids: incineration. Apprehended by neighbours as he was in the
process of burning his son's body in a barrel of petroleum, Dr
Price was subsequently arrested, and tried before Mr Justice
Stephen at the Glamorganshire Assizes, Cardiff. Resting his
judgement on the cardinal rule of English law that nothing is a
crime unless it is plainly forbidden by law, Justice Stephen decreed
that,

> A person who burns instead of burying a dead body does not
> commit a criminal act unless he does it in such a manner as to
> amount to a public nuisance at common law

and

> that to burn a body decently and inoffensively is lawful, or at
> least not criminal.[55]

In order to overcome the anomaly produced by the conflict of
this judgement, and the ruling of the Home Secretary forbidding
cremation, Mr Charles Cameron introduced the Disposal of the
Dead Regulation Bill to the House of Commons. Assuming the
legality of cremation, this Bill proposed to recognize and regulate
the practice, placing it under the license and control of
Government with such precautions as would ensure its safety and
decorum, prevent its abuse, and render penal its unauthorized
performance. Although defeated on its second reading, the
minority vote was sufficiently large, and its composition sufficiently
influential, to encourage the Cremation Society to commence
cremation at Woking. On 26 March 1885 the first body was
cremated at Woking: that of Mrs Pickersgill, 'a lady well known in
literary and scientific circles who had long taken an interest in the
question.'[56] Between 26 March 1885, and May 1887, 18 bodies were

cremated, 'a considerable proportion of the bodies so disposed of being those of ladies.'[57] In 1889, 53 cremations were performed, and by 1908 the rate was up to 795 per year.

The increasing, although still somewhat limited, acceptance of cremation as a method of disposing of the dead indicated by these figures, reflects the success of cremationist propaganda in presenting the economic, sanitary, and aesthetic benefits of the practice. The arguments consciously articulated in favour of cremation, however, do not entirely account for the growing popularity of the practice. Equally important were the subconscious appeals made by cremationist writers to the individual's perception of death and dying. An examination of both pro- and anti-cremationist propaganda, for example, reveals several underlying concerns that relate less to the practical issue of disposal of the dead than to the nature of death itself. The language of the cremationists reveals their intention not only to remedy sanitary malpractice, but also, by manipulating the physical remains of the dead, to alter popular perceptions of death. Descriptions of the corpse, and of its appropriate treatment, are particularly illustrative of this tendency.

At the base of cremationist thought, and underlying the sanitary and economic motives for advocacy of this method of disposal, was a feeling of intense loathing for the physical remains of the dead. The appalling facts of water, worms, and putrefaction, although hidden under a mass of so called 'false sentiment', must, it was believed, if followed out in the imagination, lead to the condemnation of the system which permitted them. The prominent cremationist Hugo Erichsen expressed his personal, but generally felt, view: 'The more I might love my dead', he wrote, 'the less willing I should be to leave the fair form that had once held an immortal spirit to turn into putrid carrion underground, and breed a myriad of loathsome creatures out of its own rottenness.'[58]

This attitude of abhorrence for the human corpse was not new. After the Middle Ages, realistic pictorial representations of the corpse in its various stages of decomposition had on the whole been shunned.[59] The novel element in Victorian attitudes was the extension of this feeling of repugnance from that roused by the eyes, to that conjured up in the imagination. Even within the grave, hidden from sight, the corpse was felt liable to give offence to the living. The particular merits of cremation became obvious in this context:

> Undoubtedly one result of adopting generally the incinerative burial, will be a disassociation in our ideas from that existing and shocking conception of horrible bodily decay, in which almost every thought bestowed upon the dead is necessarily enveloped. . . [60]

Opponents of cremation responded to such sentiments by drawing analogies between the process of decomposition and other bodily functions, which, although unpleasant, are tolerated because not immediately obvious to the human eye.[61] Such arguments, although eminently logical and sensible, failed to respond to the nuances of cremationist thought. Cremationists experienced a loathing for the physical remains of the dead precisely *because* they were analogous with natural bodily functions. The almost universal use of euphemisms to describe the sexual and excretory functions suggests, moreover, that an attitude of distaste for these functions was felt generally throughout society, and that cremationists merely highlighted in their works an already extant tendency.

That the cultural imperative to concealment of natural physical functions was to an extent class based, however, is indicated by the failure of the cremationist cause amongst the working classes. Cremationists, and before them burial and funeral reformers, had been attempting for almost half a century to alter the funerary practices of the working classes; with little success. Several factors contributed to this failure. The status derived from the provision of a formal funeral was, for example, undoubtedly a significant factor in the maintenance of traditional funerary rituals by the working classes well into the twentieth century.[62] The element of natural human conservatism in the adherence to traditional practices was also important. The most fundamental aspect of resistance to burial reform and the introduction of cremation, however, was the essential irrelevance to the working classes of the psychological and intellectual claims made for 'improved' methods of disposing of the dead.

In the nineteenth century, the bulk of the English working classes lived their lives in an environment largely devoid of personal privacy. All human activities: eating, drinking, sleeping, childbearing and rearing, were carried out within public view.[63] Because more openly acknowledged, physical functions were not to the working classes as disturbing, or as distasteful, as they were to the middle classes. Their attitude to the dead was similarly prosaic. Constant contact with disease and death: through the 'laying out' of the corpse, through the use of 'coffin furniture' in daily life, and through familiarity with the graveyard where the dead were by no means hidden from sight, had encouraged a 'matter-of-factness' in their approach to death matched by no other sector of society. By contrast, the tendency in the middle and upper classes, and among those sections of the working class with aspirations to respectability, was towards the privatization of human activity. Destruction of the physical remains of the dead through burning may be regarded as the final stage in this process of privatization. Feeling no such abhorrence for the physical functions of the human body, either living or dead, the majority of the working class never derived that element of psychological comfort from cremation which appeared to have been so important to the middle- and upper-class supporters of the practice.

The unease experienced by the middle and upper classes at the process of physical decay was expressed in a number of ways. In the area of sepulture, for example, the trend was to replace direct representations of death – skulls, crossbones, and so on – with gentler, more sentimental images. The nineteenth century saw the proliferation of classical forms on tombs.[64] The use of urns, weeping willows, broken columns, sorrowing ladies, and the like, reflected the desire to swathe the reality of decomposition in a romantic aura, masking and denying the actuality of death. Decorous language was similarly used. The word 'dead', for example, had been almost universally replaced by the euphemisms 'passed on', 'passed away', 'gone to God'.[65] Cremationists, however, went a step further in their use of the sentimental euphemism. With a fine appreciation of the poetic possibilities of the process, Sir Henry Thompson wrote:

> Never could the solem and touching words 'ashes to ashes, dust to dust', be more appropriately uttered than over a body about to be consigned to the furnace; while, with a view to metaphor, the dissipation of almost the whole body to the

atmosphere in the ethereal form of gaseous matter is far more suggestive of a type of another and brighter life, than the consignment of the body to the abhorred prison of the tomb.[66]

Those elements of romanticism and scientific naturalism exhibited in the above quotation appear to have combined to substitute the transformation of the human body into nature for the Christian dogma of resurrection of the dead. This tendency is evident in the following passage also:

> Burial cannot be followed out in the imagination, but with cremation, the rapid transfer of the material body to the ultimate state as part of Mother Earth, etherealised and purified, gives no food for unpleasant reflection.[67]

It was just this recourse to euphemism, this attempt to invest with a halo of poetic sentiment the redistribution of the physical elements of life, to which clerics of all denominations objected. Death was *intended* to be a spectacle: awesome and terrible, reminding each individual of his own mortality. The fear of death consequent upon the presentation of this spectacle was a powerful force for social order, and for continued adherence to the Christian faith. The authority of the Catholic Church, in particular, was seen to be threatened by the 'dying of death':

> Catholics have good reason to oppose cremation; this purification of the dead by means of fire would shake to its foundations Catholic predominance, based on the terror with which it has surrounded death. Death would then cease to be horrible, and the horror and repugnance which the grave inspires are among the most efficacious instruments of the hobgoblin machinery which Catholic rhetoric makes use of in order to humble the faithful. The *Remember thou must die* is the keystone of their dominion; strip death of this character and horror and fantastic repugnance, purify it as Gorini says, render it, as it were, amiable in the eyes of the living, and the priests are done for. The *Remember thou must die* would no longer produce its old effect.[68]

Although an attempt to undermine the 'lessons of mortality' could be interpreted as an attack on the Christian faith, the role played by fear in maintaining religious adherence was, in the increasingly secularized society of nineteenth-century Britain, of much lesser significance than in the Roman Catholic countries on the Continent. It was rather, the concept of death, of mortality itself, which was seen to be threatened by the cremationists in Britain. Cremation revealed a 'philosophical distaste for the emblems and the reality of death'.[69] It was

> a deliberate attempt to veil the dread realities of death under a cloud of sonorous but unmeaning phrases, while removing from the eyes of the living all such relics of it as tend to keep fresh in their hearts the reverent memories of those who have gone before. The tremendous lesson of mortality is, as far as possible, hidden out of sight. . . [70]

This tendency was not new, however: it may be traced to the campaign for burial reform in the 1840s and '50s. Commenting on the moves to ban intramural interment in 1855, the Rev. W. Hale had written:

> The one great object of the opponents of Intramural Burial appears to be the entire separation of the mansions of the dead from the houses of the living; the modern Hygeist advocating the measure for the sake of the public health, and the modern Epicurean, because nothing is so painful to him as the thought or sight of death.[71]

There appears then to be an ideological thread linking the otherwise disparate aims and activities of burial reformers and cremationists. These reformers all sought, in one way or another, to manipulate attitudes towards the dead, perceiving a causal relationship between these attitudes and burial practices. It was the cremationist's boast that cremation

> Removes all that morbid 'after the funeral' feeling which burdens so many Christian people. Perhaps in time the 'skull and crossbones' as a symbol of death will disappear, and a beautiful butterfly (the Grecian symbol of the fearless soul) will wing its way into favour as the truer representation.[72]

The attempt to circumvent the fear of death initiated, according to one nineteenth-century writer, a process which he labelled as the 'dying of death'.[73] By this phrase, he meant to imply not the annihilation of physical disease and death, but rather the disappearance of the thought of death as an influence bearing upon practical life.[74] This process culminated in the so-called 'death denying' society of the twentieth century.

The process of the 'dying of death' commenced in Britain during the early decades of the nineteenth century, with the campaign for the prohibition of intramural interment. Although primarily sanitary in intent, this campaign introduced new concepts of death and the 'proper' treatment of the dead; concepts which were to influence fundamentally both the ideas and actions of subsequent reformers. The feeling of abhorrence for the physical remains of the dead which characterized cremationist thought may, for example, be traced in the actions of those advocating burial reform thirty years earlier. Symptomatic of this attitude was the use of such terms as 'shocking', 'disgusting', 'disgraceful', and 'demoralizing' to describe the contact of the living with the dead, and in a similar vein, the practice of subsuming burial legislation under the general title of 'Nuisances'. Like the cremationists, burial reformers sought to remove the physical evidence of putrefaction, to remove the dead from sight.

The failure of improved burial practices to alleviate the disgust with decay shaped new responses to the troublesome confrontation with death. One response was that of embalming, a practice which, by the end of the century, had gained almost universal acceptance in North America. The aim of embalming was to preserve the human corpse. The aim of the other response – cremation – was to destroy the corpse. Despite their different methods, both processes advocated human activity in the face of death and decay, and were intended, by circumventing the stage of physical decomposition, to dispel the aura of horror surrounding death.[75] No longer was death to be associated with water, worms, and putrefaction. Instead, it was to be enveloped by the sentimental concepts of reunion and memory.

Changing patterns of sepulture within the cemetery and crematorium reflected the emphasis on the spiritual, rather than the corporeal aspects of death. Classical forms and images came to predominate, as did settings reminiscent of a rural past. The emphasis placed by cremationists on nostalgic forms and sentiments had a profoundly conservative influence in a movement early associated with innovation and radicalism. Itself one of the great conservative principles of Victorian society, sentiment, and the emotions of patriotism, local attachment, family affection and human sympathy which it embodied, were invoked as a counterpoint to the process of modernization and urbanization, thus giving the cremation movement an aspect of conservatism in its dealings with the living concurrent with an aspect of innovation in its dealings with the dead.

The changes wrought by the introduction of cremation as a means of disposing of the dead were not merely technological. Technological innovation gave scope, rather, for the valid expression of new interpretations of the meaning of death and dying. Cremationists gave prominence to the relationship between mode of disposal of the dead and attitudes towards death itself. This relationship, although alluded to in the activities of earlier reformers, had never before been fully explored and articulated. The link perceived was a causal one, and anticipated that made in the twentieth century between concealment of death and its denial. The ethos of the cremation movement, and the burial reform movement from which it had evolved, thus had a profound influence on the subsequent development of attitudes to death. The antecedents of the modern attitude of death denial may be traced not to changes initiated during the exigencies of the First World War but rather to those consciously initiated by reformers in mid-nineteenth-century Britain. If not solely responsible for the 'murder' of death, these reformers were certainly willing accessories to the act.

9

THE TWO FACES OF DEATH: CHILDREN'S MAGAZINES AND THEIR TREATMENT OF DEATH IN THE NINETEENTH CENTURY

DIANA DIXON

The nineteenth century is often regarded as the era of the periodical, and nowhere is this more true than in the provision of literature for young people under the age of about twenty. In 1800 only a handful of magazines for the young existed, whereas in 1900 at least 160 periodicals were intended specifically for children. During the period hundreds of titles had flourished and died. A few juvenile periodicals emerged during the last two decades of the eighteenth century, but they tended to be instructional, remarkably similar in format and presentation, and rarely lasted long. Typical of the genre was the *Juvenile Magazine*, aimed at 'young friends who are fond of instruction'. It saw itself as a means of improving the characters of the young with a firm desire 'to correct their little foibles, and to guide them with propriety'.[1]

It was not until the 1820s that there was a marked rise in the number of new titles appearing, and these were invariably religious in character. The reasons why this happened have been examined by J. S. Bratton[2] who places them in the context of the expansion of elementary education in the early nineteenth century and the upsurge of publishing activity especially for the young. The success of organizations such as the Religious Tract Society and the Society for the Promotion of Christian Knowledge in promoting books and tracts for instructional purposes led them to embark upon periodical publishing. At the same time, commercial publishers, Nisbet, Houlston, and Nelson, were also producing devotional literature for the newly literate. Louis Billington suggests that the growth of the Evangelical movement led to a demand for more cheap literature which could be distributed in Sunday Schools.[3] The magazines were always regarded as having a strictly evangelical and didactic purpose, and there was never any intention of entertaining their young readers. Although some of them were extremely long-lived, such as the Reverend Carus Wilson's *Child's Companion* (1824–1932), they were not considered recreational reading. Designed for Sunday reading at home or in the Sunday School, they had a moral lesson to enforce which could be achieved by stories in which sinners paid the ultimate price for their transgression, and the rewards of the righteous were in heaven.

A number of studies have been made of the early periodical press for children, of which the most important is that by Sheila Egoff.[4] She identifies three periods of importance: the 1820s, 1860s, and 1880s, in each of which there was a marked rise in the number of titles appearing. Possibly the most significant change is seen in the 1860s, when commercial publishers recognized that juvenile magazines were a potentially important area for expansion. The result was a rapid increase in the numbers of titles available for children of all ages. More important was the change in attitude of publishers to their young readers. For the first time it was acknowledged that children needed entertaining and amusing recreational reading, and in 1866 a number of titles appeared that had this express purpose: *Aunt Judy's Magazine, Chatterbox, Kind Words for Boys and Girls,* and the popular, sensational *Boys of England.* Several publishers identified the adolescent boy as a market ripe for exploitation and titles for him mushroomed after the successful launch of E. J. Brett's *Boys of England* in 1866. Most of these magazines, which retailed for a penny each, were intended to entertain and titillate their young readers with a substantial diet of fiction in which murder, crime, and violent escapades figured prominently. Because they provided the necessary diet of bloodthirsty excitement and suspense, they replaced the adult sensational penny weeklies published by Edward Lloyd and G. W. M. Reynolds that had been popular in the 1840s and 1850s. So great was their popularity with office boys, factory workers, and the like, that they attracted the almost unanimous condemnation of moralists, educators, and the religious organizations.[5] Indeed, the Religious Tract Society was so concerned about the detrimental effect of such publications upon impressionable youths that it decided to produce its own magazine for boys to counteract the pernicious effect of the penny dreadfuls. The result, the *Boy's Own Paper*, which began in 1879, was enormously successful and approved of by boys and adults alike. In essence it did not offer substantially different fare from its rivals, and death and violence featured prominently in its fiction.

The last wave of periodical publishing for the young was the 1880s and here the important feature is the number of titles of all kinds published, rather than any significant change in the contents and presentation. In the decade 1880–89 some 102 new titles for the young were started. Competition was fierce, and publishers resorted to free gifts, cheap prices, and competitions to attract readers.

For whom were the magazines intended? In the early years of the century, the magazines were devotional and directed to members of the various religious organizations via the Sunday Schools of all denominations. Circulation of such magazines varied from several hundred to thousands: in 1842 the Wesleyan *Child's Magazine* had a circulation of over 42,000.[6] This figure is comparable with S. O. Beeton's claim in 1862 that his boys' weekly, the *Boy's Own Magazine* had a circulation of 40,000 copies a week.[7] Circulation figures for periodicals in the latter half of the nineteenth century are extremely difficult to assess with any accuracy. Advertisements and claims in the magazines themselves are often extravagant and should always be treated with great caution. Into this category falls Brett's assertions of a circulation of a quarter of a million for his *Boys of England*.[8] More realistic are the advertisements in the *Newspaper Press Directory* for 1870 which revealed that the *Juvenile Instructor* had a circulation of 64,000, and that for all of its five children's periodicals the Sunday School Union claimed an overall circulation figure of 180,000 copies a month.[9] On the occasion of its 1,000th number in 1886 the *Boy's Own Paper* was alleged to have a circulation of 200,000 copies.[10] The competition from acceptable secular titles probably divided the readership and meant the circulation figures for the devotional titles did not change significantly as the century progressed.

Who were the readers of these periodicals? Billington suggests that the early religious periodicals were not intended for the masses.[11] However, the *Child's Companion* claimed in 1824 that it was 'as suitable for children in the gentleman's lodge as the cottage home'.[12] None the less, the titles were directed to the large numbers of children from middle- and lower-class homes who attended Sunday School. Later in the century, periodicals were produced by the Band of Hope, the Boys' Brigade, and the Girls' Friendly Society for their essentially urban working-class memberships.

Some titles were consciously middle-class and were priced accordingly, generally at 6d an issue. Price is a reasonable indicator of the likely readership, and a low price reflects the intention to attract a working class readership. This is seen in the case of *Chatterbox* which was priced at a halfpenny a copy to attract lower class children. Likewise, the boys' sensational weeklies cost 1d. to make them accessible to the widest possible readership.

What is interesting is the way in which boys' periodicals were much more egalitarian than those for their sisters. Despite assertions to the contrary, girls' periodicals were always very middle-class in content and attitude, and few concessions were made to lower-class readers. Boys' magazines hoped to capture their readers from among office boys, messengers, factory workers, clerks, shop assistants, and schoolboys.[13] The criticisms of the more sensational titles frequently suggested that they were responsible for leading urban, working-class youths into lives of depravity and crime.[14]

Some of the earlier publishers of magazines for boys, such as S. O. Beeton, had recognized that boys needed excitement and variety in their fiction, and tales of mystery and suspense gained in popularity. Death in various guises was soon regarded as an essential ingredient of a gripping story. Although brave heroes inevitably triumphed against incredible odds, the villains were less fortunate. Their deaths were described laconically in a matter of fact tone, and once they were dead they were never referred to again. Statements like 'then giving a wild cry, threw up his arms motionless and dead'[15] are typical of the way in which instances of violent death were treated in the fiction in boys' magazines of the nineteenth century. The difficulty of using boys' magazines of the late nineteenth century as a source of information on attitudes to death is that of an 'embarras de richesses', since even the fiction in the more respectable and wholesome titles, such as the *Boy's Own Paper*, *Chums*, and W. H. G. Kingston's short-lived periodical *Union Jack* (1880–3), was not substantially different in content from the shoddier penny weeklies from publishers such as Brett, Emmett, Rayner, Shurey, and Fox, and later in the century from Harmsworth and the Aldine Publishing House. As E. S. Turner[16] has pointed out, even the *Boy's Own Paper* was not for the squeamish, and he quotes instances of gory illustrations, with blood pouring from the trunk of a newly decapitated man or boys playing football with a severed head.

Stories of adventure often implied that human life was expendable. The settings for such stories tended to be highly fanciful, in exotic surroundings in Africa, Asia, or even Greenland, where heroes faced bizarre situations: attacks from ferocious man-eating tigers, wild Indians, or savage brigands. The death of adversaries was generally depicted as sudden, violent, and bloody. An account of an ambush by Indians in the *Boy's World* (1885) aptly illustrates this:

> For half-an-hour the fight raged furiously the Indians falling quick and fast before the sure aim and deadly knife-thrust of the white men.[17]

The style of reporting death in boys' periodicals was always terse, staccato, and unemotional. Stories of battle abounded: in some cases the setting was recent: from the Crimean War, the Afghan Wars, the Indian Mutiny, and even the Franco-Prussian War. This lack of emotion surrounding death in battle is clearly demonstrated in a story of 1880 by G. A. Henty in *Union Jack*:

> Ned caught up the musket of a man who fell dead at his side.
> Mr Stirling fell dead, Captain Murphy and Captain Macraw
> fell fighting nobly beside him, and the gallant captain
> received three bullets. For of fourteen officers, seven were
> killed and two wounded.[18]

Almost all boys' magazines of the late nineteenth century were full of similar accounts and most regularly featured serials in which death was an essential part of the action. Often stories began with a death for the hero to avenge by whatever means possible. Conversely a traitor had to be suitably punished for his perfidy. Death in such cases was always regarded as perfectly legitimate, as was the protection of damsels in distress. The adversary could as easily be a tiger as a human being, but the style of reporting did not change appreciably. A story in the *Boy's Own Paper* of 1892 records an event in which 'the result was an immediate explosion which wrecked the building and killed the man'[19] as unemotionally as one describing the death of a tiger in the *Boy's World* seven years earlier.[20]

It is interesting to note that, despite the strenuous opposition of the critics to the brutality and violence in the boys' penny weeklies, even magazines that were intended for general family reading were not free from stories of violence and death. Magazines like the *Weekly Welcome* sometimes carried fiction that could be every bit as bloodthirsty. Set in the French Revolution, a story entitled 'A Dreadful Time' (1887–8) contains a detailed description of a spy being tortured to death by vicious whipping. In this case the unfortunate victim expired as he was being nailed to a crucifix.[21]

Although well over one third of all children's magazines were directed at boy readers, a large number of periodicals were general in character. Of these, most were religious and had a strong didactic purpose. As they were cheap and were often awarded as prizes in Sunday Schools, or were freely distributed, they provided an ideal vehicle for influencing and moulding the characters of large numbers of children.

Many of the strongly evangelical religious movements produced magazines for the young and these frequently used accounts of death-bed scenes as a device to extol the benefits of a righteous and virtuous existence. Several titles carried regular features describing the last moments of blameless young readers. In such cases death was normally regarded as a friend releasing the child from a life of suffering. For twentieth-century readers these accounts seem unnecessarily detailed and harrowing, but in the early nineteenth century children were accustomed to a high rate of mortality among their peers.

Realistic accounts of death-beds were common in many of the religious juvenile periodicals. As early as 1824 the Wesleyan *Youth's Instructor and Guardian* contained a regular monthly feature entitled 'Juvenile Obituaries', as did its contemporary published by the Religious Tract Society, the *Child's Magazine, and Sunday Scholar's Companion.* Typical of all such accounts is the sad case of the exemplary Elizabeth Ann Pascoe who ' was seized with scarlet fever . . . . She suffered so much that she could not converse freely. On Saturday morning, August 4th, 1824, she exchanged earth for heaven, suffering for enjoyment, "mortality", for "life".'[22]

Death was frequently preceded by great suffering and came as a merciful release to a child who had proved his or her virtue. An example of such a case was poor Margaret Bedlington who was afflicted with a worm fever in 1824:

> Her conduct and courage through illness were worthy of imitation. During her last hour her nurse said 'Are you happy?' 'Yes' she said 'I am going amongst —'. Here she was prevented at that time from saying any more; and soon afterwards she breathed her last at the age of ten years, in these emphatic words 'Come, Lord Jesus, come quickly! Come quickly!'[23]

To a modern reader the accounts may appear unnecessarily gruesome in their detail. In 1837 the *Children's Friend* carried a particularly explicit account of the death of 'Little Robert', who was afflicted with a painful and sudden consumption:

> His patience was wonderful for so young a child. Though full of sores, he never was heard to utter a complaint, and often when his Mother expressed her surprise at his fortitude, while his bones were literally piercing through his tender skin, he would meekly observe, 'Oh! this is nothing to what my dear Saviour suffered for me.'[24]

Some of the devotional periodicals almost seemed to revel in death. Both the *Children's Friend* and the strict Baptist *Little Gleaner* carried regular features specializing in the dying moments of children. Two examples from 1877 illustrate the way in which death scenes were treated. The suddenness of death was portrayed in the case of William Shaw aged six years and five months:

> He was taken ill on Thursday and died on the next Sunday night about 7 o'clock from scarlet fever . . . . He was gone in a few minutes. He suffered much during his affliction, it was so rapid but he did not suffer many days and now it is over.[25]

In contrast Little Robert almost seems to have hastened his own death: 'But oh! how changed was little Robert. Death sat on his infant features. His eyes were closed and he breathed convulsively. Through the whole course of his illness he absolutely refused to take his medicine.'[26]

A change can be detected in the way in which magazines described the process of dying: in the earlier part of the nineteenth century readers were spared none of the physical details, however unpleasant. An account in the *Youth's Instructor and Guardian* of 1824 of the demise of seventeen-year-old Salome illustrates this forcefully: 'A sudden and copious discharge of blood indicated the rupture of some internal vessel, and the speedy dissolution of their beloved child.'[27] In similar vein is a description of the death of Eliza Jacob in the *Child's Companion* of 1842:

> The conflict of death now came on; and all we could do was weep and pray for her. Her breathing became more rapid, her thirst was excessive, and her pains agonizing.[28]

This contrasts with the much blander accounts in the same journal in 1896, where little Willie dies in his mother's arms, and Polly succumbs to diphtheria, without any of the harrowing detail that was so much a feature of earlier accounts.[29] Death was no longer envisaged as frightening, as we see in an account in *Every Girl's Annual* of 1888 whereby, 'It was over in a minute. There was nothing very sad about it. After all there is nothing very terrible in leaving sorrow and pain for everlasting gladness.'[30] The religious periodicals emphasized the spiritual aspects of dying rather than the physical details by the last years of the century and this marks a fundamental change in attitude.

An examination of the index of the annual volume of the *Little Gleaner* for 1893 clearly demonstrates the preoccupation of this magazine with death themes: stories were entitled 'I am not afraid to die'; 'Anxious to be prepared to die'; and 'Dr Watts' death-bed'. Most of the death-bed scenes in the magazines suggested that once suffering was over there was the promise of a heavenly existence, expressed in phrases like 'a child gathered to the angelic bosom'.[31] Heaven was a desirable alternative to the suffering of the world, as in the case of the boy described in 1831 as having 'left this sad and troublesome world for that happy home above the sky where all our troubles are wiped away'.[32] Although the child's last words feature prominently in such accounts, it is hard to gain much impression of who attended the dying child. Mothers were generally there, if only as a convenient person to record the last utterance of the child, as in the case of J. Twyman Hogue dying of a spinal affliction, recorded in 1866: 'During his last sickness but a few days ago, he said to his Mother, "I am going to die. I am going to heaven."'[33]

Although most of the death-bed scenes that have been discussed offered the promise of a better life the other side of the grave, for those who had sinned, death was by no means as joyful and comfortable. Poor deceitful Alfred, in the *Children's Friend* of 1893, is rewarded for his perfidy by falling off a cliff.[34] The grim consequence of illicit bathing was depicted in an 1837 issue of the same magazine, where the narrator recalls, 'As I was returning from afternoon service, I met in the street a mournful procession of a lad drowned because he went to bathe instead of attending divine worship.'[35] Likewise, in 1892 the *Little Gleaner* carried a particularly moving account of little Bobbie's wretchedness in his final conversation with his Mother, in which he confessed he was tormented by the fact that his illness was caused by his disobedience.[36] Vanity and selfishness were regarded as unacceptable traits of character, and were rewarded, in a story of 1893, with a suitably unhappy end for a young girl, who bitterly reproached her mother for encouraging her love of fine clothes.[37]

Scenes like this are typical of numerous stories intended to demonstrate that sinners must suffer the consequences of their misdeeds by paying the ultimate price. Parents also sinned, and had to be punished for their transgressions. Drunkenness was a serious social evil and it was not uncommon for fiction to mete out an appropriate punishment to a drunken parent, as in a story in *Juvenile* in 1853, when an inebriated father was run over and killed.[38] Early in the twentieth century, the *Girl's Home* carried numerous harrowing tales of foolish young girls eloping with unsuitable partners and reaping the consequences of drunken husbands, poverty, and the deaths of beloved children.[39]

Although it was a criminal offence, sometimes suicide was the only honourable solution to a sinful life. Children's periodicals rarely carried stories about suicide, but in 1876 the *Morning of Life* used it as a device to reinforce a moral. Improvident, extravagant, and vain, Alice squanders all the money her husband has saved on pretty clothes. Her moment of truth comes when the husband announces he has found a house to buy and needs the money. Faced with no alternative, Alice hangs herself, leaving a farewell letter:

Now how vain it seems. To leave my husband and child wrings my heart with agony. Yet I dare not live. I cannot meet my husband's just anger, neither can I ask God to forgive me, for my doom is wilfully brought on.[40]

On the whole, although death was an essential part of all children's magazines, once the character had died there was little interest in the ritual of death. We have already seen that in the boys' magazines death was a necessary part of a story, but that once it had occurred, that was the end of the matter: obsequies were rarely considered necessary to the action. Most magazines for children ignored funerals, mourning, and grief.

In some cases, however, funerals and mourning were considered worthy of attention. The *Girl's Own Paper* was noted for all matters concerning etiquette and correct behaviour, and inevitably it had to consider mourning attire. In 1887 a lavishly illustrated article discussed appropriate clothing:

Mourning dress follows much more closely than it used to in the steps of the fashion of the day. Tucks have gone out of favour and crape is usually put on in panels, wide or narrow, as the case may be and the depth of the mourning requires . . . . A perfectly plain dress of Scarborough serge, with no crape trimmings, yet looks very deep in its dull black tones. The same may be copied in crape cloth.[41]

Writing to a correspondent in 1880, the paper had informed a young reader: 'Very little children are not "put into mourning" as it is termed, that is, very little crape is used for their dress, none in fact, save on the hat.'[42] In 1888 'a lady dressmaker' informed readers that widows need not wear a mourning cap and veil after the first six months but that a large muslin collar should be worn for a year.[43]

The *Girl's Own Paper* discussed matters like mourning dress in strictly factual terms and saw itself as a provider of essential social information for its middle-class readers. Fictional allusions to mourning and funerals are extremely unusual in children's magazines, and this is somewhat strange when death is so freely described. A rare description of mourning is found in the Church of England magazine *Boys' and Girls' Companion* in 1886:

In the room on the right-hand side of the passage were two women dressed in very respectable mourning. It was a bare room, for the chairs they sat upon were the only ones it possessed, for every piece of furniture that could be spared had gone to pay the [funeral] expenses of Archibald Williams' wife.[44]

This periodical was much less middle-class, and it was able to underline the importance attached to a decent funeral by the poor. There is also an allusion to the poverty that many families faced as a result of providing a respectable funeral, even if in some cases it was positively meagre. The account of a pauper's funeral in *Peter Parley's Annual* for 1868 is particularly touching and is unusual for the amount of detail it conveys:

In a few days the corpse of the poor woman was put into a shell and taken away to the common burial ground at the expense of the parish. It was carried in a chimney sweeper's cart. There was mourning only of the sooty kind. There were no pall bearers.

In this case the corpse was lowered into a deep hole full of water reserved for parish paupers.[45]

Towards the end of the century it was unusual to find any discussion of funerals and mourning in this sort of fiction. A rare example can be found in a heart-rending story entitled 'Seven years for Rachel' in the *Girl's Own Paper* (1884) in which the heroine's father slowly wastes away and finally dies. What is interesting is the amount of detail given to the funeral preparations for the deceased, who was a member of the Ivorites, and over two pages of the story are devoted to the ceremonies.[46]

Much more typical of the attitude to funerals was that of the devotional children's magazines of the 1830s and 1840s. Children were allowed to ask questions about death and funerals, but parents tended to gloss over details and be evasive, concentrating on the spiritual happiness of the deceased child.[47]

Just as the magazines consciously avoided funerals wherever possible so, too, did they eschew grief. To dwell on grief was contrary to the message they wished to convey that the victim was an innocent whose reward was in heaven. Consequently, grieving was an emotion that was avoided wherever possible. None the less, a few editors recognized that it was an inescapable consequence of death and mentioned it in their editorials, if not in the stories. The New Year's message for 1888 in *A.1. Annual* recognized that some of its young readers would be mourning departed friends and relatives:

> and yet my instinct leads me to think of the young hearts that are also heavy hearts, of tears that gather slowly in dulled eyes .... The pealing bell will waken many sad memories and emphasize the desolation of many a vacant chair. But in this season of the year the great healer of all sorrows seems specially present.[48]

Much earlier in the century a story in the *Nursery and Infants School Magazine* of 1831 carried a story about grief. 'He cried indeed, very much for the loss of his dear little companion, yet he knew that he was gone to a happy place and he hoped he should meet him there again.'[49]

Certainly in the first half of the nineteenth century the magazines were much more concerned with grief and mourning than later in the century. Instructional periodicals, as for instance the *Juvenile Forget-Me-Not*, often carried stories of deaths of mothers and brothers and sisters and grief was a necessary part of the plot. Thus, in 'The Indian Island' (1833) we are told, 'Mournful indeed did the first sad weeks pass away without Michael – incessant were Marion's inquiries when he would return. It is so difficult to give a child an idea of death.'[50]

In the *Boy's Journal* of 1863 a child is threatened with death and the author predicts the anticipated anguish of the mourners: 'if the catastrophe predicted by the surgeon actually came to pass – pretty Alice lying dead in her coffin – their grief would I knew find frantic expression in loud wailing, wringing their hands and the like tokens of distraction.'[51] Such a graphic description of the mechanics of grief is itself an unusual statement and one infrequently found in periodicals for children.

There is no doubt that later boys' weeklies would have regarded such a description as unmanly, and one which would be more appropriate to a magazine for girls or women. However, even in periodicals for young women, the chances of finding such references are remote. A rare example is found in the *Girl's Own Paper* for 1884:

> There are feelings of grief that lie deep, deep in the heart, and that are far beyond the search of human scrutiny. They have no vent in words, therefore words cannot paint them. They are confined to no rank of life but exist as painfully in the breast of the cottager as of the prince.[52]

As the nineteenth century progresses it becomes evident that expressions of grief appear less often in the magazines. In the early part of the century, the magazines reflect a recognition that grief was a necessary part of mourning and of the process and ritual of death, but towards the last part of the century it seems that grief became an emotion to be concealed, and one which could only be expressed through the formal trappings of correct mourning attire.

Of course, in cases where a child's actions might have contributed to the death of another, grief could be regarded as a justifiable penance and was therefore acceptable. This is clearly demonstrated in a story in the devotional *Children's Friend* (1895): 'Poor Lionel's grief was inconsolable. Mrs Moore did not know how to deal with this violent remorseful grief. She could comfort Lena but Lionel half frightened her with his passionate sobs and self reproaches.'[53]

If the religious periodicals did not allow any indulgence in grief, they were extremely assiduous in reminding their young readers of their imminent mortality. The editorials in the annual volumes of some of the more strictly evangelical magazines, such as the *Little Gleaner*, the *Children's Friend*, and the *Morning of Life* carried constant reminders of the transitory nature of human life. The editorial in the *Little Gleaner* for 1892 was typical of the genre, as it advised its readers: 'sickness and death prevail around us, beloved ones are being removed from around us.'[54]

Some editors almost seemed to relish the prospect of the mortality of their young readers. In 1876 the editorial for *Morning of Life* was quick to remind readers that for some:

> Before the New Year's morn shall dawn on the frozen earth, their life journey may have ended, they will know that inscrutable mystery, death, and while the happy greetings of the season are passing from lip to lip, their tongues may be silent, and their bodies shrouded in the lonely grave. Reader, it may be you. Are you ready?[55]

The devotional periodicals maintained the traditions set much earlier in the century which informed the young of the uncertainty of human existence, and the need to be prepared for death. One of the earliest magazines, *The Child's Companion or, Sunday Scholar's Reward* had in 1824 begun by advising its readers to

Reflect on that terrible place which will be the end of all sin where wicked children must go . . . . Which of you can tell how soon you may be called away? You may not live until the end of the year just begun.[56]

Just as the texts of the stories and features of nineteenth-century children's magazines revealed the sad and the exciting aspects of death, so too did the illustrations. Boys' magazines revelled in numerous pictures of tension and suspense and were not above depicting mutilated corpses with blood pouring from them. Pictures of boys strapped to railway lines in the paths of oncoming trains, heroes hanging perilously on to cliffs and defending themselves from the fangs of lions and tigers all added to the excitement and encouraged prospective purchasers. In contrast, the devotional and religious press specialized in haunting images of wan, pathetic children sitting by the bedsides of their consumptive, dying parents.

Children's magazines of the nineteenth century reflect two very different approaches to death. The boys' periodicals demonstrate the manly, unemotional attitude in which death is often violent and necessary, but is never accompanied by unbridled excesses of mourning and grief. On the other hand, the religious press of the first eighty years positively wallowed in death-bed scenes, especially when the victim was a child. Pathos and bravery shine through their pages as the young sufferers await their just rewards in heaven.

This diversity in treatment can partially be attributed to the fundamental difference in purpose between the moralistic and didactic religious periodicals and the magazines for boys that were intended to entertain and amuse their young readers. Even the religious periodicals showed a change in their attitude to death by the end of the century. Death-bed scenes were not described in such physical terms and regular juvenile obituaries, common in the earlier part of the century, were abandoned. Most periodicals recognized that young readers needed entertainment as well as instruction, and with very few exceptions tried to present the message they wished to instil in a more attractive and less threatening way. This change is partly the result of a fundamental shift in religious teaching away from frightening children into a righteous life, and also to the changes in attitudes towards death, grief, mourning, and funeral ceremonies, all of which are reflected in the pages of the magazines. More importantly it reflects a change in attitude to children. This change is seen in the way in which magazine editors consciously tried to present a more approachable and chummy attitude to their readers through the editorials and correspondence columns in the last decades of the century. The old image of the authoritarian editor was replaced in almost all magazines by a much more friendly, avuncular attitude. At the same time it is this shift in emphasis towards amusement that leads to the glossing over of death later in the century, in all but a few of the strictest Nonconformist titles.

10

VICTORIAN UNBELIEF AND BEREAVEMENT

MARTHA MCMACKIN GARLAND

Among the literate upper or upper-middle classes of late-Victorian England a thin, somewhat wavering, but nevertheless perceptible line divided the religious landscape into two territories: a district populated by the believing faithful, and the newly colonized land of religious doubt and unbelief. The Christian part of the former kingdom was large, encompassing orthodox Roman Catholics, ritualistic High-Church Anglicans, evangelical low-church Anglicans, and various kinds of Nonconformists. The land of doubt was smaller, but it was inhabited by some admirable folk: writers, educators, artists, scientists, and former clergymen who for a variety of reasons – and often at considerable cost to themselves – had decided that they could no longer honestly profess the faith of their fathers.

The intellectual origins and consequences of this widespread loss of faith have been quite thoroughly studied,[1] but the emotional impact on the personal lives of individuals has been much less well understood. In almost all societies one of religion's most important roles has always been to comfort and sustain individuals and the community during the significant 'passages' of life.[2] Thus a comparison of Victorian believers and unbelievers facing some of life's most difficult crises – in the case of this chapter, the death of a loved one – should provide a useful case study in what John Stuart Mill called the 'utility of religion'.[3] If 'Christian comforts' really did provide comfort, then we would expect to see Victorian agnostics experiencing bereavement differently and perhaps more painfully than would their still Christian contemporaries.

We have good information about the bereavement experiences

151

of quite a number of late Victorians; and if we use people from relatively similar backgrounds – in this case, upper- or upper-middle-class, well-educated Britons – who are divided into two groups only on the question of whether or not they had 'lost their faith', it should be possible to understand something about what believers had kept and what agnostics had set aside. Of course, the very division into categories of belief and unbelief is fraught with peril, especially when dealing with sophisticated and subtle thinkers; but if the focus is on operational rather than intellectual definitions, such a division does seem possible. Unbelievers were people who identified themselves as having lost their faith. They may have had heated disagreements within their families as they turned away from their religious upbringings, or resigned a post requiring religious orthodoxy as a condition of employment. They may have written articles attacking the plausibility of Christianity or given talks arguing against the existence of God, or of the immortal soul. And in their private correspondence they may have made sceptical reference to religion or earnestly discussed their reasons for disbelief.

Believers, on the other hand, would have remained at their religious posts. Their public articles or speeches would have treated theological issues positively and dealt with matters of church governance or doctrine as serious topics. And in their private correspondence they would have used religious language to advise or comfort one another and would have portrayed themselves as people who participated in religious services or who regularly prayed.

From the perspective of intellectual history, of course, such a rough-hewn division may seem unsatisfactorily simplistic. Such people as George Eliot, F. D. Maurice, T. H. Huxley, or Charles Kingsley had subtle and complex ideas about many subjects, including religion. But whether or not such people honestly felt they could use religion in their daily lives was a question which they undoubtedly could answer about themselves. They also tended to be able to answer it about each other; and from their biographies, letters, and published writings, we can answer it about them, too, at least at this practical, operational level.

Another complexity can come into such an analysis: Christian comforts, of course, could have been of many types, ranging from the ritualism of the High Church through the emotionalism of

Evangelicalism and even including the purgatorial doctrines of Roman Catholicism. In order to make the comparison as straightforward as possible it is appropriate to draw Christian examples only from the experiences of people whose intellectual orientation (and, usually, social background, economic level, and educational experience) made them most similar to their apostate contemporaries: the members of the liberal, flexible, non-literalist 'Broad Church', just barely back over the boundary line into orthodoxy.

At first glance, liberal Christians and unbelievers seem to have confronted grief in very similar ways. At a formal level, nineteenth-century rituals of mourning – funeral services, black bordered letter paper, condolence notes, mourning clothing – appear to have been employed in ways which were neither Christian nor non-Christian but merely Victorian.[4]

Believers and unbelievers both turned to 'Duty' or 'Work' for consolation in time of bereavement. A. P. Stanley, for example, a Broad Churchman and later the Dean of Westminster, was on a tour of the Middle East as a companion and tutor to the Prince of Wales when his beloved mother died; as his Victorian biographer says of him, 'It was, he believed, his duty to continue the expedition. It was, he knew, his mother's wish that he should do so. To throw himself into the work that lay immediately before him with all the force of his nature was at once the wisest and the most unselfish course.'[5] And such unbelievers as Thomas Carlyle, John Addington Symonds, or George Eliot found the strength to face life in part through completing a project or editing the papers of the lost love.[6]

Another common characteristic of Victorian grief, whether Christian or agnostic, was the establishment of a permanent memorial of some sort. Victorian cemetery monuments were as elaborate and expensive as mourners could manage, no matter what the faith of the deceased; William Morris, for example, was a thoroughgoing unbeliever, but his architect friend Philip Webb designed a complicated roofed structure for his tombstone, elevated on short stone stilts.[7] A more poetic commemoration, of course, was Tennyson's Christian (or nearly Christian) *In Memoriam*, written in honour of his friend Hallam. And one need look no further than to the large number of hefty volumes of 'Lives and Letters', written by the admiring sons, widows, and nephews of believers and unbelievers alike, to find evidence of a general urge to eulogize and in some sense immortalize the beloved.

Even the emotional responses of believers and unbelievers displayed at least superficially many of the same characteristics: Christians as well as agnostics felt anger about death, guilt toward the lost one, at least temporary desolation at being left alone, and a wish to deny the reality of the loss.[8] However, despite these common threads which run through Victorian grief, close inspection reveals real differences between the bereavement experiences of Christians and unbelievers.

The very rituals of consolation were employed with subtle changes; in particular, the language used in condolence letters sent to unbelievers was different from that directed toward Christians. Benjamin Jowett, the Master of Balliol College, Oxford, and a believing though very liberal Christian, provides a number of useful cases. Jowett lived to be seventy-six years old and saw many of his acquaintances experience bereavements, so that the last chapters of his *Life and Letters* are filled with condolence notes sent to his friends. When the bereaved was a Christian, Jowett always made reference to religious consolations; here are some characteristic phrases: 'I do not doubt that she is with God, and that all this has not passed away.' Or, 'our greatest comfort must ever be that the departed are in the hands of God.' Or, 'May God, who can alone heal such sorrow as yours, give you peace and rest.'[9]

On the other hand, when he wrote to a non-Christian, though he showed much human compassion and psychological perception, Jowett carefully avoided religious phrasing. Here is the letter he wrote to George Eliot on the death of George Henry Lewes:

I hardly know how either to write to you, or not to write to you after the sad news which I read in this morning's paper. I am afraid that the blow must be to you an overwhelming one, and that for years you will feel the dreariness and isolation caused by it.

I am so glad that I knew him and was able to appreciate him. [Jowett then goes on to discuss a number of concrete strengths of Lewes' work.]

And now as a sad duty to his memory you must bear up under the greatest trial of life, and make the most of the years which remain to you. It would not be worthy of you who have done so much for others just to pine away because your best friend is taken from you. Dear Mrs. Lewes, it seems hard to say this to you just now, but you must know how deeply I feel with you.

I should like to come and see you sometime when it is suitable and pleasant: If there is anything I can by any possibility do for you, will you let me know?

In fact, no one who wrote to George Eliot used religious language, whether the consolers were such doubters as Herbert Spencer, Frederic Harrison, or John Morley, or such believers as Tennyson, Browning, or Annie Thackeray Ritchie. Furthermore, scattered throughout most of the condolence letters to 'Mrs. Lewes' were particularly despondent phrases like 'heard with deep horror', 'calamity', 'irreparable loss', 'helpless sympathy', and 'grieving most bitterly', so that the tone of this correspondence seems especially desolate, even though Lewes had been ill for some time and both he and the author were in their sixties.[10]

Occasionally a believer confronted an unbeliever directly, using the condolence letter to press a theological case, as when Charles Kingsley wrote to the agnostic scientist T. H. Huxley at the death of the latter's young son. But such examples are rare, and even Kingsley – an enthusiastic Broad Churchman and one of the founders of 'muscular Christianity' – knew enough to be tentative and almost metaphorical in his consoling language:

To have lived a few years, even a few days, with one's child – is it not a gain pure and simple? Has it not enlarged our whole character & being? Can we ever be what we were before, & no more? And even if the loss have left a void, are we not still the larger by that void? But if, as I believe, that void will be refilled somewhen, somehow, somewhere; if no thought of God – as our child is – can finally perish, must be fulfilled hereafter, in due course of things – shall we not be, if not content, at least resigned, to wait? & strive meanwhile to make ourselves worthy of the re-union, & great enough to take in the greater being wh[ich] that child will have by then become?[11]

Unbelievers writing to unbelievers, on the other hand, were forced to fall back on strictly practical consolations so that even when written with obvious fellow-feeling and sympathy, their letters often seem extremely bleak and tragic. Herbert Spencer thus wrote to console Huxley at the loss of an adult daughter who died after a long and debilitating illness:

> I coincide with the feeling that you expressed that, considering the hopeless state in which she has long been, and the probability of continued painful decay, it was better that the end should come as it did. But it is sad to think of so promising a career so early blighted – such successful and enjoyable achievement, joined, as one may infer, with a great deal of domestic happiness, closing so early after so much suffering.[12]

And when Huxley himself died this was the best that Spencer could write to his widow:

> If recovery had become hopeless, longer continuance of life under such suffering as has of late been borne was scarcely to be desired, and this thought may be entertained as in part a consolation in your bereavement. A further consolation, and one which will be of long duration, is derivable from the contemplation of his life having been model – exemplary in the capacities of husband, father, citizen and teacher.[13]

If condolence letters posed problems, funeral services presented even greater difficulties to nonbelievers. The very words of the traditional service not only failed to comfort, they actually exacerbated the pain of bereavement. Leslie Stephen, an articulate and dedicated agnostic, bitterly described

> what is called our 'sublime' Funeral Service [which contains] the strange chapter from St Paul's Epistle to the Corinthians, where the one noble outburst of rhetoric has to be rushed through strange tortuous special pleadings, arguments from superstitious practices, [and] false analogies . . . Standing by an open grave . . . we all must feel that . . . the Apostle is desperately trying to shirk the inevitable, and at best resembles the weak comforters who try to cover up the terrible reality under a veil of well-meant fiction. I would rather face the inevitable with open eyes.[14]

156

Huxley, too, vehemently objected to the funeral service, especially the passage in which Paul says, 'if the dead rise not again, let us eat and drink for tomorrow we die'.

> I cannot tell you how inexpressibly [these words] shocked me
> .... What! because I am face to face with irreparable loss . . . I
> am to renounce my manhood, and howling, grovel in
> bestiality? Why, the very apes know better, and if you shoot
> their young, the poor brutes grieve their grief out and do not
> immediately seek distraction in a gorge.'[15]

For their own services and for their loved ones, unbelievers naturally sometimes made modifications in the traditional service so as better to reflect their beliefs. But these modifications themselves could cause additional distress, in part, of course, because the circle of sympathetic friends would not always entirely share in the sceptic's views. George Henry Lewes' funeral, for example, was conducted by the Unitarian minister, Thomas Sadler; one of the attenders rather waspishly described the sermon as a half-hearted apology 'for suggesting the possible immortality of some of our souls'.[16]

Furthermore, for unbelievers of great public eminence the place of burial itself sometimes caused an additional wrench for the bereaved: while such Christian literary figures as Browning or Tennyson were buried with loving ceremony in Westminster Abbey, George Eliot, despite the efforts of some of her friends, was interred in the unconsecrated section of Highgate Cemetery. As Huxley explained, the Abbey was not just a national monument but a Christian church; neither in her 'practice in regard to marriage [nor] in theory in regard to dogma' was George Eliot orthodox. 'One cannot have one's cake and eat it too.'[17]

In practice, a number of unbelievers came strongly to dislike funeral services and to avoid them whenever possible. Carlyle had his wife and ultimately himself buried essentially without a service and refused to attend the services for either his father or his brother. Leslie Stephen wrote to a friend in 1881 that he did not go to Dean Stanley's funeral 'because I find funerals so painful that I only go when it is a question of not hurting somebody's feelings.' Herbert Spencer explained his views in his *Autobiography:* 'As my beliefs are at variance with those expressed in burial-services, I do not like attending funerals, and giving a kind of tacit adhesion to all that is said.' And George Eliot even failed to attend the service for Lewes.[18]

But it was not just with respect to the ritual of mourning that believers and unbelievers varied; at a basic emotional level there also seem to have been differences between the two groups. The intensity of Christian anger and despair usually was somewhat muted, almost always moderated by countervailing references to God's purposes, or to hope in His mercy. The anger and despair of unbelievers, on the other hand, especially in the early stages of bereavement, were met with no softening consolations and often bordered on rage. We know that at the death of G. H. Lewes George Eliot's cook 'spoke indiscreetly of her mistress's self-control breaking down entirely – her screams heard throughout the house'.[19] And Virginia Woolf has recorded a gripping description of her father, Leslie Stephen's, behaviour in the months following her mother's death:

> Against all his expectations, his wife had died before him, [and] he was like one who, by the failure of some stay, reels staggering blindly about the world, and fills it with his woe. But no words of mine can convey what he felt, or even the energy of the visible expression of it, which took place in one scene after another all through that dreadful summer. One room it seemed was always shut, was always disturbed now and then, by some groan or outbursts. He had constant interviews with sympathetic women, who went in to see him nervously enough, and came out flushed and tear-stained, confused as people are who have been swept away on the tide of someone else's emotion . . . and there were dreadful mealtimes when, unable to hear what we said, or disdaining its comfort, he gave himself up to the passion which seemed to burn within him, and groaned aloud or protested again and again his wish to die.[20]

It is also true that immobilizing grief seemed to last a long time with unbelievers; Stephen really never recovered his emotional balance, although he lived another nine years. The same can almost be said for George Eliot; certainly it was more than a month before she could write even to her closest friends, and then only in the most fragile tones: 'I bless you for all your goodness to me, but

I am a bruised creature, and shrink even from the tenderest touch. As soon as I feel able to see anybody I will see *you*.'[21]

This reaction can be compared to that of Robert Browning, a believer, at the death of his wife Elizabeth. Although theirs had been another of the great, almost notorious loves of the nineteenth century and Browning was no doubt deeply grieved, nevertheless he was able within a very few weeks of his wife's death to describe his loss calmly and to use religious language as if to mute the intensity of his pain:

At four o'clock there were symptoms that alarmed me, I called the maid and sent for the doctor. She smiled as I proposed to bathe her feet, 'Well, you *are* determined to make an exaggerated case of it!' Then came what my heart will keep till I see her again and longer – the most perfect expression of her love to me within my whole knowledge of her. Always smilingly, happily, and with a face like a girl's – and in a few minutes she died in my arms; her head on my cheek. These incidents so sustain me that I tell them to her beloved ones as their right: there was no lingering, nor acute pain, nor consciousness of separation, but God took her to himself as you would lift a sleeping child from the dark, uneasy bed into your arms and the light. Thank God.[22]

At about the same time he wrote to another friend: 'I shall go away from Italy for many a year – to Paris, then London for a day or two just to talk with her sister – but if I can see you it will be a great satisfaction. Don't fancy I am "prostrated", I have enough to do for the boy and myself in carrying out her wishes.'[23]

A further example of the Christian moderation of grief can be seen in the case of Lady Tennyson at the poet's death. Tennyson died on 6 October 1892; within five days his wife was able to write to her sister and niece that although 'I am unable to have anyone with me except my Hallam [her son]. . . . [h]e and I feel that we live with Him still and that in this is our best hope of a fuller life in God. I have indeed much beyond words to be thankful for.' And in a letter dated 15 October she wrote that she would not have wanted her husband to live on suffering and with 'no enjoyment of life. But for our hope of another [life] the void would be unendurable.'[24]

It is common in the early stages after a death for bereaved

people to attempt to deny the reality of the loss,[25] and in a sense, it can be said that what Victorian mourners, both Christian and unbelieving, were seeking was an effective system of denial. For the orthodox, the essence of the funeral service lay in the 'sure and certain hope of a blessed resurrection', in the phrase, 'O death, where is thy sting? O grave, where is thy victory?' To be sure, most liberal Christians of the Broad Church tradition hardly insisted on literalness in their interpretation of these words; Jowett, Stanley, F.G. Maurice, and Kingsley were all frank enough to admit that they did not know exactly what to expect from life eternal or from God's mercy.[26] But when confronted with grief even very liberal Christians used formulaic language about eternal life, resurrection, and union with God in ways which seemed to provide other believers with comfort.

For sceptics, on the other hand, such theological denial systems simply could not work. Even if they understood the desirability of such comforts they could not accept them in Christian form. Again, let Leslie Stephen's words provide the analysis:

> We cannot and we will not believe in the loss of those whose lives seemed to be part of our essence . . . . You ask me for consolation under a blow which has wrecked your happiness. The only consolation which would satisfy you would be the assertion that the blow has not really fallen. We try to make such an assertion.[27]
>
> [Yet] who, that has felt the burden of existence, and suffered under well-meant efforts at consolation, will deny that such consolations are the bitterest of mockeries? Pain is not an evil; death is not a separation; sickness is but a blessing in disguise. Have the gloomiest speculations of avowed pessimists ever tortured sufferers like those kindly platitudes? Is there a more cutting piece of satire in the language than the reference in our funeral service to the 'sure and certain hope of a blessed resurrection'?[28]

Stephen in effect denied himself denial, in principle calling for resignation and the 'transmuting' of sorrow into nobler feeling, in practice grieving angrily and inconsolably for years.

Other sceptics, however, sought comfort – denial if you will – in other ways. Occasionally a case clearly bordered on the pathological, as when the painter Rossetti, distraught at the loss of his wife, called the doctor back on the third day because he thought that she was somehow still alive.[29] Much more typical, though, was turning to some theoretical or practical alternate system.

The Positivist 'Religion of Humanity' appealed to some English unbelievers. This system, devised mainly by Auguste Comte and disseminated in England by Frederic Harrison and Richard Congreve, emphasized the dependence of human beings on one another. After death individuals continued to be important, to 'live again', in the memories of their fellows. George Eliot's poem, 'Oh May I Join the Choir Invisible' came to represent almost an informal confession of faith for this philosophy:

> Oh may I join the choir invisible
> Of those immortal dead who live again
> In minds made better by their presence: live
> In pulses stirred to generosity,
> In deeds of daring rectitude, in scorn
> For miserable aims that end with self,
> In thoughts sublime that pierce the night with stars,
> And with their mild persistence urge man's search
> To vaster issues.
> So to live is heaven:
> To make undying music in the world [30]

A touching letter from Frederic Harrison about the recently dead wife of a friend illustrates how the positivist position was perceived to work in practice:

> To have her lying beside her old home will be a consolation unspeakable to him. What her life was before death, an active life of work in that quiet village, such her life will be after death. I mean her memory, and all the nameless influence of her doings, feelings, and thoughts, working still around her, amongst those who have known her . . . . Now every memory will be sealed up with all that dwells most deeply on his mind respecting her, her memory will be one unbroken thread of images of the past, and will irradiate his life.[31]

But positivists were never very numerous in England,[32] and in any case, as Martha Voegler points out in her excellent article on Eliot's poem, this position contained a certain sterility. Not only did the religion of humanity ignore 'the causal connection between sin and suffering, while entertaining that between goodness and bliss' but 'there is nothing in the poem of the pain that joining the Choir Invisible inflicts on the living – pain of the sort George Eliot herself experienced during months of harrowing anguish over Lewes's death.'[33]

A much more popular movement in late-Victorian England was spiritualism, the practice of communicating with the dead through mediums, spirit-writing, or other devices.[34] Belief in the authenticity of such communications was remarkably widespread, growing in part, most modern analysts believe, from a general concern that materialist philosophies were driving the soul, the spiritual element, out of contemporary life. For Christians – and a surprising number of its practitioners were Christians – spiritualism seemed an actual support to the old religion. With its experimental 'proof' of at least a kind of immortality and its ostensibly scientific approach, 'spiritualism appeared [in the words of Janet Oppenheim] to solve that most agonizing of Victorian problems: how to synthesize modern scientific knowledge and time-honoured religious traditions concerning man, God, and the universe'. Christian spiritualists, therefore, seemed confident, 'exuded an air of complacency',[35] for whether through their old religious beliefs or because of their communications with the spirits of the departed, their hope for personal immortality was reinforced.

Bereaved unbelievers, on the other hand, came to spiritualism more with a sense of desperation, doubting profoundly, yet – in their grief – hoping for some kind of reassurance. F.W.H. Myers, one of the founders of the Society for Psychical Research, provides a good example. He had been involved in an almost certainly Platonic love affair with his cousin's wife, Annie Marshall, and when she died in 1876 he was left in despair. His religious development had included a stage of committed Christian belief, then a loss of faith, and finally a turning to spiritualism. In an autobiographic essay, published privately after his death, Myers spelled out the relationship he saw between religion, love, and immortality.

The process of disillusionment, [with Christianity] I say, was slow; and in its course I passed through various moods of

philosophical or emotional hope . . . . These hopes faded
likewise from lack of evidence,and left me to an agnosticism
or virtual materialism which sometimes was dull pain borne
with joyless doggedness, sometimes flashed into a horror of
reality that made the world spin before one's eyes, – a shock
of nightmare-panic amid the glaring dreariness of day. It was
the hope of the whole world which was vanishing, not mine
alone. [Gradually he began to believe that only general
immortality could restore hope.] If there were indeed some
progressive immortality, then were the known evil of the
universe so slight in proportion to infinity that one might
trust in a possible explanation which should satisfy every soul.
But if there were nothing after death, then no argument
could reconcile the moral sense to the fact that so many
innocent creatures were born to unmerited and unrequited
pain.[36]

While she was alive Annie Marshall had been much interested
in psychic phenomena and particularly responsive to seances and
other spiritualistic influences. She and Myers had become involved
with each other during the period in which he was turning to
spiritualism, and her interest in the topic may well have been part
of her attraction for him. Three years after her death Myers felt,
although not too confidently, that he had received messages from
her. He continued to be interested in spiritualist phenomena and
to investigate them energetically, and in 1899 – twenty-three years
after Annie's death – he attended a series of seances in which he
was certain that he had made contact with his lost love, who came
to the medium as a 'spirit almost as bright as God; brighter and
higher, at any rate, than any she had thus far seen.' He described
his feelings in a letter to the philosopher William James (also
much interested in spiritualism):

You know that destiny brought me into the nearness of a spirit
who assuredly is immeasurably far from the highest, but who
nevertheless, is as high as aught that my own limited heart &
mind can grasp: – is to me indeed for all practical purposes a
satisfactory object of worship, & in herself an eternal hope.

May I not feel that this adoration has received its sanction,
& that I am veritably in relation with a spirit who can hear &
answer my prayer?[37]

The religious views of the poet and critic John Ruskin are not easily categorized, but it is fair to say that in his middle years he turned away from the literalist doctrines of his evangelical upbringing and became, as he described himself to a young friend, something of a 'pagan'.[38]

The great love of Ruskin's life was Rose La Touche, a girl he met when she was only ten, he thirty-nine. He proposed marriage when she reached eighteen, but her family objected and Rose herself had great doubts, mainly because of his religious heterodoxy. Theirs was a very troubled though intense relationship which never reached any real resolution; and when she was twenty-three (May 1875), Rose died, overcome by tuberculosis and nervous prostration.

A rather thorough record of their relationship and of his reaction to her death is provided by Rose's diary and Ruskin's letters,[39] and it is clear that her loss caused him to grieve deeply. Shortly after his father's death a decade before, Ruskin had been introduced to spiritualism, although at that time he had remained rather sceptical. After Rose's death, however, he was more receptive; at a seance arranged for him by his friend Lady Mount-Temple, he himself felt Rose's presence 'overwhelmingly' and the medium saw the figure of Rose bending protectively over him. Another mystical sign which affected him greatly came in the form of candle wax; 'At an Abingdon inn where he often retreated from Oxford he left the door open one evening in November, and noticed that the currents blew the melting wax of his candle into the configuration of *R*.'[40] These experiences convinced him of the reality of a spiritual world and of the immortality of the soul, and although he never became strictly orthodox in his beliefs he did thereafter feel more charitable toward Christianity.[41] More importantly for our purposes, through these mystical events he found comfort in his bereavement; as he wrote shortly thereafter to a friend: 'I feel quite well, chiefly because my dear little ghost seems to be looking at everything I want in all my books for me, as if she were really here, and Librarian. It's almost come to the point of my telling her to fetch me the books.'[42]

The Pre-Raphaelite painter Dante Gabriel Rossetti provides another example of an unbeliever who turned to spiritualism for comfort in his bereavement. His wife Elizabeth Siddal Rossetti died, almost certainly a suicide, in 1862. Rossetti felt both grief-stricken and guilty toward 'Lizzie', to whom he had on several occasions been unfaithful, and it is possible that his despair was exacerbated by his sense of responsibility. In any case, although he had been an unbeliever throughout his adult life, he seems to have turned quickly to the idea that he might in some way meet Lizzie again in a future existence. Close to the time of her death he wrote to a friend that he would not 'attempt any vain conjecture whether it may ever be possible for me . . . to meet her again',[43] but within a couple of years at the latest Rossetti was experimenting with various spiritualist techniques – especially table-tipping – in an attempt to communicate with his dead wife. Over the next few years he confided to friends that Lizzie was 'constantly appearing (that is, rapping out things) at the seances in Cheyne Walk . . . [And his brother William affirmed] that the things so communicated [were] such as only she could know.'[44] Lizzie long continued to exercise a morbid fascination for Rossetti. For years he was troubled by serious insomnia; in his brother's words:

> I consider that painful thoughts, partly but not wholly
> connected with his wife and her death, were at the root of it
> . . . . His active imagination gave him no respite; and to be
> sleepless was to be agitated and miserable and haggard as
> well. Haunted by memories, harried by thoughts and
> fantasies, he tossed and turned on the unrestful bed.

And seven years after her death he found a dead chaffinch lying in the road and picked it up, claiming that it was the soul of his lost Lizzie.[45]

A thread running through these spiritualist experiences of bereaved unbelievers is an extreme idealization of the lost beloved, amounting almost to an obsession. It is as if the bereaved – faced with a loss which in its devastating finality seemed to deprive life of its meaning – must provide the dead love with some man-made, self-created kind of immortality. It is true, of course, that Victorians in general showed respect for the departed, and that in their grief Christians, too, often exaggerated the virtues of the lost one.[46] Still, such admiration usually did not approach the near-hysteria which caused the people about whom we have been talking to view their really very ordinary loves as virtual saints.

To both Ruskin and Rossetti it seemed appropriate to compare the lost love with Beatrice, Dante's guide to spiritual understanding. Rossetti had made a number of sketches of Lizzie before her death and over the next decade he used them as the basis of a portrait of her as 'The Blessed Beatrice'. And Ruskin referred to Rose regularly as 'his Beatrice',[47] although a year and a half after her death he identified her more completely with the martyred St. Ursula, especially as portrayed in the Venetian painting by Carpaccio. Ruskin saw in his joined vision of Rose and St. Ursula another mystical sign, believing himself to be 'under supernatural guidance' so that 'in his mind Rose had achieved a kind of apotheosis, a tutelary force with the same revelatory power as the myth of St. Ursula'.[48] And we have seen that Frederic Myers thought it appropriate to see Annie Marshall as an object of veneration and even 'worship'.

Even when their adoration was emotionally more controlled or channelled in ways more socially acceptable, unbelievers seem to have used extravagant images to describe their lost loves. Leslie Stephen compared his wife Julia to 'the Sistine Madonna or any other representation of superlative beauty',[49] and used her life as a text for a secular sermon he preached to an Ethical Society within a few months of her death.[50]

Fundamentally, however, none of the alternative denial systems used by Victorian unbelievers seem to have worked very well. George Eliot died within two years of Lewes' death, hardly yet reconciled to her loss; Stephen, as mentioned above, remained bitter to the end of his days. Carlyle and Myers continued depressingly focused on their lost loves. And Ruskin's biographer notes that his subject and Rossetti were 'curiously similar . . . in their tragic fate. Secretly linked in prolonged and unaltered suffering, each, at last, was to be hounded across the very borders of sanity by the ineffaceable image of a dead woman.'[51]

To understand why bereaved Christians could find comfort while unbelievers, despite confidence in their own rationality, seem often to have come to the brink of despair, we need not engage in a philosophical debate about the truth or falsehood of the two groups' literal beliefs. Nor – for that matter – is it necessary to use intellectual history to try to examine the consistency or integrity with which they held their views; although it probably should be noted that 'logic', 'scientific evidence', and 'intellectual honesty' were exactly the kinds of term which the Victorian participants themselves used to conduct their ongoing debate.[52]

Instead let us turn to modern theories about grief and the role of religion in emotional life.

Scholars in this area, for example, have noted that one of the very widely observed phenomena of early grief involves an effort to resist change, to deny that the lost person is really gone.[53] In this denial stage Victorian Christians could talk to one another in terms of immortality and resurrection, so that the continued existence of the loved one was felt to be at least a poetic or metaphorical, perhaps even a literal, reality. Charles Kingsley, for example, comforted his dying wife by speaking

> of an eternal reunion and the indestructibility of that married love which, if genuine on earth, can only be severed for a brief moment . . . . And when the dreary interval before reunion was mentioned, he spoke of the possibility of all consciousness of time being so abolished that what would be long years to the survivor might be only a moment to the separated soul that had passed over the River of Death.[54]

The new unbelievers, on the other hand, were left with no persuasive language to use in helping themselves achieve any kind of denial or resistance to change. For many of them it was not merely that the old phrases about resurrection and eternal life were not literally true; they actually viewed them as an active deception, a lie. Angered at what they saw as religion's attempt to trick believers with a false comfort, they were unable to accept the Biblical tradition in even a metaphorical sense. Whereas Broad Church believers could use Christian formulae to affirm, at least at a poetic level, that life has meaning which transcends death, the new agnostics said essentially, 'If it is not true literally, then it is not true at all. And since it is not true, death must be seen as total annihilation, as a negation of life, even of life's meaning.' Thus we see Herbert Spencer near the end of his own life in intense despair, looking forward 'merely to extinction, that is a mere negative'. And even the usually cheerful Thomas Huxley at age fifty-eight confided to his friend John Morley that

> [i]t is a curious thing that I find my dislike to the thought of extinction increasing as I get older and nearer the goal. It flashes across me at all sorts of times with a sort of horror that in 1900 I shall probably know no more of what is going on

167

than I did in 1800. I had sooner be in hell a good deal – at any rate in one of the upper circles, where the climate and company are not too trying. I wonder if you are plagued in this way.[55]

Unwilling or unable to find reassurance in Christian terms, a number of the new unbelievers turned as we have seen to such apparently more bizarre systems as spiritualism or a nearly obsessive memorializing of the lost love. Extended, almost hysterical focus on the beloved seemed comparatively common among the bereaved unbelievers we have examined; George Eliot's behaviour after Lewes' death, for example, including her very peculiar marriage to John Cross, can perhaps be understood as an attempt to establish something of a cult to her husband's memory.

Modern analysts have also noted that, especially in the early stages, guilt and anger are common components of grief, presumably arising from the ambivalence involved in any ongoing relationship. When one of a pair is removed from the interaction and can no longer argue for his or her own position, the negative feelings of the remaining partner do not disappear but remain to confuse and to inspire guilt.[56] Bereaved Victorians, both Christian and agnostic, did experience such emotions: the believer F. D. Maurice, for example, wrote guilt-ridden letters on the death of his wife, saying 'I feel much more oppressed with the sense of sin than of sorrow . . . it is most mournful to think what I might have been to her and what I have been.'[57] And raging anger or guilt were obviously elements in the grieving of Leslie Stephen and George Eliot, as well as of Carlyle, Ruskin, and Rossetti. While we cannot prove that Christian beliefs helped believers deal with their guilt, it should be noted that Maurice (and other Christians) in guilty letters usually go on to express the hope that God will be forgiving. And it seems most reasonable to assume that a religion whose central message deals with the expiation of sin and with reconciliation would provide a generally comforting context. That among unbelievers anxious guilt so often was so prolonged seems to confirm this surmise.

At a social level, modern scholars have frequently noted that death produces potentially disruptive dispositions which may need to be channelled, controlled, and limited in intensity for the sake of social stability.[58] Again, differences presented by the two kinds of Victorian experience seem illuminating. It is useful to consider the consolatory language of Victorian Christianity as a means for controlling and directing emotion, for the social guidance of grief. Whereas condolence notes to George Eliot talked about 'dreariness', 'isolation', and 'deep horror', Christians used ritualized language and forms to tell each other how much grieving was too much. Consider this comparatively characteristic letter sent by Charles Kingsley to a friend whose mother had just died:

> I am not going to tell you impertinent commonplaces as to how to bear sorrow. I believe that the wisest plan is sometimes not to try to bear it . . . but to give way to sorrow utterly and freely . . . . If we say simply, I am wretched – I ought to be wretched; then we shall perhaps hear a voice, 'Who made thee wretched but God? Then what can He mean but thy good? And if the heart answers impatiently, 'My good? I don't want it, I want my love;' perhaps the voice may answer, 'Then thou shalt have both in time.'[59]

Or this letter sent by Jowett to a friend:

> To indulge in a life-long sorrow is not natural, nor quite right. We ought, I suppose, to be first resigned to the will of God and then cheerful again after a time . . . . Is there not a real danger that . . . we may be unthankful to God for the many blessings which He has left, because He has taken away one of them? . . . and I venture to ask you whether sorrow should not work in some way – in a diffused care and love of all, taking the place of an absorbing affection for one – in an absolute trust of God, though He has left us so very dark?[60]

It could, of course, be argued that turning to resurrection beliefs is in no way inherently more 'sane' than other kinds of coping mechanisms, that spiritualism is no more 'bizarre' than is a belief in bodily immortality, and that it is essentially unfair or at least illogical for consolers to claim a knowledge of God's will when what they are fundamentally exercising is social control. Logically such assertions may be sound, but at an emotional and social level, they are irrelevant. In Victorian England, it was Christianity, including beliefs, rituals, and consolatory language, which provided the kind of emotional and social structure that almost all human societies seem to find necessary. Unbelievers, determined to be rational, cut themselves off from much more than a set of myths and superstitions. They moved outside the societal psychological support framework of their time. They then had to 'make it up as they went along', to devise alternative comforts. But substitute supports did not have the authenticating stamp of the social context; in fact, sometimes their substitutes brought them into direct hostile conflict with the larger society, making them feel isolated as well as bereaved.[61]

Logically it may have been completely appropriate for the new unbelievers to argue – as so many of them did – that the Christian faith no longer seemed to rest on solid rational ground. Science, both in its content and in its method called the Biblical message into question, as did Biblical scholarship itself. And a commitment to rational inquiry and intellectual honesty may have legitimately seemed to require a setting aside of old beliefs.[62] In terms of individual, personal emotions, however, agnosticism was adopted at considerable cost. 'Without God, without creed'[63] could also mean 'without community, without comfort'. At the time of bereavement, this was often a rather lonely position in which to be.

11

DEATH, GRIEF, AND MOURNING IN THE UPPER-CLASS FAMILY, 1860–1914

PAT JALLAND

Despite the increasing interest in death as a suitable subject for historical analysis, death in Victorian Britain has been surprisingly neglected. Those few writers who have commented on the Victorian way of death have been generally critical of nineteenth-century practices, starting with a series of attacks towards the end of the First World War. Dr Robert Mackenna, C.E. Lawrence and Edward Mercer argued that people increased the fear of death by the 'pageantry of funereal gloom' surrounding it, rendering it 'black, mysterious and awesome'. In their view the dismal pomp of funeral and mourning rituals evoked false and morbid emotions, which encouraged extravagant commercialism and excessive gloom.[1] Bertram Puckle's book on *Funeral Customs* in 1926 also denounced the 'ugly trappings' and 'vulgar madness' of Victorian ceremonial; such excessive manifestations of grief were the outcome of self-indulgence.[2]

After a silence of almost half a century, several writers have taken up these anti-Victorian themes again. John Morley in 1971 wrote of the 'congealed and morbid romanticism' of the nineteenth century, when a show of exaggerated grief was a mark of gentility.[3] Two books on mourning costume have emphasized the expenditure and elaborate etiquette accompanying nineteenth-century death, as well as the snobbery, social climbing and profits of the mourning industry.[4] David Cannadine has recently condemned the Victorian celebration of death as 'a bonanza of commercial exploitation . . . more an assertion of status than a means of assuaging sorrow, a display of conspicuous consumption rather than an exercise in grief therapy'. He argues that excessive mourning robbed the bereaved of the will to recover and condemned them to an unhealthy obsession with death in their remaining years. Yet he admits that 'we still know quite extraordinarily little' about nineteenth-century attitudes towards death.[5]

To some extent, the more recent critics of the Victorians have been responding to an alleged crisis in the twentieth-century way of death, first documented in 1965 by Geoffrey Gorer, a social anthropologist. Gorer stated that half the deaths in his British sample of 359 bereaved people took place in hospital, less than a quarter of the bereaved were present at the death, and most people had no social or religious ritual to help them cope with mourning. The bereaved tried to hide their grief, and mourning was treated as a weakness rather than a psychological necessity. Gorer concluded that such denial of death and repression of grief were liable to cause physical or psychological suffering – a verdict subsequently sustained by psychologists.[6] This perceived crisis in the twentieth-century way of death has led some historians to consider whether death was more terrible in the past or the present. Philippe Ariès and David Stannard preferred the past, though chiefly in the context of French and American history; but historians of modern Britain seem to prefer death today, and perhaps their perspective on the Victorians alters accordingly.[7]

The arguments of the critics have also inevitably reflected the nature of their evidence. This has tended to emphasize prescriptive advice manuals on mourning dress and etiquette, funeral accounts of wealthy people, undertakers' records and parliamentary papers concerning the burial system. Historians need to know far more about the private and family experience of grief in the nineteenth century to achieve a more balanced view of the subject.

My aim in this chapter is to examine the experience of sorrow rather than its formal expression, and to consider whether Victorian mourning was indeed so excessive and unhealthy that it prolonged the normal process of grief. My chief focus is on the Victorian and Edwardian family, and the manner in which family members came to terms with dying and grieving; my interest lies more in experience and feeling than ritual, expense, costume and ceremony. My richest sources have been the correspondence and diaries of more than sixty upper-middle- and upper-class families, for the period 1850 to 1920. My emphasis is on the death of a husband or wife, since the loss of a spouse involves one of the most severe forms of grief.

Queen Victoria has frequently been cited as the archetypal Victorian mourner and therefore she provides a useful starting point. She appears several times in John Morley's study, and in the various books on mourning fashion, to illustrate general aspects of Victorian grief and mourning. Cannadine argues that the unhealthy Victorian obsession with death was 'exemplified most spectacularly in the case of Queen Victoria'.[8]

Queen Victoria's experience of sorrow merits closer consideration, to compare it with that of other Victorian and Edwardian widows, and to attempt to determine how far her grief was either typical or normal.[9] Queen Victoria's father died when she was a baby and her search for a father-figure included Lord Melbourne and culminated in the Prince Consort. Her love for Albert was overwhelming, involving powerful emotional dependency, even in matters of state. Victoria was highly emotional, prone to what Albert called 'combustibles' and temperamental nervousness. Her mother's death in March 1861, aggravated by guilt and remorse, led to a nervous breakdown. She nursed her sorrow in isolation, her 'unremitting grief' arousing rumours that her mind was unbalanced. Albert died suddenly of typhoid in December 1861 when Victoria had barely begun to recover from her mother's death. The doctors concealed the gravity of Albert's illness from the Queen, so 'this frightful blow has left her in utter desolation', as Mary Ponsonby noted.[10]

Victoria's mourning involved the 'mummification' of Albert, leaving his rooms and belongings undisturbed, as if he might return from the dead at any time, having his clothes laid out each day with hot water and a towel. Soon after his death Victoria told the King of the Belgians: 'I live on with him, for him; in fact I am only outwardly separated from him, and only for a time.'[11] She confessed to Lord Canning:

> To lose one's partner in life is . . . like losing half of one's body and soul, torn forcibly away. . . . But to the Queen – to a poor helpless woman – it is not that only – it is the stay, support and comfort which is lost! To the Queen it is like *death* in life! . . . and she feels alone in the wide world, with many helpless children . . . to look to her – and the whole nation to

nation to look to her – now when she can barely struggle with her wretched existence![12]

Victoria was only forty-two on Albert's death, but she continued to pine for the next twenty years, instead of the two or three which her subjects would have understood and which etiquette rules endorsed. She shut herself away with her family and household, seeing her ministers as little as possible. A prolonged depression led her to fear that the pressure of business on top of her grief was literally driving her mad. Rumours circulated that she was indeed insane, and the press increasingly condemned her seclusion and neglect of public obligations. The Queen's subjects generally considered her response to death so exaggerated as to be shocking and most certainly abnormal. The campaign against her seclusion reached its peak by 1869–70, eight years after Albert's death, fuelled by yet another refusal to open Parliament. The Queen's gradual recovery in the 1870s was aided by her adoption of the role of matriarch to her enormous family, and encouraged by Disraeli.

There is no doubt that Victoria suffered intensely during the dozen or so years after her bereavement. She experienced chronic and prolonged depression which left her afraid for her sanity. She was quite literally crippled by grief. The first decade of bereavement was characterized by persistent 'nervous' ill-health and physical disorders such as exhaustion, irritability and gout. Those close to her differed as to the remedy, but agreed about the gravity of the debility. The Queen's physician, Sir William Jenner, contended in 1871 that 'these nerves are a form of madness, and against them it is hopeless to contend'. Victoria's lady-in-waiting, Lady Augusta Stanley, considered the Queen self-indulgent and neurotic, rather than mad: she was best when 'taken out of herself – taken out of Doctors and maladies and nerves.'[13]

Psychologists today would conclude that Victoria's was a classic case of chronic grief – an obsessive preoccupation with the dead person, causing severe depression many years after bereavement. Psychiatrists and anthropologists such as Colin Murray Parkes, Geoffrey Gorer and John Bowlby have studied chronic grief among random samples of 'ordinary' people, as opposed to psychiatric patients. They concluded that chronic grief was a pathological disorder, characterized by prolonged grief, intense pining and severe distress, sufficient to impair working capacity and cause social withdrawal. Approximately ten per cent of Gorer's sample, and thirteen per cent of the London widows studied by Parkes, were still in a state of chronic despair and incapacitating depression more than a year after bereavement. Other studies report 'no less high an incidence'.[14] Such studies suggest that certain antecedent influences help to determine peoples' reactions to bereavement. Among the pre-determinants of an unfavourable outcome, Parkes includes childhood losses of close family, the death of a spouse in a dependent relationship, and a sudden, untimely death with no previous warnings. He found that younger women were more likely to experience difficulties in dealing with bereavement, especially if they were 'grief-prone' and had previously responded to death with excessive grief.[15] Judged by such criteria, Queen Victoria should be regarded as 'the exemplar of chronic grief',[16] criticized and misunderstood by contemporaries for her excesses. She was certainly not the archetypal Victorian mourner nor the model widow. Nor can we blame elaborate mourning rituals for her condition – that is to confuse grief with mourning. The explanation probably lies in the pre-determinants, such as her lonely childhood, her dependence on Albert, her extreme reaction to her mother's death, and the sudden, premature death of her husband. Jenner's diagnosis of 'a form of madness', ten years after Albert's death, was not far removed from today's psychological verdict.

My study of sixty Victorian and Edwardian families revealed remarkably few examples of chronic grief other than Queen Victoria, and certainly no incidence as high as ten or thirteen per cent. The rare cases I found were usually famous men in public life, comparable with Queen Victoria in certain obvious respects, if not in gender and royal status. Lord Aberdeen, for example, had a lonely and disturbed childhood; his father died when Aberdeen was only seven and he lived with strangers from the age of eleven. His beloved wife, Catherine, died in 1812 after seven years' mutual contentment and total commitment. Aberdeen, at the age of twenty-eight, was devastated and grieved for his idolized Catherine throughout his life. He believed that her ghost visited him almost daily and for a year recorded her appearances in Latin. An unhappy second marriage made it harder to bear the deaths of his three young daughters by Catherine, while his political career also suffered severely.[17] There are some similarities with Joseph

Chamberlain's experience. He lost his first two wives in childbirth, the first in 1863 and the second twelve years later. Chamberlain was left mourning two wives, with six motherless children. His prolonged sorrow and bitterness evidently exacerbated his cold reserve, acid temperament and introspection.

Ramsay MacDonald suffered similarly after his wife's death in 1911. He was in a state of shock for some weeks, followed by 'a horrible reaction'.[18] As he explained to friends, he was 'one of those unfortunate people who sorrow alone'. And as David Marquand noted: 'there was no catharsis; the wound never healed.' The reserved, aloof parts of MacDonald's personality predominated in the absence of his wife's warm companionship. When asked by an insensitive acquaintance why he never remarried, he replied: 'My heart is in the grave.' This grief and loneliness marred his children's home life, while he tried to find forgetfulness through work. His son, Malcolm, remembered his father's grief as 'absolutely horrifying to see . . . . This terrible tear-stained agony of grief' haunted the first anniversary of her death, and many afterwards.[19] Like Lord Aberdeen a century earlier, MacDonald's lonely, insecure childhood, without family life and comfort, made him exclusively dependent on a loving wife and more vulnerable to chronic grief on her death. The elevated political position of people like Victoria, Aberdeen, Chamberlain and MacDonald perhaps also left them more personally isolated on the death of a spouse.

Victoria, Aberdeen and MacDonald suffered chronic and abnormal grief, which was a highly unusual response to death in the sixty or so families examined. I will turn next to consider, by contrast, the far more typical and normal process of grief and recovery experienced by the vast majority of widows and widowers in these families. The evidence suggests that the basic psychological and emotional responses to the loss of a spouse were similar for men and women, but attempts to cope with their disrupted life varied according to gender. The two major differences between widows and widowers related to work and remarriage. Young and middle-aged widowers were positively encouraged to return to work, and later to seek solace in a second marriage. Dr John Gladstone, Professor of Chemistry, for example, lost his first wife and two children in 1864. According to an obituary written after his own death many years later: 'This [misfortune], however, seems to have been followed by only temporary suspense of activity, social and scientific.'[20] Six years later he remarried a woman seventeen years younger, who was happy to become mother to his four children. When Lord Cromer heard of Lady Grenfell's death in 1899, he wrote: 'Poor Francis. I hope he will stick to his work, though he will find it a hard struggle.'[21] Cromer himself 'stuck to his work' in Egypt after his wife's death in 1898, and remarried exactly three years later. Katharine Bruce Glasier was twelve when her own mother died and experienced 'no home happiness at all' until her father married again three years later; 'his grief and loneliness put out the sunshine for us children.'[22] The Count de Franqueville, well over sixty years old, wrote to Lord Selborne in 1916 to justify his second marriage, only a year after the death of his first wife, Selborne's sister. De Franqueville was increasingly depressed, found it painful to be alone in the 'big house', and was 'becoming neurasthenic': 'Unfortunately no one of my children was either able or willing to live with me .... Such being the case, I asked a lady friend to become the companion of my last days .... She is quite free and able to take care of me.'[23] A widow could scarcely expect to justify a second marriage on the same grounds. Dying wives and their friends frequently encouraged husbands to remarry in the interests of motherless children, as well as the assumed male need of 'sympathy and support.'[24] Most of the widowers in my sample seem to have taken this advice to heart.

Alfred Lyttelton deserves closer scrutiny because his experience of grief was not only more representative of widowers in these families than was that of Aberdeen or MacDonald, but it was also better documented than many. Alfred's first wife, Laura Tennant, died in 1886 after a difficult labour and after only a year of idyllic married life. Mary Drew thought Alfred 'desperately wounded. He can never be quite the same again.'[25] Alfred tried to cope day by day through work and routine. Two weeks after the funeral he commented: 'I can't write at all tho' I can work, and have got to a certain extent back into routine. The silence grows so intolerable.' He admitted that he found some comfort in the numerous condolence letters which reminisced about Laura's life. Three months later he wrote to his sister:

> I get along pretty well when I have active work, and when I am with others – but for me who used to love a good deal of solitude, it is strange and sad enough to dread my own company. For when I am alone I feel sometimes almost despair . . . [weakened] by the intense suffering I have borne.[26]

Alfred decided to take a holiday abroad at this point, in the hope that a complete change might do him good, especially in treating 'the mere bodily depression'. He believed 'there is strength, and beauty, and glory, to be won from these awful events, if only one is man enough to struggle bravely'. Six months after Laura's death, Alfred returned from America far more at peace with himself:

> I *am* the better for [the holiday] in all ways. The quick return to work after April, though the right thing to do, was a frightful strain in my state of mind then. But it was absolutely necessary to have the obligation of other men's affairs to look after in order that part only of the day should be spent in the agonising thoughts of fresh grief. But as you get a little bit away and the wounds begin to close a little, it is good to have the long days to oneself and to books, when one can travel back over every day of the sunny time.[27]

Alfred married again six years after Laura's death. His second wife, Edith Balfour, had initially seen him as a man set apart, sanctified by the loss of both wife and child, but she was delighted to discover that 'love of the dead need not be lost in love of the living'.[28] Alfred's grief for wife and child was intense, but never obsessive, endured with resignation and courage, aided by a deep religious faith and disciplined adherence to his professional occupation.

Widows generally had an even tougher time than widowers, with no paid occupation to divert their time, and no social expectations of re-marriage, except for the very youngest and prettiest. The emotional trauma of widowhood and the stages of grief for widows in these Victorian families generally followed the patterns described by modern psychologists. The state of alarm or panic at the loss of security and protection, and the fear of new circumstances, were very marked. Many nineteenth- and early twentieth-century widows experienced an utter helplessness, both practical and emotional. May Harcourt found George Bentinck's widow in a 'dreadful state' after his sudden death in 1909: 'Poor,

poor woman – What will she do? She has no interests and no occupation', after a life devoted to her husband's career and well-being.[29] Marion Montagu's father died in 1911, having been the mainspring of family life for years: 'all dear mother's actions were dependent on him'.[30]

Most widows recorded an initial stage of numbness, shock and disbelief. Harriet, Baroness de Clifford, lost her husband very suddenly in 1877 after twenty-four years' marriage: 'It was all so awfully, awfully sudden that even now when I *know* it is true I don't in the least believe it and try in vain to wake up from what I hope is some horrible dream.'[31] During the first three months, many experienced severe panic attacks, like Edith Lyttelton in 1913: 'Sometimes I wonder how I *can* go on without him – I suffer every now and then from a storm of panic.'[32] Most felt dislocated, disorientated and unutterably alone, as illustrated by Lady Wantage in 1905: 'one's whole past life seems as it were swept away; nothing can mitigate the feeling of solitude and desolation'.[33] Most experienced the intense psychological pain of acute and episodic pangs of grief in the early months. Blanche Balfour lay 'ill and distraught' for several weeks after her husband's death in 1856, so that relatives feared for her sanity. After her recovery, 'never again did she lose that iron self-control that was so marked a feature of her character as a widow and a mother'.[34] Lady Minto suffered 'intense anguish' for many weeks after her husband's death in 1914:

> [She kept] seeing him in my mind lying suffering in my bed or in my chair by the fire – the agony of the loneliness is almost more than I can bear . . . . He speaks to me from every nook and corner . . . . His presence is everywhere. I see him resting on his shooting stick looking at the cutting and levelling in the church garden.[35]

Mary Drew felt 'physically wounded' in 1910, with no hope of treatment, since 'half of me has been taken away'.[36] Many widows endured this characteristic search for the dead husband, the attempt to locate him in his favourite chair. Most of them saw no option but to 'go on, day by day, and try to do the right thing'. Most found it a 'terrible effort', exacerbated by lack of food and sleep; they could not concentrate or keep account of time; there was 'a numbing sense of utter indifference to things and people, events and books'.[37] All these symptoms of grief were experienced and recorded within the first year of bereavement.

Most of these behavioural characteristics are noted by psychiatrists who have studied the response of groups of widows in recent years. The only significant difference was crucial, in that very few of the Victorian and Edwardian widows experienced a pattern of prolonged, chronic, and obsessive grief. Most of these widows endured severe anguish to varying degrees during the first year of bereavement, and struggled to cope with loneliness and practical problems during the second. They learned how 'to tread the path of life alone', 'living from day to day' as apathy turned slowly into acceptance. In the course of the second year the 'numbing sense of utter indifference' faded, and an attempt to build a new life began.

If we ask why these Victorian and Edwardian widows seemed to cope more readily with grief than the groups of widows examined by psychologists in recent years, there are two possible types of explanation. First, support networks of family, friends, and religious beliefs were more effective before 1914. These widows found different forms of consolation in their grief, but religious belief was the most significant. This is well illustrated in Winifred Byng's letter to her father after her bereavement in 1887: 'Yes, indeed, God is the only refuge in such misery as this. He alone can send the comfort, and He does . . . I am quite convinced that God allows [Alfred's] soul to speak to mine . . . [Religion] is *the* link that binds us together still. We can meet in God, if nowhere else.'[38] The support of their families, combined with love of children and grandchildren also helped to provide a positive purpose for life.

The second explanation is crucial to any understanding of Victorian mechanisms for coping with grief. Nineteenth-century mourning rituals met the psychological needs of the bereaved by reducing the terrifying aspects of death, and structuring the grieving process within a coherent set of customs. These rituals also performed a valuable function in rallying the support networks of family, friends, and neighbours, and enabling them to operate effectively within a defined framework. Some critics of the Victorian way of death have seemed to confuse mourning with grief, but these are not identical and the distinction is vital. Grief is the experience of deep sorrow, whereas mourning implies the expression of sorrow.[39] My evidence suggests that mourning customs provided opportunities for the bereaved to express their sorrow in a manner that made the grieving experience easier to endure and to complete. Mourning rituals held therapeutic benefits which could outweigh the disadvantages for those who suffered most.

A brief examination of some of the more significant mourning customs should substantiate my argument. A vast number of comments testified to the value of condolence letters. In 1878 Lady Portsmouth reminded her brother, Lord Carnarvon, to write to the Cadogans on the death of their son: 'people in great trouble are easily touched or easily wounded'.[40] Violet Cecil, twenty years later, shared this view: 'It is not very much trouble and makes all the difference at such a time'.[41] Lucy Cavendish in 1882, after her husband's assassination, experienced a sense of falling into an abyss, and yet at the same time she was sustained, and 'protected and wrapped round as with soft cotton wool with the sense of love and sympathy all round'.[42] Constance Flower thanked Marion Bryce for her letter of condolence on her husband's death in 1894: 'the love shown to him does help me . . . I long and cling to those who cared for him.'[43] Mary Herbert wrote on the death of her father, Lord Acton, in 1902: 'It *does* help to see how much his friends mourn with us.'[44] On her mother's death in 1903, Mary Bryce wrote: 'We have received over 100 letters and cards, and there is such a wonderful spontaneity of feeling about the sympathy – a real genuine feeling of admiration and reverence for her that is very touching . . . . One does feel grateful for so much sympathy.'[45] Lavinia Talbot noted in 1913 that the numerous condolence letters proved a source of comfort to her bereaved sister-in-law, Edith Lyttelton: 'their love and passionate feeling for him, and through him for her and his children, cannot but be wrapped round in a real glow of affection, and keep her in the "dark times"'.[46] Lucy Cavendish commented on these same condolence letters for her brother: 'How one *loves* the personal recollections and actual words quoted – like *living* things amid all sad regrets.'[47] An extraordinary sensitivity and understanding of grief often founded on personal experience marked most of the thousands of condolence letters in these family papers.

Memorials and memorabilia of the dead were also important for the Victorians, but are often perceived today as particularly morbid and distasteful. Therefore it is vital to consider Victorian responses to such memorabilia, rather than assuming that their attitudes were the same as ours. The psychological explanation for the value of mementoes is not hard to find. The phase of grief described by psychologists as the 'searching period' involves locating the dead person in specific places, such as the grave or favourite chair. These locations become shrines which help to mitigate grief during a temporary period of intense anguish. Similarly, familiar mementos evoke a sense of closeness to the dead person which can be rewarding during the 'searching' phase and sometimes subsequently.

Photographs or portraits of the deceased lying in the coffin were a fairly common form of remembrance which seems to have been much appreciated by the bereaved family. After Lord Frederick Cavendish was brutally murdered in Dublin in 1882, Lord Spencer arranged that photographs be taken immediately in the hospital, once the nurses arranged flowers around the bed. Lord Spencer intended the photographs as a surprise for the grief-stricken widow, who thought them 'too beautiful – such a deep comfort'; she had them framed in soft velvet and sent numerous copies to close relatives and friends. A lock of Lord Frederick's hair was cut off in Dublin by Lord Spencer and enshrined in a diamond locket which Lucy treasured.[48] Widows often wanted a bust or a statue of their dead husband, as well as portraits and photographs. On the death of her husband in 1885, Lady Charlotte Phillimore reported – in an unusual turn of phrase: 'I have had a cast taken of his beautiful face and hope for a successful Bust.'[49] In 1891 the newly widowed Gertrude Gladstone told the family she would like a 'recumbent statue' of William in Hawarden Church, but her father-in-law, W. E. Gladstone, considered this inappropriate in the small church. Gertrude persisted with the Grand Old Man: 'I do long for there to be some little memorial of Him in the Church, near where we sit. Do you see any objection to our getting some designs for a Tablet?'[50]

Another form of memorial which evidently helped to assuage the grief of the survivors was the written record of the deceased person's life and death. Such memoranda were usually seen as therapeutic to the writer, as well as providing a precious recollection for other members of the family. Lady Minto proposed to the recently widowed Katharine Elliot in 1865 that she write 'a little account of my dear husband', partly 'with a view of its being some little occupation to myself in my loneliness and also one which would be in harmony with my feelings'.[51] In 1910 Edward Talbot was writing and crying over 'the wonderful account' of his brother's life, which was expected to bring great 'comfort and thankfulness' to Johnny's widow.[52] Memorials of this kind were usually written only for the immediate family; sometimes several family members contributed, especially in compiling detailed daily records of the last illness and death. These testimonials were often copied out lovingly by relatives and friends, to be bequeathed in their informal wills. There is considerable evidence, then, that these various forms of memento served a genuinely useful function in satisfying the needs of the survivors for tangible memories of the dead.

The value of Victorian mourning dress and etiquette is a more complex question, in part because far more evidence survives about the formal requirements than about people's attitudes to them. Also, twentieth-century writers have subjected these rituals to such criticism that it is difficult to see beyond these to the Victorians' own experience and response. Victorian mourning dress and etiquette rules were based on traditional customary judgement concerning the most appropriate time needed to work through grief. A widow was required to wear full black mourning for two years, gradually changing into the colours of half mourning, such as grey and lavender, for the last six months. The dress also implied social isolation, since no invitations could be accepted in the first year and public places of resort were to be avoided. Mourning of a parent for a child, and vice-versa, was twelve months, while six months was stipulated for a brother or sister. It was assumed that in normal grief the period of mourning dictated by society would roughly approximate to the period of grief. The etiquette of mourning dress undoubtedly had its disadvantages, especially for women. Modern critics have dwelt on the potential for commercialism, extravagance and social emulation, while contemporary 'authorities' on mourning fashion, such as the *Gentlewoman* and the *Queen*, were capable of absurd refinements.

By contrast, my research into the personal experience of grief, rather than its formal expression, suggests that mourning dress was not necessarily a burden for those in deep sorrow. Advice books acknowledged that it soothed the sorrow of many widows to express it outwardly. *Manners and Social Usages*, in 1884, recognized the value of wearing black as 'a shroud for ourselves . . . a wall, a cell of refuge', while deploring 'ornamental mourning'. The wearing of black in moderation could be therapeutic and was usually a genuine expression of grief, helping especially 'to break the first fierce flow of sorrow'.[53] Modern psychologists argue that 'in so far as [mourners] feel heavy-hearted it may help them if society recognizes this.'[54]

People in these Victorian families who suffered intense grief scarcely ever mentioned mourning clothes in their correspondence or diaries. Black dress was taken for granted, and was usually the least of their concerns. Mourning dress fulfilled a useful function in reminding friends and relatives that those most closely affected by the bereavement were likely to be in a state of depressive withdrawal for a number of months. For example, in 1896 Elizabeth and Agnes King were in deep mourning for their mother, who died two months before their niece's wedding. They wished to attend the wedding, 'black dresses and all', but did not feel 'quite up to joining any gathering of friends' afterwards. Their thoughts would be with the bride's dead grandmother, so that 'I think we should either break down altogether or else be too cold and quiet, like dampers to the happiness of others.'[55]

Discussion of the practical details of mourning dress was more common among relatives further removed from the immediate family. Even then, there are many more examples of moderation, common sense, and 'making do', than of fashionable extravagance. Agnes Anson had to wear black in 1888, 'as public mourning is desired, but I can so manage that it will not cost us much'.[56] On the death of her uncle in 1906 Elsa Bell commented: 'We are hardly going to make any difference in our doings except dressing in black.'[57] Victoria Dawnay had 'no black whatever' on Uncle Harvie's death in 1887, 'but I do not think that will matter – my clothes are all dark'.[58] The chief expressions of irritation at the etiquette of mourning related to public ceremonial mourning required for royalty. In May 1910, Audrey Wallas hoped that King Edward VII would not die 'at an inconvenient moment', though she had no intention of wearing more than 'a little black', whenever the moment came.[59] Ceremonial public mourning was not related to private feelings for most people; therefore it could be either an imposition or an occasion for the kind of extravagant fashionable excess so often condemned.

Finally, the vexed question of extravagant funeral and mourning expenditure deserves comment. Surely the crucial point here is that people with wealth have committed part of their money to their own, or their family's deaths throughout the ages. Marvellous monuments of pagan antiquity were devoted to the housing of the dead, such as the pyramids of the Pharaohs and the splendour of Tutankhamen's tomb. Clare Gittings has demonstrated that late-medieval wills often divided the estate into three, with one-third earmarked for the testator's soul. Expenditure on the funerals of the nobility rose markedly from the late fifteenth century; the funerals of Henry Percy in 1489 and the second Duke of Norfolk in 1524 each cost more than £1,000.[60] Lawrence Stone believed the early modern period marked the zenith of extravagant aristocratic expenditure on funerals.[61] The emphasis on personal glory increased with the Renaissance, and with it the grand displays over the grave, such as Henry VII's chapel in Westminster Abbey. Professor McManners has shown that it was customary in eighteenth-century France 'to spend more, rank for rank, than was reasonable by any provident standard.'[62] Throughout recorded time there is abundant evidence that people received the funerals and memorials they were willing and able to pay for.

The Victorians seem to have differed little from their predecessors in this respect. The increasing wealth and numbers of the middle classes explain rising expenditure on funerals and mourning dress, especially in the first half of the nineteenth century. Many Victorian deaths were, indeed, costly. The 1843 Report on 'Interment in Towns' found that the average funeral expenses of titled people varied from £800 to £1,500, and those of the upper gentry from £200 to £400. The Duke of Wellington's funeral in 1852 was the highpoint of Victorian funeral extravagance; the triumphant funeral car alone cost £11,000, while the *Observer* calculated that £80,000 changed hands for seats for the funeral.[63] But Wellington's funeral was remarkable precisely because it was so extraordinary.

It would be as valid to applaud the Victorians for reforming funeral excesses as to condemn them for promoting such extravagance. The vogue for ostentatious display reached its peak in the 1850s, and the Victorians were themselves responsible for curbing it. As early as the 1840s the case for the reform of funeral ceremonies was already recognized, as was the need to create new cemeteries and to close down the unsanitary, overcrowded churchyards. Societies like the National Funeral and Mourning Reform Association were established to encourage moderation and simplicity. In mid-century Roundell Palmer's will directed that:

> my body may be buried in the plainest, commonest, and least expensive way, in a single coffin, made of elmwood, and in a common grave . . . . And I would have no tablet or other monument erected to my memory in the Church.[64]

Wellington's 1852 funeral was widely criticized and contrasted markedly with Gladstone's simpler and more dignified state funeral in 1898. By the 1880s the highly complex mourning conventions were being relaxed and many more people were expressing wishes for more modest funerals. In 1894 the *Lancet* stated that 'the cost of funerals has been very greatly reduced among the upper and upper-middle classes. It is found that the expenditure of £10 to £15 will allow of everything being completed in good taste and reverence, but without any excess.'[65] The Victorians would appear to have been no better and not much worse than the people of earlier centuries in the matter of funeral extravagance, pomp and display. The numbers of the wealthy willing to spend their money on death had vastly increased, but the Victorians were themselves responsible for significant reforms in funeral excesses.

A reassessment of death, grief and mourning in nineteenth-century Britain is overdue. My own contribution is an attempt to understand more about the experience of death and grief in dozens of families, in order to relate the mourning rituals to the actual experience of grief and loss. The incidence of chronic and obsessive grief appears to be higher today than it was in the century before 1914. There were probably fewer Widows of Windsor then than now. Religious belief undoubtedly brought more comfort to the bereaved in the nineteenth century than it does today. Probably equally important was the complex framework of death and mourning rituals, which seemed to comfort the dying and helped to meet the psychological needs of survivors. The evidence from these Victorian and Edwardian families suggests that mourning rituals, familiarity with death, and understanding of the process of grief, helped the bereaved come to terms with their loss, and contributed to the process of healthy grieving. If the Victorians were indeed morbidly obsessive about death, as some modern critics claim, then perhaps Victorian obsession is more healthy than modern repression. The Duke of Wellington's funeral and the sad excesses of the Widow of Windsor have misled us for too long. We should be fair to the Victorians about death and grief as well as love and sex. Above all, we need to distinguish more clearly between grief and mourning, directing as much historical attention to the former as the latter.

12

THE LANCASHIRE WAY OF DEATH

ELIZABETH ROBERTS

The title for this chapter was chosen because it is based almost entirely on primary evidence taken from Lancashire sources, namely 170 elderly people from the towns of Barrow, Lancaster and Preston whom I interviewed at length in the years 1971–81.[1] The chapter makes no claim to discuss customs associated with the dying, the dead and bereaved in other areas of Great Britain although common sense would suggest that some if not all the customs could be found elsewhere. However an alternative title might have been 'Lancashire ways of death' because there were variations in customs between different families. Some of these differences were related to religious denomination, for example only Roman Catholic families mention praying for the dead. It has been more difficult to discern differences in custom caused by the passage of time. The younger witnesses (some of whom are quoted in this paper) describe patterns of behaviour which were very similar to those recounted by previous generations. There is a strong sense of continuity in accounts of the social and familial lives of perhaps a rather conservative working class before the Second World War. When changes are discernible mention is made in the text. All the people interviewed were of working-class origins. A rather simplistic definition of 'working-class' was adopted, that is the father or widowed mother of the family worked with his or her hands, was paid weekly, and was an employee rather than an employer. Obviously this group included skilled, semi-skilled, and unskilled workers. Families' levels of income were different but they shared the same aspirations of having the 'best' funerals possible for their dead relatives. However it is clear from the evidence that some funerals were 'grander' than others, and that such questions as the number of coaches and horses in the procession were indicators of status and financial standing in the community.

The problems of interpreting evidence are ever present for historians. Sometimes however the difficulties appear to be more acute than is usual. This is indeed the situation for the present writer when considering evidence on the Lancashire way of death. The respondents in the oral history surveys talked about many aspects of their familial, social, and working lives and were in fact only asked two questions specifically about death. These were 'What do you remember about funerals?' and 'At what ages did your immediate family die?' (It should be noted that they usually spoke about their own families' funerals but they also described funerals as neighbourhood events and spectacles. When the evidence is atypical mention is made.) These questions and others about, for example, the roles of the extended family and of neighbours, generated a substantial amount of information which provides the evidence for this chapter.

These data however present major difficulties in interpretation. Some of the difficulties arise from the nature of the original research. Its aim was to collect evidence on many aspects of working-class life which otherwise would not be recorded. This broad approach has the obvious advantage of providing contexts, interrelationships, and corroboration for data on any particular topic. For example the interconnections between family, neighbours, religious beliefs, poverty, budgeting, and status can be looked at as the context for a specific examination of death, ritual and bereavement. The disadvantages of a general approach are that very specific questions about some topics were not asked, as indeed will become apparent in this chapter. However there are more serious problems of interpretation. The meanings firstly of what so many respondents said in their interviews and secondly and perhaps more importantly what they did in the earlier part of this century, often eluded me and, in fairness, appear also to have eluded them. Certainly those who described rituals virtually never gave any view as to their meaning and purpose. Like so much of late-nineteenth-century and early-twentieth-century social life, much was taken for granted, was unquestioned and done because 'it was the thing to do.'

Definitions of ritual found in a dictionary of sociology include 'ritual is a mode of communication from person to person and from age to age', and 'Ritual makes explicit the social structure, the system of socially approved "proper" reactions between individuals and groups, ritual is all action symbolic of important social values.'[2] These definitions when considered in the light of the Lancashire evidence simply produce many questions but few answers. Precisely what were the rituals surrounding death communicating and to whom? Which social structures and social values was ritual making explicit or at least symbolizing? Did ritual have any meaning at all? Analysis is difficult and this chapter as a result is rather descriptive.

One thing is however clear; judging from the time, money and attention lavished on the dying, the dead and the bereaved, death was a very important part of working-class life in north Lancashire in the period 1890–1940. It is also apparent that even if the precise significance of each ritual was never made explicit by the respondents, the carrying out of the various rituals was important and appeared to provide comfort and support for the bereaved. Funeral rituals were also to do with status and prestige and the cost of working-class funerals had long been commented upon. Sir Edwin Chadwick noted in 1843: 'The desire to secure respectful interment of themselves and their relatives is, perhaps, the strongest and most widely diffused feeling amongst the labouring classes of the population. Subscription may be obtained from large classes of them for their burial when it can be obtained neither for their own relief in sickness nor for the education of their children nor for any other object.'[3]

Certainly there was only one family in the sample who did not pay death insurance for each family member and who suffered the indignity of the mother having a pauper's funeral. The money was usually paid through a large industrial insurance company but sometimes through a small, locally organized death or funeral club. On the other hand only a relatively small minority could afford voluntary health insurance (usually through a friendly society). A splendid funeral for the dead appears to have been more important than health care for the living. Again funerals were much more expensive and assumed a greater importance than weddings although by the 1930s there are signs that in more prosperous working-class families, weddings were beginning to have special clothes, transport, and celebrations. The usual explanation for working-class families saving so hard for funerals was the dread of a pauper's funeral. Robert Roberts wrote: 'To have a body put away on the parish was to bear a lifetime's stigma.'[4] The woman who remembered her mother having a pauper's funeral continued to be distressed throughout her life because her mother's grave was unmarked and therefore there was nowhere to go to grieve for her mother or to lay flowers. Having such a focal point for grieving continued to be very important during this period.

And yet questions of status and cost were not the only factors determining the arrangements surrounding death. Many rituals cost very little but were still important.

Different rituals and different procedures were followed at different stages from the person's death to the long aftermath of the funeral. Each appears to have had a different function and a different significance.

It is important to understand the part played by death in the socialization of working-class children.[5] It became a familiar part of their lives from an early age: siblings, grandparents, parents died and almost inevitably at home. Children both observed and participated in the rituals surrounding death. These experiences inevitably affected their adult attitudes to death, ritual and bereavement, although it would be unwise to assume that they were all affected in the same way.

The experiences of the first respondent in the early years of the century can in many ways be described as totally atypical. She was the only child in the sample asked to dispose of a still-born baby, this usually being performed by the midwife or the parent. In other ways however Rose's attitude and behaviour were typical; she was not afraid of the dead body, she was confident about handling it and knowledgeable about the 'correct' way to make a coffin however economically. She demonstrates the familiarity with death so often observable in children from that era (i.e. in Edwardian England). Rose must have seen a body before but she was not asked that question. Her very practical approach and absorption in the detail of what she was doing were characteristic of the neighbourhood 'layer-out' of the period. It is not perhaps too surprising to find Rose fulfilling this role as an adult.

Mrs Armstrong (A3B)

R: No, when the baby was born we could hear . . . we used to
know how fat mam was getting but we didn't know
anything. Then I heard a noise one night and I got up
and I thought m'mamma must be bad and I went in the
room and said, 'Is m'mamma bad?' Dad said, 'No, go and
get yourselves back into bed m'lass she'll be alright till
morning'. When I got up in the morning and I went in
she'd had this little baby and it was still born. She said,
'You're not going to school today Rose'. I said 'Aren't I?'
She said, 'No, you'll have to stay at home I want you to do
something for me'. I said, 'What's been the matter with
you mamma?' She said, 'Well I've got a baby'. I said
'Where is it?' She said, 'It's just there', and it was on a
wash stand, on a pillow with a cover over it. When I
looked at it it was like a little doll, very small. She said, 'I
want you to go to a shop and ask for a soap box'. I said 'A
soap box Mam'. She said, 'Yes'. I said 'What's it for?' She
said, 'To put that baby in'. I brought this soap box back
and I called on the road to my friend, a young girl I went
with, so I told her and she went with me. She said, 'I'll
come down to your house with you'. She came and we
had a look at this little doll and my friend said, 'Let us
line this little box with wadding'. We lined this box with
this bit of wadding and then m'mamma put this wee baby
in it and the lid fastened down like the boxes do today, no
nails. She said, 'There's a letter here' . . . They didn't call
them midwives then, just ladies and it used to be half a
crown or five shillings to come and deliver a baby . . . She
gave me a letter. 'Now you've got to go up to the cemetery
and give this letter to the grave digger, any grave digger
you see in.' I said, 'I can't take it wrapped up in paper', so
I went in the back and saw an old coat of m'dads. I ripped
the black lining out of this coat and we wrapped this little
box in this lining and put some string round it, put it
under our arms and off we went to the grave digger. I give
him this letter and he read it. He said, 'Oh yes, just take it
over in the church porch love. You'll see a few parcels in
that corner just leave it there'. Me being inquisitive said,

'What are you going to do with it?' He said, 'Well we have public graves, everybody don't buy graves, they haven't the money, when the public graves get nearly full up we put one in each grave'. 'Oh that's what you do', I said. He said, 'Yes. Tell your mammy it'll be alright', and we turned back home.

ER: Did it upset you at the time?

R: Yes because we thought it was like a little doll. It wasn't really developed, just small.

ER: How old would you be then?

R: I'd be about twelve.[6]

The great majority of working-class people died at home and were attended by various members of their family. However only a few death-bed scenes were remembered. This one is from a family of devout Roman Catholics of Irish descent living in Barrow.

Miss Thompson (T2B)

R: Dad was only fifty-six when he died but it was the mill flour got on his chest. He got angina pectoris. He died a very good death and when he was dying he called them all around, all of them, all of us and said that if he'd ever done anything to hurt us or anything that was wrong would we forgive him and ask God to forgive him and pray for him when he was dead. I remember dadda.[7]

Mr Blackburn said 'My father was very poorly before he died and he sent for Dick and Tom. He said to them. "Always be good to your mother." And they were that! All ten of us were round her bed when she died!'[8] It is interesting how one important aspect of being good to one's mother is assumed to be being at her death-bed.

The death itself appears to have been a time for the family, for the giving and receiving of the dying person's last wishes and mutual comfort for the living.

Very soon after death, however, before *rigor mortis* set in, the body had to be laid out. This duty was sometimes carried out by a female relation, a wife, sister or daughter, but more usually by a 'layer-out' from the neighbourhood. These women were known and respected throughout the small communities in which they lived and could be called upon at any time. They were, especially before the 1902 Midwives Act, very often the area's untrained, but experienced, midwife. None was remotely like Dickens' Sarah Gamp who would go to a lying-in or a laying out with equal zest but it is clear that they were part of a long tradition. John Hawkins Miller wrote: 'Victorian midwives had their roots in ancient folk traditions and it was not unusual for them to preside over the rituals of both birth and death.'[9] In Lancashire these traditions continued well into the twentieth century for the 1902 Midwives Act did not of course prevent unqualified midwives from working, providing that they were registered. As late as 1917 the Lancaster Medical Officer of Health reported that almost one third of all the babies born in the previous year had been delivered by the same unqualified midwife.[10] The presence of these women to usher into life the newly born and to provide some of the last services for the dead seem to symbolize women's significance in the two most important *rites de passage* in life, that is birth and death. Certainly there are echoes in the rituals performed for the newly born and the newly dead.[11] Pennies were placed on the navels of the babies and on the eyes of the dead; a binder was tied round the child's abdomen and also round the chin of the corpse. As the century has progressed women have lost something of their traditional dominance in the rituals surrounding birth and death, the former now being likely to be presided over by a male obstetrician and the latter by a male undertaker.

Laying out did something to demystify death, the bereaved had something practical and detailed to think about, for example what the dead person would wear. Layers-out were practical women, often humorous, always kindly. Some were paid, some accepted presents, others refused all recompense, seeing the laying out as part of their neighbourly, perhaps religious duty.

Mrs Morrison shows how laying out tended to run in families, how it was seen as part of the obligation of helping neighbours and the usual attention to practical details. The time she refers to was just after the First World War.

Mrs Morrison (M3P)

ER: Did she (i.e. her mother) ever lay people out when they were dead?

R: Oh yes. So did I. Not many but I have. I've laid two out. I was with one and then I did the other myself. Oh I did another one.

ER: How did you know what to do? Did your mother tell you?

R: My mother didn't tell me how to lay anyone out. But an old lady across the way used to go to lay people out and I was asked to go. I said 'Well Mrs B. will go if you'll go and help her.' So she showed me what to do. When it came that I had to do, I could do it.

ER: Did you used to put pennies on their eyes?

R: Yes. And cotton wool up their noses and backpassage and a nappy on and a pair of stockings. There's many a man gone with a pair of silk stockings on when we couldn't find anything else.

ER: And a night-shirt?

R: A night-shirt or shirt or whatever they had. My husband was in pyjamas. We would generally put them a clean one on. Because my husband, the nurse (male) changed him and just laid him ready. I said 'Do you want anything?' and he said 'No love, his clean clothes are here. I'll just put them on. He's just right for taking away.'

ER: And did you used to tie a cotton round the chin?

R: Or put a book, a prayer-book under their chin to hold it. And if they had any teeth, get them back in if you could.

ER: When babies used to be born do you ever remember them putting pennies on their tummy-buttons?

R: Yes. And a binder round and a binder round you! They don't do that today? (The binder was to support and flatten the mother's stomach).

ER: No, they don't. Where did your mother learn about laying people out?

R: I wouldn't know! Unless her mother?

ER: Did her mother used to do it as well?

R: Grandma used to do it oh yes, she was the old woman of the village. The doctor always came for her whenever anything wanted doing.[12]

Mrs Armstrong, who has already been heard of as the child Rose, was her street's layer-out as an adult.

Mrs Armstrong (A3B)

R: Really they were better friends than what they are. They're good friends today but they're more for themselves. In the olden days it was sisterly love and more motherly love. I used to be knocked up time out of time when anybody died. They used to come and knock at the door at midnight and say, 'Will you come and lay the baby out? Will you come and lay so-and-so out?' I used to go and lay them out.

ER: Do you remember how old you were when you first laid somebody out?

R: Oh, I'd be about twenty. I would have loved to have been a nurse but my mother made me go as a cook. One night I had a knock at midnight and I'd three little girls and I got up and an old lady up the street had passed on and they asked me if I'd go and lay her out. I said 'Just give me time to get dressed.' I got dressed and when the children got up in the morning to go to school they said, 'Who was that man knocking the door again through the night?' 'It was only Grandma Houldsworth had passed away and they asked if I'd go and lay her out'. Mabel turns round and said, 'Why don't you put a blinkin' card in the window: "Laying-out taken in"? Not "Washing taken in", "Laying out taken in"!' We never used to take anything off them, never bothered, but now today everything is altered and the undertaker does all that.

ER: Would people give you a present, were they grateful for what you did, or just take it for granted?

R: No, they would ask you and try to offer you summat or buy you summat. They hadn't the money and we used to say 'No'. I never took nothing off them and it used to be our good deed for them, we were good neighbours.[13]

For some men and women laying out was somehow seen as a metaphor for relationships within and obligations to the neighbourhood. It is tempting to relate the decline in the custom of laying out with changes in neighbourhood relationships. A Preston woman, married in the inter-war period, had been a layer-out before marriage. However after marriage, her husband, who in many other ways did as he was told by his wife, expressed a wish that she did not continue as a layer-out as 'he did not want her bothered'. (Perhaps echoing the sentiments of Mrs Armstrong's daughter). 'Distancing' between neighbours would also lead to a reluctance to ask anyone to perform such an intimate task as laying out. As Ruth Richardson has pointed out, no one was compelled to seek the services of the undertaker for this work. They chose to do so.

However the local layer-out was active and her services usual in Lancashire before 1940. After the laying out the corpse became the focus of attention. The body was almost inevitably kept at home if the person had died there and those dying in hospital were usually brought home. The body was placed in a coffin without the lid, in a downstairs room. The curtains were drawn and a Catholic family may well have had candles round the coffin. However, despite the large number of Prestonians of Irish Catholic origins, the only mention of a wake came from a man from an Irish Catholic family who had spent his childhood in Cleator Moor on the West Cumberland coast. This extract is included because it is one example of the black humour surrounding the various aspects of death. Mr Foster gives this account as if he were telling a very funny story. The role of humour in the rituals surrounding death is as yet unexplored but for some people it appears to have been important.

Mr Foster (F1P)

ER: What about funerals when you were young?

R: Well, in Cleator Moor, of course, funerals were a big thing because they had the wake beforehand, you know. The wake went on until the corpse was nearly smelling.

ER: Did you ever go to a wake?

R: Yes. Once or twice.

ER: And what happened?

R: I mean, I didn't realise that they were wakes, I thought they were having a party or something.

ER: And what happened at them?

R: They would all be sat down telling tales and laughing like hell. Poor corpse was lying in the coffin there with his rosary beads round his hands. I remember, it was an uncle of mine that were dead and I remember looking at him and I said, 'By God they've washed him!' It was the first time that I had ever seen him clean! I had never seen him clean.[14]

Perhaps one should add that the uncle had been a miner.

Wakes were uncommon but viewing the body was completely usual. Far more people visited bodies than went to funerals. Indeed it was unusual for children to attend a funeral unless it was that of a close relative. But it was very common for children as well as adults to view bodies. It is not always easy to discover why this was done. Certainly some children or young people went because they were 'persuaded' to do so by older relatives or neighbours. We do not know why the older people thought this viewing was essential. However, it is possible that in the reluctance of some of the young to view bodies, can be seen the seeds of the future decline in this custom. Mrs Peters was about ten years old in 1908 when this incident took place. Her sister had died with peritonitis in hospital.

Mrs Peters (P1L)

R: They brought her back home and she was in the front room, the coffin was on the chairs. A dreadful time, I was scared stiff. The neighbours came and the children from school as well. You didn't seem to want to deprive them of it. I only had one look and I thought, well, it's not my sister. She must have been in pain, torn at her little face. They'd put cotton wool in her nostrils and granny said, 'You must go in'. Fancy making you do things like that in those days, and she said, 'Now just touch her'. I remember putting my hand on her forehead and it was stone cold. I remember shuddering. I didn't ever go in again. They collected at school and we were all dressed up in little black dresses.[15]

There is a similar feeling of revulsion in the evidence of Mr Terry who was eighteen when this event occurred.

Mr Terry (T2P)

R: In 1921 I think there was a cotton strike on and I came home from St Helens and a pal of mine Jack Nimmo and I went swimming in the river. We got caught in the Spring tide and he panicked and drowned and they compelled me to go and have a look at him in the coffin. I didn't want to but the law was the law and I well remember going in. I remember his mother getting hold of his clothes and putting them on the fire to burn them.

ER: Who suggested that you went to see him?

R: I think it was some of the elderly neighbours. I can remember her, Old Mother Barnes, as we called her. She insisted that I went.[16]

Mr Terry's comment that 'the law was the law' could presumably be interpreted as the 'custom was the custom'. Thus in these cases visiting the body could well be ascribed to reluctantly bowing to moral or social pressure. But very many other cases of visiting the corpse occurred for apparently different reasons. Some children visited voluntarily, perhaps to seek and find emotional release in weeping in a group. Mrs Booth remembered when she was at school before the First World War.

Mrs Booth (B1P)

R: When I was at school girls used to die and you'd think, oh, suchabody's ill and she's died. And you would go and knock at the door and 'Please can I see your Annie?' They'd have gone off in consumption quick, you know. It was dreadful.

ER: When you went to see them they were at home in their coffin?

R: Oh it was a highlight. A band of us would go from the school and knock at the door and you went in to see them, and crying our eyes out you know. Well that's not done now.[17]

Other children also found viewing the body 'a highlight' but found it perhaps more exciting and enjoyable an occasion than an emotional one. Mrs Calvert grew up in the inter-war period. Her experiences, like those of many respondents, suggest that the custom of viewing the dead remained a common one.

Mrs Calvert (C5P)

ER: You are younger than a lot of the people I talk to but when you were a little girl had the habit died out of going to see dead people?

R: Yes, we used to go. Me and my mate used to go and we

would knock on the door and say, 'Please, can we have a look at 'em?' They would open the door and let you in you see. We would go in and have a look and then we would go out and then we would be there for the funeral because they always gave you a bit of cake. Even now I say, 'Isn't that funeral cake good?' We used to go that often and once me and m'mate went and we knocked at the door and when they opened the door we asked if we could have a look at 'em and they said 'Who?' We said, 'Them that's dead!' They said, 'There's nobody dead at all.' We just said, 'Well, your curtains is drawn.' She just said, 'We're washing our lace curtains.' After that m'mother got to know and I never went again.

ER: How old would you be?

R: Happen about eleven or twelve.

ER: When you saw the bodies did you touch them, did they expect you to touch them?

R: Now I would touch them as it wouldn't trouble me now but then I would never touch them but yet I never dreamt about them.

ER: It wasn't just young people, it was anybody?

R: It was anybody, all round our neighbourhood and people we knew would tell us that suchabody was dead. If I thought it was near enough I used to say 'Nellie, suchabody is dead, can we go?' We would go and that were it.

ER: Why did you like going?

R: I don't know why I liked going. Unless they are a relation now I won't go and see anybody dead.

ER: Quite a lot of people used to go and look at bodies.

R: Yes. And yet my daughter today, she'll not go and see anybody dead, yet she works at the Infirmary.[18]

Like Mrs Booth, Mrs Calvert is very aware of customs changing but has no clear idea of why she behaved as she did when she was eleven. Was it ghoulish interest? Was it the inter-war equivalent of going to a horror film? We can only make surmises. She mentions not touching them and yet not dreaming of them. There was a very old superstition that if you touched dead people you did not dream of them.

In general it was assumed that visiting the dead was a way of neighbours showing respect. It must have been of comfort to the bereaved although no respondent actually said that. There were other ways too in which neighbours showed respect and gave support. Money was often collected for a wreath with, in some areas, the surplus going to help with the family's expenses. On the day of the funeral neighbours drew their curtains and came out into the street again 'to pay their last respects'. A few women in the street undertook to prepare the funeral tea. The bereaved family provided the food but the women got it ready, cutting up sandwiches, setting out cups and saucers, boiling kettles and so on. Occasionally if there was a need they might loan china or even a good hearth rug. In some areas they even wore black dresses with white broderie anglaise aprons. They did not stay for the tea as guests, only as helpers. The only people outside the family who appeared to gain anything tangible from a funeral were the neighbourhood's children who attended the door of the house to be given some sort of funeral bread or cake (already referred to by Mrs Calvert). Its actual form varied from town to town and district to district.

Mrs Shuttleworth (S3L)

R: The tea was always at home. When you went to the funeral you always got a funeral biscuit wrapped in paper. It was like a sponge. I know a little girl died. Our Tom said, 'Will we be going to the tea party and getting a biscuit?' He was only thinking about the biscuit. They used to give it to you in the house. You'd go to the door and they'd be giving biscuits out.[19]

Of all the accounts left by respondents about funerals none speak, of the religious service, or the role of the priest, minister or vicar. Admittedly they were not asked specifically about these matters, simply about their memories of funerals. This omission of a religious dimension to funerals is very curious as so many of the respondents were conventional and/or convinced Christians, who continued as life-long Church-goers. What is remembered is the pomp and pageantry of the funeral procession which added colour and drama to many lives. One respondent said: 'When there was a funeral it was like going to the cinema.'[20] It also, and most importantly, both proclaimed the status of the bereaved and his family and also confirmed it. Black clothing for all the mourners, except for very small children, was 'de rigueur'.

Mr Bowker (B1B)

R: To show their respect the men always walked three or four either side of the hearse, always black ties and never brown boots. You must have black boots, everybody was in mourning. If you were very poor and couldn't afford it and had a grey suit, you were allowed to wear a black band round your arm. All the ladies must be in black and very often a funeral was more expensive than a wedding.[21]

He went on to describe the black crape which a widow wore. Sometimes the very poor borrowed clothes. Other respondents have described mourning clothes in a similar way, some deplored the arrival of navy blue and grey as substitutes for black in the 1950s. The hearse was a splendid vehicle, horse drawn until well into the inter-war period. It often was of great interest to children.

Mrs Wilkinson (W1B)

R: It was my first funeral. I remember running home and saying 'Oh there's a glass coach in the next street, and there's a big wooden box in it, oh it's like a fairies' coach'.[22]

It was also, and perhaps inevitably, a source of more black humour. One spectator said to another one as the splendid hearse passed 'People are dying for a ride in that!' The hearse and the driver and the clothes made lasting impressions on children who attended funerals.

Mrs Mitchell is remembering the 1920s:
Mrs Mitchell (M1P)

R: But still they had a funeral. They probably wouldn't have new clothes but they were always dressed in sombre black. For twelve months afterwards you didn't wear anything only black. When my father died I was ten and we were all in deep black for at least twelve months afterwards for respect. When father died it was 1923. I remember going in a carriage and pair, to the funeral. It was the old fashioned glass coach for the coffin, like the hansom cab, and the horses were black with big white plumes and the driver had his tails on and his black hat with these black ribbon streamers down the back and the whip in his hand.[23]

Adults were more aware than were children of the exact indications given by the funeral procession of the status of the family. Mr Bowker after describing the black topcoats and hats of the undertaker and the drivers went on to the crucial question of the transport itself. 'If you could afford it you had two black horses, if not just one, and then there was the question of how many carriages you'd have ... everybody to find out what kind of funeral it was used to say "how many carriages did they have?"'[24] The answer to this question tended to define the wealth and standing of the bereaved family. But status could be demonstrated in other ways. It was very important to some families to have a lot of people in a funeral procession, most of whom would walk. Mrs Mulholland's mother was a socialist activist in Barrow and when she died in the late 1920s had a very large funeral procession: 'M'mother's funeral, the unemployed turned out. I think the front end of the funeral was going into Cheltenham Street and the tail end was at the station. It was a big turn out.'[25] (The procession was probably about 300 metres long.) Ironically this family was the only one to mention the funeral service: as atheists they had a secular one!

If the bereaved had been a member of a friendly society the family could expect a large turn out at the funeral. Indeed societies tended to pay members to go and act as bearers for the coffin. In the eyes of the bereaved this attendance undoubtedly gave status to the dead person. Mr Bowker and his family were members of several friendly societies. He said 'When they got to the cemetery they'd all stand around and bury them and there was always someone there and you felt then that the person that was being buried was a proper person not just the ordinary man out of the street who didn't belong to anyone.'[26] To add the final drama and to confirm the ultimate status, a band might be hired (for about £1-10s or £2 before the First World War). Hiring a band has however only been mentioned in Barrow and again it was the focus of more black humour. Spectators approved of it heading the funeral procession to the cemetery playing the *Dead March*, however the mother of one respondent strongly disapproved of its playing (on its return) *The Girl I Left Behind Me*, especially if a lady had been buried.

Some respondents had relatives who either were killed in the First World War or who died as a result of injuries or illnesses contracted therein. Again it would appear that it was the special pomp and ceremony attached to a military funeral which was remembered.

Mrs Askew (A2B)

ER: What about funerals when you were a child?
R: I remembered m'dad's very well. He was an old army man so they had him on a gun carriage. He was a member of British Legion you see and they had a gun carriage and they fired over his grave. They sounded the Last Post and fired over his grave and I remember that very, very vividly it was on a Whit Monday and it was a blazing hot day and we were all in deep black. We had to have black. They had the horses of course then, cabs, no coaches, no cars.[27]

A final indication of status was the number of wreaths displayed on the grave. Mourners admired the flowers but also tended surreptitiously both to count the number of 'floral tributes' and to read the inscriptions on the cards. Very often neighbours collected for a neighbourhood wreath as the final gesture in the ritual of paying their last respects.

Mrs Booth (B1P)

ER: Do you remember neighbours collecting when people died?
R: Oh yes, they have done that up till a few years back.
ER: And was it just for flowers?
R: Just for flowers, but now of course, there's other things you can give to now. You give your money to church or Pat Seed (a Lancashire campaigner for cancer relief) or anything like that, which is far better. But oh you had to be loaded up with flowers. I used to say, 'You can smother me with them', but now I keep telling them 'No'. How you change.[28]

This respondent like many others is aware of her own changing attitudes. The possible reasons for these changes will be looked at later.

The bereaved were helped by various rituals following the funeral. Firstly the funeral tea was a time for family solidarity with stories and reminiscences about the dead person and about the wider kinship group. Secondly for a considerable time after the death the bereaved family was in mourning. Before the First World War the length of the mourning period has been quoted as a year. It is possible that in the inter-war period this period was somewhat reduced. Unfortunately no respondent mentions how long the period of mourning was in the 1920s and 1930s and they were not asked this question. However the wearing of mourning clothes for lengthy periods survived in many families especially among older people. This tradition may well account for their appearance in the photographs of the period. They appeared to be inevitably dressed in black or in very dark colours. It was neither seemly nor economical to have light coloured garments. As both best and everyday clothes were probably black there was not usually a problem in buying expensive special mourning clothes. Mourning however not only meant wearing black clothes, it also meant refraining from too much social activity. Indeed the bereaved might well be gossiped about if they appeared to be too jolly. This might well have been seen as a constraint by some people but it had a more positive side. People were given time to grieve, indeed they were expected to grieve. There appears to have been little expectation that they should smile brightly and pretend nothing had happened. Lastly the dead were constantly remembered, they were talked about, their photographs were displayed and their graves visited. The bereaved felt no sense of embarrassment when remembering their dead relatives. Mr Boyle remembers the 1930s.

Mr Boyle (B9P)

R: The dead were a very important aspect of life. They were talked about a great deal, almost as though they were still living. There were little prayer cards in the prayer books. 'Of your mercy pray for the soul of so and so.' We went to the cemetery, what seemed like every Sunday afternoon and that seemed my only link with the countryside. My first memory of roses was the magnificent roses in the cemetery at Preston. The graves were tended and it was

what seemed like a weekly ritual. And they went on living,
so to speak, in conversation and memory for some
considerable time. So there was that sense of continuity.[29]

Many old people might wonder why an historian should want to
record what to them seemed an obvious part of every day life.
Others will suggest that within recent years they have experienced
at least some of these customs surrounding funerals. But it would
seem that for the majority of people funerals are not what they
used to be. In some ways changes in funerals and their attendant
customs can be seen as a metaphor for what has happened to other
aspects of working-class life. Death has been taken over by the
professionals: hospital staff, district nurses, the undertaker and his
staff. As well as professionalization death has experienced
rationalization: it is judged preferable to spend money on the
living than the dead (notice Mrs Booth's comments on flowers);
and old customs judged to be superstitious like visiting and
touching the dead body have been abandoned. Death like family
life has also become a much more private affair than it was
formerly, much less frequently are neighbourhood curtains
drawn, passers-by's hats removed or the tea prepared at home by
willing neighbours, nor of course are the neighbourhood's
children involved. It is important to stress that these changes have
not been forced upon an unwilling working class; they have chosen
different ways from those of their ancestors. The reasons why these
choices were made and the old ways largely abandoned are not
entirely obvious and require much more research into working-
class social life after 1940.[30]

Death was central to life at the beginning of the twentieth
century. It was not an unmentionable subject, it was talked about
and experienced all too frequently. Children from their earliest
years were acquainted with it. Perhaps this familiarity explains the
way death is discussed by old people. It was there as were the rituals
surrounding it. It was accepted. Mothers did care about their dead
children, siblings missed each other as did spouses. But the
respondents gave the impression of all passion and all grief having
been spent. Only rarely does a passionate sense of loss emerge. Mrs
Gregson's mother had sixteen children and raised eleven of them.
One of the boys was two years old when he died and she missed
him dreadfully. Her daughter remarked: 'She said that every baby

she saw she wanted to snatch. She would have stolen anybody's baby to fill that want. She had all those but she wouldn't spare one.'[31] Another woman remembered her stepmother's youngest son being killed in the First World War and remarked: 'Well it killed her. She died after that'. [32] But in general the attitudes of working-class people in the period 1890–1940 towards death were rather different from those of their descendants.

The mother of a Preston woman died in a diabetic coma aged 44. Her daughter later discovered that an insulin injection cost 10 shillings. At the time she was earning 12 shillings a week as a domestic servant. She added: 'I've consoled myself, I've composed myself. If mum had come out of the coma we just couldn't have afforded it. She would have had to die.'[33] There was no railing against the unfairness of not being able to afford this treatment, no bitterness against the 'system'. And yet this was and indeed remained a deeply loved mother. This acceptance, coupled in many cases with a sense of fatalism and allied to the comfort given both by performing long established rituals and by receiving the help and support of kin and neighbours, seem to have helped our predecessors to cope with death.

Finally there is the mystery of the missing religion. Funeral rites seemed to owe more to cultural traditions and social needs than to religious beliefs. And yet there was much genuine religious belief among the respondents. Perhaps underpinning and ultimately explaining the working-class attitude to death and bereavement was a belief that the dead wife, husband, child or parent was going to a better place. But that belief was rarely made explicit and it was my failure as an oral historian that I did not ask about it. In the final analysis we can describe but not perhaps fully understand the Lancashire way of death.

NOTES

1 INTRODUCTION

1 W. Shakespeare, *Hamlet*, I. ii. 72.
2 R. Huntington and P. Metcalf, *Celebrations of Death. The Anthropology of Mortuary Ritual*, Cambridge, 1979; J. Whaley (ed.), *Mirrors of Mortality: Studies in the Social History of Death*, London, 1981; L. Stone, *The Crisis of the Aristocracy, 1558–1641*, Oxford, 1965, 572–81; C. Gittings, *Death, Burial and the Individual in Early Modern England*, London and Sydney, 1984.
3 H. Brémond, *Histoire littéraire du sentiment religieux en France depuis la fin des guerres de Religion*, IX, Paris, 1932; M. C. O'Connor, *The Art of Dying Well*, New York, 1942; N. L. Beaty, *The Craft of Dying: A Study in the Literary Tradition of the* Ars Moriendi *in England*, New Haven and London, 1970.
4 E. A. Wrigley and R. S. Schofield, *The Population History of England, 1541–1871: A Reconstruction*, London, 1981, 528–9 (quinquennial estimates produced by back projection).
5 A. F. Sillitoe, *Britain in Figures: A Handbook of Social Statistics*, 2nd edn, Harmondsworth, 1973, 30–3; T. H. Hollingsworth, 'The demography of the British peerage', supplement to *Population Studies*, XVIII (2), 56, 59; Wrigley and Schofield, op. cit., 250; M. Anderson, 'The emergence of the modern life cycle in Britain', *Social History*, 10 (1), 78.
6 Wrigley and Schofield, op. cit., 332–6, 667–70; P. Slack, *The Impact of Plague in Tudor and Stuart England*, London, 1985; R. Mitchison, *British Population Change Since 1860*, Studies in Economic and Social History, London and Basingstoke, 1977, 39–57.
7 J. Le Goff, *The Birth of Purgatory*, London, 1984; D. P. Walker, *The Decline of Hell: Seventeenth-century Discussions of Eternal Torment*, London, 1964.
8 A. D. Gilbert, *Religion and Society in Industrial England: Church, Chapel and Social Change, 1740–1914*, London, 1976, 175–87; J. Jacobs, 'The dying of death', *Fortnightly Review*, LXXII (392), 264–9.
9 D. Cannadine, 'War and grief, death and mourning in modern Britain', in Whaley (ed.), *Mirrors of Mortality*, 191–2.

10 P. Ariès, *Western Attitudes toward Death from the Middle Ages to the Present*, Baltimore, 1974; *Essais sur l'Histoire de la Mort en Occident du Moyen Age à nos jours*, Paris, 1975; *The Hour of Our Death*, Harmondsworth, 1983.

11 Gittings, op. cit., esp. 9–14.

12 M. Vovelle, *Piété Baroque et Déchristianisation en Provence au XVIIIe Siècle*, abridged edn, Paris, 1978, esp. 322–6; P. Chaunu, *La Mort à Paris: 16e, 17e, 18e siècles*, Paris, 1978, esp. 187, 454–6; J. McManners, *Death and the Enlightenment: Changing Attitudes to Death among Christians and Unbelievers in Eighteenth-century France*, paperback edn, Oxford, 1985, esp. 438–65.

13 D. E. Stannard, *The Puritan Way of Death: A Study in Religion, Culture, and Social Change*, New York, 1977, 117–63.

14 Gittings, op. cit., 98.

15 This was further illustrated in a paper delivered by L. Taylor, 'The function and use of mourning dress in Britain, 1885–1925': abstract in *Social History Society Newsletter*, 12 (1), 7.

16 Cf. Whaley, 'Introduction' to Whaley (ed.), *Mirrors of Mortality*, 14.

17 'Death denied', is the title of Chapter 12 of Ariès, *The Hour of Our Death*.

18 Spiritualism could also be combined with Christianity, as Professor Garland makes clear.

19 The phrase comes from a letter written to me by Professor Garland.

2 DEATH, CHURCH, AND FAMILY IN ENGLAND BETWEEN THE LATE FIFTEENTH AND THE EARLY EIGHTEENTH CENTURIES

1 C. Gittings, *Death, Burial and the Individual in Early Modern England*, London and Sydney, 1984.

2 R. L. Greaves, *Society and Religion in Elizabethan England*, Minneapolis, 1981, chapter 16.

3 A. J. Collins (ed.), *Manuale ad vsum percelebris ecclesie Sarisburiensis*, Henry Bradshaw Society, XCI (1958), 97–118; F. E. Brightman, *The English Rite*, 2 vols, London, 1915, II, 818–47; T. Becon, *The Sicke Mannes Salue*, in J. Ayre (ed.), *Prayers and other Pieces of Thomas Becon S. T. P.*, Parker Society, 1844, 87–191; N. L. Beaty, *The Craft of Dying: A Study in the Literary Tradition of the* Ars Moriendi *in England*, New Haven and London, 1970, 154.

4 For two vivid and very different accounts of death-beds in funeral sermons, see J. Chadwich, *A Sermon preached at Snarford in Lincolnshire at the Fvnerals of Sir George Sanct-Pavle Knight and Baronet*, London, 1614, 25–9, and R. Wroe, *Righteousness Encouraged and Rewarded with an Everlasting Remembrance in a Sermon at the Funeral of the Right Worshipful Sir Roger Bradshaigh of Haigh, Knight and Baronet*, 1684, 19–20.

5 P. S. Seaver, *Wallington's World: A Puritan Artisan in Seventeenth-century London*, London, 1985, 27.

6 E. Kübler-Ross, *On Death and Dying*, London, 1970, esp. 235.

7 R. Bird (ed.), *The Journal of Giles Moore, Sussex Record Society*, 68 (1971), 288–90.

8 M. C. Cross, 'The Third Earl of Huntingdon's death-bed: A Calvinist example of the *Ars Moriendi*', *Northern History*, XXI, 80–107.

9 J. Evelyn, *The Life of Mrs Godolphin*, ed. H. Sampson, London, 1939, 76–8.

10 Ibid., 12; J. Horsfall Turner (ed.), *The Rev. Oliver Heywood B.A., 1630–1702; His Autobiography, Diaries, Anecdote and Event Books* Brighouse, 1881–5, II, 281.

11 E.g. J. O. Halliwell (ed.), *The Autobiography and Correspondence of Sir Simonds D'Ewes, Bart*, 2 vols, London, 1845, I, 111; S. Clarke, *A Collection of the Lives of Ten Eminent Divines*, London, 1662, 472.

12 L. Stone, *The Family, Sex and Marriage in England 1500–1800*, London, 1977, 207.

13 J. Taylor, *The Rule and Exercises of Holy Dying*, London, 1929, 94; B. Grosvenor, *Observations on Sudden Death*, London, 1720, 28–9.

14 H. Alford (ed.), *The Works of John Donne, with a Memoir of his Life*, 6 vols, London, 1839, VI, 228. (I owe this reference to Dr Kenneth Fincham.)

15 Taken from Reading, Berkshire Record Office D/A1/1, 1A, 2 35–41, 43–5, 47–9, 51–9, 61–4 and Norwich, Norfolk and Norwich Record Office, Norwich archdeaconry will registers Fuller alias Roper, Aleyn, Bastard, and the will registers for 1648–52, 1699–1700 and 1746.

16 F. Pollock and F. W. Maitland, *The History of English Law before the time of Edward I*, 2nd edn, 2 vols, Cambridge, 1968, II, 314, 326, 356–8; M. Spufford, *Contrasting Communities: English Villagers in the Sixteenth and Seventeenth Centuries*, Cambridge, 1974, 320–34; K. Wrightson and D. Levine, *Poverty and Piety in an English Village: Terling 1525–1700*, New York, San Francisco and London, 1979, 151–2.

17 For some examples of continuing overt concern that the soul should benefit from pious benefactions, see Norfolk and Norwich Record Office register Aleyn, ff. 213b^v–214^r, 235^v–236^r, 246^r, 260^r–261^r and Berkshire Record Office D/A1/39/172a, 181a, D/A1/51/165a, and cf. Gittings, op. cit., 161–3.

18 J. Raine (ed.), *Depositions and other Ecclesiastical Proceedings from the Courts of Durham, Surtees Society*, 21 (1845), 214.

19 Spufford, op. cit., 334; Wrightson and Levine, op. cit., 158.

20 Berkshire Record Office, D/A 2/C 155, ff. 117^r, 47^v–49^r.

21 Cf. R. T. Vann, 'Wills and the family in an English town: Banbury 1550–1800', *Journal of Family History*, 4(4), 360.

22 Brightman, op. cit., 828–9; T. Hall, *A Sermon Preached … at the Funeral of Robert Huntington Esq.*, London, 1684, 28; Taylor, op. cit., 109; Berkshire Record Office, D/A 2/C 155, 96^r–97^v.

23 H. Swinburne, *A Briefe Treatise of Testaments and Last Willes*, London, 1590, 23^{r-v}; D. Cressy, *Literacy and the Social Order. Reading and Writing in Tudor and Stuart England*, Cambridge, 1980, esp. 142–74.

24 Cf. Wrightson and Levine, op. cit., 93.

25 Collins, op. cit., 152–62; Brightman, op. cit., II, 848–79.

26 J. G. Nichols (ed.), *The Diary of Henry Machyn, Camden Society*, 42

(1848), xxi–iv; see also some of the funerals which took place immediately before and after the implementation of the Elizabethan religious settlement, ibid., 174, 188–190, 193, 211–12, 244–5, 307; Gittings, op. cit., 162–3; Greaves, op. cit., 706–8.

27 Ibid., 700–3, 706–16; L. Stone, *The Crisis of the Aristocracy, 1558–1641*, Oxford, 1965, 576–7; Gittings, op. cit., 166–215.

28 Ibid., 162–4, 241; Greaves, op. cit., 720–1.

29 Wrightson and Levine, op. cit., 134–7; Gittings, op. cit., 155–61, 240; cf. D. E. Stannard, *The Puritan Way of Death: A Study in Religion, Culture and Social Change*, New York, 1977, 110–15.

30 J. T. Rosenthal, *The Purchase of Paradise: Gift Giving and the Aristocracy, 1307–1485*, London, 1972, 16, 22.

31 See the very revealing remarks made on his death-bed by Thomas Pepys, the diarist's brother, in R. C. Latham and W. Matthews (eds), *The Diary of Samuel Pepys. A New and Complete Transcription*, 11 vols, London, 1970–83, V, 87.

32 A recent excellent study of change in a conservative region is R. Whiting, '"For the health of my soul": prayers for the dead in the Tudor south-west', *Southern History*, 5, 68–94. But see also Greaves, op. cit., 706–8.

33 G. Ferebe, *Life's Farewell, or A Funerall Sermon Preached at Saint Iohns in the Deuises in Wiltshire, the 30 of Avgust last 1614 At the Fvnerall of John Drew, Gentleman*, London, 1615, 27; Greaves, op. cit., 704–6; F. S. Boas (ed.), *The Diary of Thomas Crosfield*, Oxford, 1935, 55, 60; T. Gataker, *Certaine Sermons, first preached and after published at severall times*, London, 1637, 211, 255; C. Scot, *The Saints Priviledge or Gain by Dying*, London, 1673, 24: P. Collinson, '"A magazine of religious patterns." An Erasmian topic transposed in English Protestantism', in D. Baker (ed.), *Renaissance and Renewal in Christian History, Studies in Church History*, 14, 242–8.

34 E. Gibson, *Codex Juris Ecclesiastici Anglicani*, 2 vols, Oxford, 1761, I, 453.

35 Greaves, op. cit., 697, 701, 703.

36 F. Burgess, *English Churchyard Memorials*, London, 1963, 27–9; J. G. Hurst, 'A review of archaeological research to 1968', in M. Beresford and J. G. Hurst (eds), *Deserted Medieval Villages*, London, 1971.

37 My impression that such requests became less common from the later sixteenth century onward contrasts with that given by Gittings, op. cit., 87.

38 In Norwich a college of priests was attached to the charnel founded by Bishop Salmon (d. 1325). The clean bones of those dying in the city might be brought there, to be 'decently reserved till the last day'; it was granted to the city in 1548 and apparently emptied. See F. Blomefield and C. Parkin, *An Essay towards a Topographical History of the County of Norfolk*, 11 vols, London, 1805–10, III, 261; IV, 55–6.

39 Gittings, op. cit., 114, 240 (though our explanations for the spread of coffin burial are different); Burgess, op. cit., 27, 116–7; R. Parkinson (ed.), *The Autobiography of Henry Newcome, M. A.*, 2 vols, *Chetham Society*, 26, 27 (1852–3), 52.

40 J. T. Cliffe, *The Puritan Gentry: The Great Puritan Families of Early Stuart England*, London, 1984, 131–3; Greaves, op. cit., 732–3.

41 F. P. and M. M. Verney, *Memoirs of the Verney Family during the Seventeenth Century*, 2 vols, London, 1907, I, 530–3.

3 THE GOOD DEATH IN SEVENTEENTH-CENTURY ENGLAND

1 L. M. Beier, *Sufferers and Healers: The Experience of Illness in Seventeenth-Century England*, London, 1987.

2 R. S. Schofield and E. A. Wrigley, 'Infant and child mortality in England in the late Tudor and early Stuart period', in C. Webster (ed.), *Health, Medicine and Mortality in the Sixteenth Century*, Cambridge, 1979, 61–96; E. A. Wrigley and R. S. Schofield, *The Population History of England 1541–1871: A Reconstruction*, London, 1981.

3 J. Graunt, *Natural and Political Observations Made upon the Bills of Mortality*, in P. Laslett (ed.), *The Earliest Classics*, Gregg International, 1973, (first published, 1662), 14, 32, 76–7.

4 R. Latham and W. Matthews (eds), *The Diary of Samuel Pepys*, London, 1970–82, IV, 285 and IX, 381.

5 A. Wilson, 'Participant or patient? Seventeenth century childbirth from the mother's point of view', in R. Porter (ed.), *Patients and Practitioners: Lay Perceptions of Medicine in Pre-Industrial Society*, Cambridge 1985, 129–144.

6 P. Ariès, *The Hour of Our Death*, trans. H. Weaver, London, 1981, 5–28, 297–312.

7 E. S. de Beer (ed.), *The Diary of John Evelyn*, London, 1959, 8–9.

8 M. E. Lamb, 'The Countess of Pembroke and the art of dying', in M. B. Rose (ed.), *Women in the Middle Ages and the Renaissance: Literary and Historical Perspectives*, Syracuse, NY, 1987, 207–26.

9 The London surgeon, Joseph Binns, routinely kept patients with fractured legs in bed for two months or more. See British Library Sloane MS 153.

10 A. Macfarlane (ed.), *The Diary of Ralph Josselin, 1616–1683*, London, 1976, 110, 112.

11 Sister Mary Catharine O'Connor's *The Art of Dying Well: The Development of the* Ars Moriendi, New York, 1942, provides a catalogue and analysis of continental and English manuscripts and printed works. Nancy Lee Beaty's *The Craft of Dying: A Study in the Literary Tradition of the* Ars Moriendi *in England*, New Haven and London, 1970, organizes discussion around selected sources in order to identify changes and continuities in the literature.

12 N. L. Beaty, ibid., 197.

13 R. Hill, *A Direction to Die Well*, London, 1613, 112.

14 Ibid., 118–19.

15 Ibid., 122–3.

16 Ibid., 182.

17 Ibid., 147.

18 Ibid., 176–80.
19 R. Brathwaite, *The English Gentleman...*, London, 1630, 440.
20 W. Gouge, *Of Domestical Duties*, London, 1622, 470–81, 560–78.
21 Quoted in M. E. Lamb, op. cit., 211.
22 D. M. Meads (ed.), *The Diary of Lady Margaret Hoby 1599–1605*, London, 1930.
23 E. Joceline, *The Mother's Legacy to her Unborn Child*, London, 1894 reprint of the 1632 edition, from 'The Approbation', no pagination.
24 J. Aubrey, *Brief Lives*, A. Powell (ed.), London, 1949, 39.
25 P. Ariès, op. cit., 6–10.
26 C. Jackson (ed.), *The Autobiography of Mrs. Alice Thornton of East Newton, Co. York, Surtees Society*, 62 (1875), 23.
27 Ibid., 34–5.
28 H. W. Robinson and W. Adams (eds), *The Diary of Robert Hooke 1672–1680*, London, 1968, 312.
29 *The Diary of Ralph Josselin*, 201, 203.
30 W. L. Sachse (ed.), *The Diary of Roger Lowe of Ashton in Makerfield Lancashire*, London, 1938.
31 *The Diary of John Evelyn*, 8–9, 14–16.
32 R. Hill, op. cit., 140–1.
33 J. Graunt, op. cit., 23–4.
34 *The Diary of Samuel Pepys*, V, 84–6.
35 F. Boas (ed.), *The Diary of Thomas Crosfield M.A., B.D., Fellow of the Queen's College, Oxford*, London, 1935, 59.
36 *The Diary of Ralph Josselin*, 394.
37 Ibid., 424.
38 W. Shakespeare, *Hamlet*, Act I, Scene v.
39 Ibid., Act III, Scene iii.
40 This subject is well covered by Clare Gittings in her *Death, Burial and the Individual in Early Modern England*, London, 1984.
41 Quoted in B. Langston, 'Essex and the art of dying', *The Huntington Library Quarterly*, February 1950, 111.
42 Ralph Houlbrooke tells me that descriptions of the death-beds of comparatively obscure people exist in depositions taken down in testamentary causes.

4 GODLY GRIEF: INDIVIDUAL RESPONSES TO DEATH IN SEVENTEENTH-CENTURY BRITAIN

I am grateful for the comments of those who heard this paper at the 1987 Social History Conference, especially those of Dr Mary Prior and Dr Ralph Houlbrooke.

1 L. Stone, *The Family, Sex and Marriage in England 1500–1800*, paperback edn, Harmondsworth, 1979, 88.
2 ibid., 80.
3 M. Mitterauer and R. Sieder, *The European Family*, 1977, trans. K. Oosterveen and M. Horzinger, Oxford, 1982, 61.

4 H. Walker, *Spirituall Experiences of Sundry Beleevers*, London, 1651, 60–1.

5 B. J. Todd, 'The remarrying widow: a stereotype reconsidered' and Mary Prior, 'Women and the urban economy: Oxford 1500–1800', in M. Prior (ed.), *Women in English Society 1500–1800*, London, 1985.

6 Stone, op. cit., 46; M. Anderson, 'The emergence of the modern life cycle in Britain', *Social History*, 10 (1), 78–9.

7 Anderson, op. cit., 70, 73, 75.

8 A. Macfarlane (ed.), *The Diary of Ralph Josselin 1616–1683*, *British Academy Records of Social and Economic History*, III, 1976; R. Bird (ed.), *Journal of Giles Moore, Sussex Record Society*, Lewes, 1971.

9 P. S. Seaver, *Wallington's World. A Puritan Artisan in Seventeenth-Century London*, London, 1985, 69, 84.

10 Especially M. Chaytor, 'Household and kinship: Ryton in the late sixteenth and early seventeenth centuries', *History Workshop*, 10, 25–60; D. Cressy, 'Kinship and kin interaction in early modern England', *Past and Present*, 113, 38–69.

11 Cressy, op. cit., 44–53 is helpful in trying to disentangle some of the problems of considering early modern kinship groups.

12 A. B. Appleby, *Famine in Tudor and Stuart England*, Liverpool, 1978.

13 R. Parkinson (ed.), *The Autobiography of Henry Newcome, Chetham Society*, 26 & 27, 1852, I. 73.

14 R. Harré, *The Social Construction of Emotions*, Oxford, 1986, 123, 122.

15 R. J. Kastenbaum, *Death, Society and Human Experience*, St Louis, 1977, 243–6.

16 *The Holy Life of Mrs Elizabeth Walker*, London, 1690, 99.

17 Anderson, op. cit., 78.

18 *Newcome's Autobiography*, I, 53.

19 *Josselin's Diary*, 112–16.

20 *Life of Elizabeth Walker*, 63.

21 F. R. Raines (ed.), *The Journal of Nicholas Assheton, Chetham Society*, 14, 1848, 81.

22 *Josselin's Diary*, 204.

23 Francis Bamford (ed.), *A Royalist's Notebook, The Commonplace Book of Sir John Oglander*, London, 1936, 108; Edinburgh, National Library of Scotland MS 34.5.19, p. 61.

24 *Newcome's Autobiography*, I, 97.

25 J. Rogers, *Ohel or Beth-shemesh. A Tabernacle for the Sun*, London, 1653, 403.

26 *Josselin's Diary*, 207, 210.

27 C. Jackson (ed.), *The Autobiography of Mrs Alice Thornton, Surtees Society*, 62, 1875, 126, 151.

28 Edinburgh, National Library of Scotland, Adv MS 32.4.4, pp. 28–9.

29 Edinburgh, National Library of Scotland, MS 1037, ff.9v, 21.

30 Edinburgh, National Library of Scotland, MS 34.6.22, p. 61.

31 Edinburgh, National Library of Scotland, MS 1037, f.21.

32 Walker, *Spirituall Experiences*, 26.

33 K. Sutton, *A Christian Womans Experiences of the glorious workings of Gods free grace*, Rotterdam, 1663, 5.

34 *Some Remarkable Passages in the Holy Life and Death of the late Reverend Edmund Trench*, London, 1693, 77.

35 Seaver, *Wallington's World*, 87.

36 *Life of Elizabeth Walker*, 116.

37 Edinburgh, National Library of Scotland, MS 34.6.22, p. 74.

38 *Newcome's Autobiography*, II, 253–4.

39 *Royalist's Notebook*, 81, 181.

40 *Josselin's Diary*, 568.

41 *Newcome's Autobiography*, I, 101.

42 J. O. Halliwell (ed.), *The Autobiography of Sir Simonds D'Ewes*, London, 1845, I, 111; *Thornton's Autobiography*, 113.

43 Rev. F. W. Bennett (ed.), *The Diary of Isabella, Wife of Sir Roger Twysden*, *Archaeologia Cantiana*, 51, 1940, 128–9.

44 Seaver, *Wallington's World*, 75.

45 F. P. Verney, *Memoirs of the Verney Family*, London, 1892, II, 120.

46 P. Laslett cited in R. A. Houlbrooke, *The English Family 1450–1700*, London, 1984, 208.

47 C. Jackson (ed.), 'The life of Master John Shaw', in *Yorkshire Diaries*, Surtees Society, 65, 1877, 149.

48 N. H. Keeble (ed.), *The Autobiography of Richard Baxter*, London, 1974, 249.

49 *Letter-Books of John Hervey, First Earl of Bristol*, Wells, 1894, I, 50–51.

50 *Verney Memoirs*, II, 415.

51 *Royalist's Notebook*, 107.

52 Edinburgh, National Library of Scotland, MS 1037, f.10.

53 *Newcome's Autobiography*, I, 5.

54 *A Narrative of God's Gracious Dealings with that Choice Christian Mrs Hannah Allen*, London, 1683, 7–8

55 *Thornton's Autobiography*, 172, 176.

56 Walker, *Spirituall Experiences*, 61, 34.

57 *Newcome's Autobiography*, I, 5: E. S. de Beer (ed.), *The Diary of John Evelyn*, London, 1959, 12.

58 *Observations upon the London Bills of Mortality More Probably by Captain John Graunt*, in C. H. Hull (ed.), *The Economic Writings of Sir William Petty*, Cambridge, 1899, II, 342, 351.

59 Oxford, Bodleian Library, Ashmole MS 193, f.190.

60 Oxford, Bodleian Library, Ashmole MS 227, f. 128.

61 M. Macdonald, *Mystical Bedlam*, Cambridge, 1981, paperback edition 1983, 159, 103.

62 F. N. L. Poynter and W. L. Bishop (eds), 'A seventeenth century doctor and his patients: John Symcotts 1592–1662',*Bedfordshire Historical Record Society*, 31, 1951, 69.

63 Quoted in P. Crawford, 'Attitudes to pregnancy from a woman's spiritual diary 1687–8', *Local Population Studies*, 21, 44.

64 John Sym, *Life's Preservative against Self-Killing*, London, 1637, 91.

5 DEATH AND THE DOCTORS IN GEORGIAN ENGLAND

1 For discussion see D. Jarrett, *England in the Age of Hogarth*, London, 1974, 210f., 228.

2 Roy Porter, 'The patient's view: doing medical history from below', *Theory and Society*, 14, 175–98.

3 W. Jones, *The Diary of the Reverend William Jones, 1777–1821*, ed. O. F. Christie, London, 1929, 63.

4 Quoted in A. Doig, 'Dr Black, a remarkable physician', in A. D. C. Simpson (ed.), *Joseph Black, 1728–1799*, Edinburgh, 1982, 37–43, 38.

5 Quoted from Burns' 'Death and Dr Hornbook', in F. P. Weber, *Aspects of Death and Correlated Aspects of Life in Art, Epigram and Poetry*, London, 1918, 317.

6 P. Linebaugh, 'The Tyburn Riot against the surgeons', in E. P. Thompson *et al.* (eds), *Albion's Fatal Tree*, London, 1975, 65–118; S. Leblond, 'The anatomists and the resurrectionists in Great Britain', *Canadian Medical Association Journal*, 93, 73–8, 113–20; H. Cole, *Things for the Surgeon. A History of the Resurrection Men*, London, 1964.

7 J. Boswell, *London Journal*, ed. F. A. Pottle, London, 1951, 105.

8 For discussion on hospitals see John Woodward, *To Do the Sick No Harm*, London, 1974; for 'gynecide', see M. Daly, *Gyn/Ecology*, London, 1979, 69, 260.

9 G. Holmes, *Augustan England. Professions, State and Society, 1680–1730*, London, 1982, 166–236; Irvine Loudon, 'The nature of provincial practice in eighteenth century England', *Medical History*, 29, 1–32; idem, *Medical Care and the General Practitioner 1750–1850*, Oxford, 1986.

10 Peter Gay, 'The enlightenment as medicine and as cure', in W. H. Barber (ed.), *The Age of the Enlightenment. Studies Presented to Theodore Besterman*, Edinburgh, 1967, 375–86, esp. 385. For a critique see Roy Porter, 'Was there a medical enlightenment in eighteenth century England?', *British Journal for Eighteenth Century Studies*, 5, 49–63.

11 P. Razzell, *The Conquest of Smallpox*, Firle, Sussex, 1977; Genevieve Miller, *The Adoption of Inoculation for Smallpox in England and France*, Philadelphia, 1957.

12 L. Clarkson, *Death, Disease and Famine in Pre-Industrial England*, Dublin, 1975.

13 M. M. Verney (ed.), *Verney Letters of the Eighteenth Century from the MSS at Claydon House*, 2 vols, London, i, 44.

14 Jones, op. cit., 267.

15 A point negatively made in E. A. Wrigley and R. S. Schofield, *The Population History of England, 1541–1871*, London, 1981. Cf. T. McKeown, *The Role of Medicine*, Oxford, 1979.

16 P. Ariès, *Western Attitudes Towards Death*, trans. P. N. Ranum, London, 1974; idem, *The Hour of Our Death*, trans. H. Weaver, London, 1981; J. McManners, *Death and the Enlightenment*, Oxford, 1981; C. Gittings, *Death, Burial and the Individual in Early Modern England*, London, 1984; F. Lebrun, *Les Hommes et la Mort en Anjou aux 17e et 18e Siècles*, Paris,

1971; E. Morin, *L'Homme et la Mort*, Paris, 1970; R. G. Olson, 'Death', in P. Edwards (ed.), *Encyclopedia of Philosophy*, New York, 1967, ii, 307–9.

17 J. Huizinga, *The Waning of the Middle Ages*, Harmondsworth, 1972, esp. ch. 11; L. P. Kurtz, *The Dance of Death and the Macabre Spirit in European Literature*, New York, 1934; J. M. Clark, *The Dance of Death in the Middle Ages and the Renaissance*, Glasgow, 1950; T. S. R. Boase, *Death in the Middle Ages: Mortality, Judgement and Remembrance*, New York, 1972; G. and M. Vovelle, *La Vision de la mort et de l'au-delà en Provence après les autels des ames du purgatoire XVe–XXe siècles, Paris, 1970*.

18 See D. Stannard, *The Puritan Way of Death. A Study in Religion, Culture and Social Change*, Oxford, 1977; there are some valuable pages in A. Wear, 'Interfaces. Perceptions of health and illness in early modern England', in Roy Porter and Andrew Wear (eds), *Problems and Methods in the History of Medicine*, London, 1987, 230–55.

19 Quoted in Andrew Wear, 'Puritan perceptions of illness in seventeenth century England', in Roy Porter (ed.), *Patients and Practitioners. Lay Perceptions of Medicine in Pre-Industrial Society*, Cambridge, 1985, 55–100, 64; cf. Stannard, op. cit., 77.

20 W. Sherlock, *A Practical Discourse Concerning Death*, London, 1690, 351.

21 Jeremy Taylor, *The Rule and Exercises of Holy Dying*, 4th edn, London, 1654, 326–8.

22 Oliver Heywood, *Autobiography and Diaries*, ed. J. H. Turner, 4 vols, Brighouse, 1872–85.

23 Lewis Robinson, *Every Patient His Own Doctor, or the Sick Man's Triumph over Death and the Grave*, London, 1778. See also M. C. O'Connor, *The Art of Dying Well: The Development of the Ars Moriendi*, New York, 1966.

24 M. MacDonald, *Mystical Bedlam*, Cambridge, 1981.

25 P. Henry, *An Account of the Life and Death of Mr Philip Henry . . . ,* London, 1699, 11.

26 Cf. H. Cook, *The Decline of the Old Medical Regime in Stuart London*, Ithaca, N.Y., 1986.

27 'Tom Thumb, his life and death', in J. Ritson (ed.), *Ancient Popular Poetry*, London, 1884, 96.

28 R. H. P. Crawfurd, *The Last Days of Charles II*, Oxford, 1909.

29 C. R. Hone, *The Life of Dr John Radcliffe*, London, 1950, 58; compare Sir Thomas Browne, 'To a friend, upon the occasion of his intimate friend', in *Religio Medici and Other Works*, ed. L. C. Martin, Oxford, 1964, 179.

30 R. Cook, *Sir Samuel Garth*, Boston, 1980, 37.

31 K. Dewhurst (ed.), *Willis's Oxford Casebook (1650–52)*, Oxford 1980, 99.

32 Robert James, *Medicinal Dictionary*, 3 vols, London, 1743–5; cf. E. H. Ackerknecht, 'Death in the history of medicine', *Bulletin of the History of Medicine*, 42, 19–23.

33 Barry Supple, *The Royal Exchange Assurance: A History of British Insurance 1720–1970*, London, 1970.

34 *Gentleman's Magazine*, 63, 1217. See the wider discussion in Roy Porter, 'Lay medical knowledge in the eighteenth century. The evidence of

the *Gentleman's Magazine*, *Medical History*, 29, 138–68, esp. 157f.

35 *Gentleman's Magazine*, 62, 869.

36 For Johnson, see Roy Porter, '"The Hunger of Imagination": Approaching Samuel Johnson's melancholy', in W. F. Bynum, Roy Porter and Michael Shepherd (eds) *The Anatomy of Madness*, 2 vols, London, 1985, i, 63–88; J. Hagstrum, 'On Dr Johnson's fear of death', *ELH: A Journal of English Literary History*, 14, 308–19.

37 James Boswell, *Boswell's Column*, ed. M. Bailey, London, 1951, 83–102, esp. 91, 98 (death is 'immediately an evil').

38 N. Spinckes, *The Sick Man Visited* . . . , London, 1712, 93, 102, 132, 190, 344.

39 Sir J. Stonhouse, *Friendly Advice to a Patient* . . . , London, c. 1750, 3, 12, 13, 24, 25, 30.

40 P. Slack, *The Impact of Plague in Tudor and Stuart England*, London, 1985.

41 Changing attitudes towards smallpox inoculation are exemplary. See above ref. 11.

42 Illuminating is I. Illich, *Limits to Medicine*, London, 1976, 147f.

43 E. C. Mossner, *The Life of David Hume*, Oxford, 1970, 589f.

44 Quoted in G. Williams, *The Age of Agony*, London, 1975, 277.

45 See above all S. E. Sprott, *The English Debate on Suicide from Donne to Hume*, London, 1961; C. Noon, 'On suicide', *Journal of the History of Ideas*, 39, 371–86; M. MacDonald, 'The secularization of suicide in England', *Past and Present*, 111, 50–100.

46 Ariès, op. cit.; Illich, op. cit., 174f.

47 D. P. Walker, *The Decline of Hell*, London, 1964.

48 P. Smithers, *The Life of Joseph Addison*, Oxford, 1968, 560.

49 Quoted in John Ferriar, *Medical Histories*, London, 1792, 9.

50 Cf. A. L. Lytton Sells, *Thomas Gray: His Life and Works*, London, 1980.

51 B. Rush, *Medical Inquiries and Observations upon the Diseases of the Mind*, New York, 1962, first edn, 1812, 326.

52 Cf. J. S. Lewis, *In the Family Way. Childbearing in the British Aristocracy, 1760–1860*, New Brunswick, N. J., 1986; L. Stone, *The Family, Sex and Marriage in England 1500–1800*, London, 1977; R. Trumbach, *The Rise of the Egalitarian Family*, New York, 1978.

53 McManners, op. cit.; P. Ariès, *Images of Man and Death*, Cambridge, Mass., 1985, 100.

54 Jones, op. cit., 276.

55 Journal of Lucy Warren, Wellcome Manuscripts Collection. There is much illumination in J. Morley, *Death, Heaven and the Victorians*, London, 1971; J. S. Curl, *The Victorian Celebration of Death*, Newton Abbot, 1972.

56 Illich, op. cit., 189f.

57 L. H. Hawkins, 'The history of resuscitation', *British Journal of Hospital Medicine*, 4, 495–500; J. P. Payne, 'On the resuscitation of the apparently dead: A historical account', *Annals of the Royal College of Surgeons*, 45, 98–107; P. J. Bishop, *A Short History of the Royal Humane Society*, London, 1974.

58 For today's dilemmas, see J. Glover, *Causing Death and Saving Lives*, Harmondsworth, 1977.

59 Ferriar, op. cit., 10. See also R. Noyes, Jr, 'The art of dying', *Perspectives in Biology and Medicine*, 14, 432–447.

60 T. Forbes, *Surgeons at the Bailey. English Forensic Medicine to 1878*, New Haven, Conn., 1986.

61 T. Percival, *Medical Ethics*, ed. C. D. Leake, New York, 1975, 95; compare [J. Gregory], *Observations on the Duties and Offices of a Physician*, London, 1790, 34:

> Let me here exhort you against a barbarous custom of some physicians, the leaving your patients when their life is absolutely despaired of, and when it is no longer decent to take fees. It is as much the business of a physician to alleviate pain, and to smooth the avenues of death, as to cure diseases. Even in cases where his skill as a physician can be of no further avail, his presence and assistance as a man and as a friend may be highly grateful and useful, both to the patient and to his nearest relations. Neither is there any propriety in his going out at one door when the clergyman enters at the other; a quaint conceit of some of our faculty, more expressive of impiety than humour.

62 Ferriar, op. cit., 262.

63 Ferriar, op. cit., 273.

64 Gittings, op. cit., 14f.

65 Recorded by James Boswell, in F. Brady (ed.), *Boswell in Search of a Wife*, London, 1957, 316. The date is 19 September, 1769.

66 W. Munk, *The Life of Sir Henry Halford*, London, 1895, 262. It is no accident that Munk also wrote *Euthanasia, Or Medical Treatment in Aid of an Easy Death*, London, 1887.

67 Munk, op. cit., 264.

68 Munk, op. cit., 184.

69 Munk, op. cit., 264.

70 Munk, op. cit., 265.

71 Munk, op. cit., 97.

72 W. Buchan, *Domestic Medicine*, London, 1772, 143–4.

73 A. Fremantle (ed.), *The Wynne Diaries*, 3 vols, London, 1940, iii, 1.

74 Jones, op. cit., 128

75 Rush, op. cit., 324.

76 Ferriar, op. cit., 265.

77 See Guy Williams, *The Age of Agony*, London, 1975.

78 See V. Berridge and G. Edwards, *Opium and the People*, London, 1981; T. Parssinen, *Secret Passions, Secret Remedies*, Manchester, 1983; A. Hayter, *Opium and the Romantic Imagination*, Berkeley, 1974; M. Lefebvre, *Samuel Taylor Coleridge, A Bondage of Opium*, London, 1974; G. Lindop, *The Opium Eater, A Life of Thomas De Quincey*, London, 1981.

79 See Parssinen, op. cit.

80 J. Jones, *Mysteries of Opium Reveal'd*, London, 1700; see also J. Worth

Estes, 'John Jones's *Mysteries of Opium Reveal'd*: Key to historical opiates', *Journal of the History of Medicine*, 34, 200–09; J. C. Kramer, 'Opium rampant: medical use, misuse and abuse in Britain and the west in the seventeenth and eighteenth centuries', *British Journal of Addiction*, 74, 377–89.

81 G. Young, *Treatise on Opium*, London, 1753.

82 S. Crumpe, *Inquiry into the Nature and Properties of Opium*, London, 1797.

83 Cf. G. Risse, 'The Brownian system of medicine: its theoretical and practical implications', *Clio Medica*, 5, 45–51.

84 Rush, op. cit., 318–19.

85 D. King-Hele (ed.) *The Letters of Erasmus Darwin*, Cambridge, 1981, 257, 245 and *passim*.

86 For the spread of these medicines see W. F. Bynum and Roy Porter (eds), *Medical Fringe and Medical Orthodoxy 1750–1850*, London, 1986, and the literature cited there.

87 Parssinen, op. cit., 16, quotes an early nineteenth-century source confirming its profitability: 'This is a very profitable business, the returns sometimes cent. percent, and seldom less than fifty; but it requires a capital of from £500 to £2000'.

88 Jones, op. cit., 27.

89 Parssinen, op. cit., 27.

90 Rush, op. cit., 327.

91 B. Z. Paulshock, 'William Heberden and opium – some relief to all', *The New England Journal of Medicine*, 308, 53–6, 54.

92 Mrs Paget Toynbee (ed.), *The Letters of Horace Walpole*, 15 vols, Oxford, 1903, iii, 421.

93 Quoted in John Wain, *Samuel Johnson*, London, 1980, 376.

94 H. Dittrick, 'Devices to prevent premature burial', *Journal of the History of Medicine*, 3, 161–71; T. K. Marshall, 'Premature burial', *Medical and Legal Journal*, 35, 14–24.

6 THE BURIAL QUESTION IN LEEDS IN THE EIGHTEENTH AND NINETEENTH CENTURIES

1 The calculations of interments and burial ground capacities contained in this paper are based on my forthcoming MPhil thesis 'The burial problem in Leeds in the eighteenth and nineteenth centuries' (University of Leeds). Capacity is estimated using a formula derived from the discussion by Edwin Chadwick in his *Report on Interments (Parliamentary Papers (PP* hereafter), 1843 (XII), 128–9).

2 This characterization of the Church of England and the comments in the penultimate paragraph are based on A. D. Gilbert, *Religion and Society in Industrial England*, London, 1976.

3 I calculate the parish churchyard's capacity at just over 2,000 p.a. but at least 8,000 p.a. were buried during the decade 1811–20.

4 Leeds Archives Department, Leeds Parish Church Records, Vestry

Minutes 1716–81, 27 March 1776. Churchwardens' Accounts, 10 September 1801. Vestry Minutes 1813–28, 15 September 1814.

5 Burial registrations at the parish churchyard fell by 6 per cent between 1801–10 and 1811–20 but rose by 54 per cent in 1821–30; defective registration during 1811–20 must be the explanation for this.

6 *Quarterly Review*, September 1819, 380.

7 J. S. Curl, *The Victorian Celebration of Death*, London, 1972, 49–50.

8 G. A. Walker, *Gatherings from Graveyards*, London, 1839, 76–90 and 149–87.

9 Curl, op. cit., 55–7.

10 H. Mellor, *London Cemeteries*, London, 1981.

11 Chadwick estimated that they buried 7 per cent of the capital's dead in the early 1840s. (*Report on Interments*, 133).

12 R. F. Fletcher, 'The history of the Leeds General Cemetery Company 1833–1965' (unpublished MPhil thesis, University of Leeds, 1975).

13 For the wider dimensions of these controversies see O. Chadwick, *The Victorian Church*, London, 1971, 60–95.

14 For the background to the campaign see D. Fraser, 'The Leeds churchwardens 1828–1850', *Publications of the Thoresby Society*, LIII (1970), 1–22.

15 *Leeds Intelligencer* (*LI* hereafter), 17 July 1828.

16 *Leeds Times*, 6 February 1841 – a later enunciation of the Liberal position.

17 This section is based on Fraser, op. cit. and R. G. Wilson, *Gentlemen Merchants*, Manchester, 1971, chap. 8.

18 D. Fraser, 'Politics and society in the nineteenth century' in D. Fraser (ed.), *A History of Modern Leeds*, Manchester, 1980, 273.

19 *LI*, 20 October 1825.

20 *Leeds Mercury* (*LM* hereafter), 20 October 1825 and 28 October 1827.

21 Leeds Archives Department, Leeds Parish Church Records, Vestry Minutes 1828–44, 18 December 1828.

22 Fraser, op. cit., 5–10.

23 In 1840 there were 474 interments at the cemetery; these were reported to the annual general meeting as 474 investments and a dividend of 5 per cent was declared! (*LM*, 28 March 1840).

24 Walker, op. cit.

25 *Select Committee on Interments* (*PP* 1842 X).

26 ibid., Q2659.

27 ibid., Q2510.

28 *Report on Interments* (*PP* 1843 XIII).

29 ibid., 96–107.

30 This section is based on R. A. Lewis, *Edwin Chadwick and the Public Health Movement*, London, 1952, 238–78.

31 Burial Acts, 15&16 Vic. cap. 85 and 17&18 Vic. cap.134.

32 A man discovered that his son's body had been moved to another grave in the interests of 'managing' the churchyard (*LM*, 16 January 1841).

33 Fraser, op. cit., 10–16.

34 *LM*, 30 January 1841.
35 *LM*, 18 December 1841.
36 *LM*, 27 November 1841.
37 *LM*, 18 December 1841.
38 ibid.
39 House of Lords Record Office, Committee Book H.L. 1842 vol.2 ff.309–11, 7 July 1842. For the background to this development see D. Fraser, 'Improvement in early Victorian Leeds', *Publications of the Thoresby Society*, LIII (1970), 71–81.
40 Burial Grounds Act, 5&6 Vic. cap.104. *LM*, 18 November 1843. Leeds Civic Hall Strong Room, Burial Act Committee Minute Book, I passim.
41 *LM*, 11 and 18 November 1848.
42 *LM*, 11 December 1854.
43 J. Carvell Williams, *The Present Position of the Burials Question*, London, 1879; R. Fletcher, *The Akenham Burial Case*, London, 1974.
44 P. T. Marsh, *The Victorian Church in Decline*, London, 1969, 242–63.
45 See the evidence and report of the *Select Committee on Burial Grounds* (*PP* 1898 VIII) for a review of this complex issue. The Burial Act, 63&64 Vic. cap. 15 followed the Committee's recommendations closely.
46 Curl, op. cit., 164.
47 Fletcher, thesis cit., 45.
48 *LM*, 23 May 1840.

7 WHY WAS DEATH SO BIG IN VICTORIAN BRITAIN?

1 As far as I am aware none of the standard works, i.e.: B. S. Puckle, *Funeral Customs*, London, 1926; J. Morley, *Death, Heaven and the Victorians*, London, 1971; nor J. S. Curl, *The Victorian Celebration of Death*, Newton Abbot, 1972, nor any other commentator on the Victorian celebration of death has registered what I perceive as the historical significance of bodysnatching.
2 B. S. Puckle, op. cit., 273–5.
3 R. Richardson, *Death, Dissection and the Destitute*, London, 1988.
4 See Charles Darwin's description of a riot in Cambridge in c.1830 in F. Darwin (ed.) *Charles Darwin*, London, 1892, 22. See also R. Richardson, op. cit., 87–90.
5 R. Richardson, op. cit., 90–3, 263, 372.
6 R. Richardson, op. cit., 59, 86, 106.
7 V. Gammon, 'Singing and popular funeral practices in the eighteenth and early nineteenth centuries', *Folk Music Journal*, 1988, 5(4), 412–47. For evidence of mediaeval influence on popular death imagery in early nineteenth century, see R. Richardson, op. cit., 10–11, 299.
8 R. Richardson, op. cit., 84, 222. Prof. Beverley Raphael, a specialist on grief and its therapy, has agreed with my own supposition that normal grief processes could be materially disturbed by bodysnatching (personal communication).

9 For Astley Cooper's evidence, see *Report of the Select Committee on Anatomy*, London, 1828, Q.50.
For others' views, see R. Richardson, op. cit., 127.

10 R. Richardson, op. cit., 272–5.

11 R. Richardson, op. cit., 273.

12 R. Richardson, op. cit., 578.

13 B. B. Cooper, *The Life of Sir Astley Cooper*, London, 1843.

14 J. C. Loudon, *On The Laying Out, Planting and Managing of Cemeteries*, London, 1843.

15 R. Richardson, op. cit., 245.

16 J. Morley, op. cit., 87.

17 ibid., chapter 7.

18 ibid., 202.

19 R. Richardson, 'Death in the metropolis', unpublished, 1978; 'Edwardian post-mortem customs', unpublished, 1978. For a brilliant analysis of the Victorian celebration of death and its demise, see David Cannadine's 'War and death, grief and mourning in modern Britain' in J. Whaley (ed.), *Mirrors of Mortality*, London, 1981, 187–242.

20 A. Wilson and H. J. Levy, *Burial Reform and Funeral Costs*, London, 1938, 61.

21 Tom Laqueur's 'Bodies, death and pauper funerals', *Representations*, 1983, 1(1), 109–30, provides a fine analysis of the social meaning of the Victorian pauper funeral.

22 R. Richardson, *Death, Dissection and the Destitute*, London, 1988, 271.

23 My own work shows that fear of the pauper funeral remains common among elderly working-class urban dwellers. During interviews undertaken since 1976 my interviewees have often recalled their own parents' solemn entreaties never to permit them to be buried as a pauper, and the utter contempt with which individuals who had failed to protect family members from such a fate were held in working-class communities. See R. Richardson, 'The nest egg and the funeral: fear of death on the parish among the elderly', in A. and S. Gilmore (eds), *A Safer Death. Proceedings of the First International Conference on Multidisciplinary Aspects of Terminal Care, Glasgow, 1987*, New York and London, 1988, 53–8.

8 ASHES TO ASHES: CREMATION AND THE CELEBRATION OF DEATH IN NINETEENTH- CENTURY BRITAIN

1 H. Erichsen, *The Cremation of the Dead*, Detroit, 1887, 50.

2 A. Richardson, *The Law of Cremation*, London, 1893, 35.

3 Rev. H. R. Haweis, *Ashes to Ashes, A Cremation Prelude*, London, 1875, 17.

4 ibid.

5 W. Eassie, 'Dangers of our system of burial', in his *Cremation of the Dead, Its History and Bearings Upon Public Health*, London, 1875, 53–62.

6 Haweis, op. cit., 28.

7 *Report from the Select Committee on Improvement of the Health of Towns, Effect of Interment of Bodies in Towns*, 1842, British Parliamentary Papers, 1970, 468.

8 F. S. Haden, *The Disposal of the Dead: A Plea for Legislation and a Protest Against Cremation*, a paper read at the Church Congress at Manchester, 3 October 1888, passim.

9 For example, the plan to cremate the dead of Bridewell Hospital within the City of London Gas Works. c.f. Erichsen, op. cit., 53.

10 Erichsen, op. cit., 54.

11 Sir Henry Thompson, 'The treatment of the body after death', *Contemporary Review*, XXIII, January 1874, 325.

12 *The Times*, 12 January 1875, 10.

13 Thompson, op. cit., 322.

14 ibid., 323.

15 ibid.

16 *The Times*, 6 April 1874, 5.

17 *Medical Times and Gazette*, 21 February 1874, 210.

18 *Medical Press and Circular*, 7 January 1874, 15.

19 Cremation Society of England, *Cremation in Great Britain*, London, 1909, 16.

20 Government Board of Health, *Report on a General Scheme for Extramural Sepulture*, London, 1850, 123.

21 Sir W. Arbuthnot Lane, 'Cremation from the public health view', *Transactions of the Cremation Society*, XLIII, 1932, 53.

22 A. G. Cobb, 'Earth burial and cremation', *North American Review*, 135 (310), 277.

23 Lord Beaconsfield, quoted in Cobb, op. cit., 281.

24 ibid., 281.

25 Prof. Gorini, 'La Purificazione dei morti', quoted in 'Cremation and Christianity', *Dublin Review*, 3rd series, XXIII (2), 394–5.

26 A. C. Freeman, *Crematoria in Great Britain and Abroad*, London, 1906, passim.

27 M. J. Wiener, *English Culture and the Decline of the Industrial Spirit, 1850–1980*, Cambridge, 1981, passim.

28 Sir A. Wilson and Prof. H. Levy, *Burial Reform and Funeral Costs*, London, 1938, 40.

29 Eassie, *Cremation of the Dead*, 3.

30 'Cremation and Christianity', 385.

31 Eassie, op. cit., 11–12.

32 Quoted in W. Robinson, *Cremation and Urn-Burial, or The Cemeteries of the Future*, London, 1889, 86.

33 Eassie, op. cit., 12.

34 'Cremation and Christianity', 390.

35 ibid., 400.

36 *The Times*, 6 July 1874, 8.

37 Wilson and Levy, op. cit., 37.

38 Q. L. Dowd, *Funeral Management and Costs*, Chicago, 1921, 229.

39 ibid., quoted 37.

40 *Sanitary Record*, 11 July 1874, 24–25.
41 C.f. Alan Gilbert's thesis in *Religion and Society in Industrial England*, London, 1976, passim.
42 *British Medical Journal*, 8 February 1908, 339.
43 *The Times*, 12 January 1875, 10; 17 June 1875, 7.
44 F. S. Haden, *Cremation an Incentive to Crime: A Plea for Legislation*, 2nd edn, London, 1892, 16.
45 C. Cameron, 'The modern cremation movement', *Scottish Review*, 10, July 1887, 35.
46 R. T. Wylde, *A Lecture on Cremation*, Adelaide, 1890, 7. Official statistics indicate that in any year during the nineteenth century, cause of death was in many thousands of cases unverified.
47 W. Tebb and E.P. Vollum, *Premature Burial and How It May Be Prevented*, London, 1905, 285.
48 L. R., 'Murder mania', *Chambers's Edinburgh Journal*, new series, XII (301), 6 October 1849, 209 and passim. Cf. the thesis of R. Altick in his *Victorian Studies in Scarlet*, London, 1972, concerning the Victorian fascination with murder.
49 Tebb and Vollum, op. cit., 140. Note: the bibliography in *Premature Burial* lists over 400 articles, books, and theses dealing with premature burial.
50 Erichsen, op. cit., 183, also Sir Henry Thompson, *Modern Cremation, its History and Practice*, 3rd edn, London, 1899, 41.
51 Cremation Society of England, op. cit., 17. Sir Leslie Stephen, George Frederick Watts, Herbert Spencer, and Sir Edward Burne-Jones were all members of the Society at various times.
52 *British Medical Journal*, 8 February 1908, 339.
53 Quoted in Dowd, op. cit., 240.
54 Cameron, op. cit., 24.
55 quoted ibid.
56 ibid., 28.
57 ibid.
58 Erichsen, op. cit., 194.
59 P. Ariès, *Western Attitudes Toward Death from the Middle Ages to the Present*, Baltimore, 1974, chapter 2.
60 Erichsen, op. cit., 217.
61 P. H. Holland, 'Burial or cremation? A reply to Sir Henry Thompson', *Contemporary Review*, XXIII, February 1874, 482.
62 Mrs C. Chesterton, *I Lived in a Slum*, London, 1936, 15–16. Social competitiveness was not however the only, or even the principal, motive for the maintenance of traditional funerary rituals amongst the working classes. Mrs Chesterton describes the funeral, with its grandeur and pageantry, as a response to the drabness of working-class life; an affirmation of human dignity amongst dirt and squalor.
63 C.f. J. McCalman, 'Respectability and working-class politics in late-Victorian London', *Historical Studies*, 19 (74), 114. McCalman notes that privacy, the possession of a back region where washing,

elimination, dressing and the preparation of food might be performed, was one of the criteria of working-class respectability. It was this element of privacy which distinguished the lives of the 'respectable' from those of the 'rough' working classes. See also E. Goffman, *The Presentation of Self in Everyday Life*, Harmondsworth, 1971, 124–5.

64 E. V. Gillon, *Victorian Cemetery Art*, New York, 1972, passim.
65 J. Morley, *Death, Heaven, and the Victorians*, London, 1971, 52.
66 Thompson, 'The treatment of the body', 327.
67 Cremation Society of Great Britain, op. cit., 16.
68 Signor Ghisleri, *Almanacco dei Liberi Muratori*, 1881, quoted in 'Cremation and Christianity', 394.
69 Rev. W. H. Hale, *Intramural Burial in England Not Injurious to the Public Health: Its Abolition Injurious to Religion and Morals*, A Charge addressed to the Clergy of the Archdeaconry of London, May 16, 1855, 2nd edition, London, 1855, 15.
70 'Cremation and Christianity', 396.
71 Hale, op. cit., 16.
72 Lane, op. cit., 53.
73 J. Jacobs, 'The dying of death', *Fortnightly Review*, new series, LXXII (392), 1 August 1899, 264–9.
74 ibid., 264.
75 James J. Farrel, *Inventing the American Way of Death, 1830–1920*, Philadelphia, 1980, chapter 5. Farrel discusses the reasons why the cremation movement failed to gain converts from the orthodoxies of embalming and earth burial in America.

9 THE TWO FACES OF DEATH: CHILDREN'S MAGAZINES AND THEIR TREATMENT OF DEATH IN THE NINETEENTH CENTURY

1 'Editor's address to her young readers', *The Juvenile Magazine*, 1788, 1, iii.
2 J. S. Bratton, *The Impact of Victorian Children's Fiction*, London, 1981.
3 L. Billington, 'The religious periodical and newspaper press' in M. Harris and A. Lee (eds), *The Press in English Society*, London, 1986, 113–32.
4 An excellent introductory survey of the history of children's magazines in the nineteenth century can be found in S. A. Egoff, *Children's Periodicals of the Nineteenth Century: A Survey and Bibliography*, London, 1951. Most studies of children's literature dismiss them but they had large circulations and attracted contributions from all the leading children's authors of the time.
5 P. A. Dunae, 'Penny dreadfuls: late nineteenth century boys' literature and crime', *Victorian Studies*, 1979, 22, 133–150, traces the history of the hostility to the boys' weeklies.
6 Billington, op. cit., 120–1.
7 Quoted in Egoff, op. cit., 16–17.

8 Quoted in *Penny Dreadfuls and Comics*, Bethnal Green Museum of Childhood, 1983, 12.
9 *Newspaper Press Directory*, 1870, 186. The titles were *Bible Class Magazine*, *Child's Own Magazine*, *Kind Words*, *Morning of Life* and *Sunday School Chronicle*.
10 *Publisher's Circular*, 1886, 1413.
11 Billington, op. cit., 120.
12 *Child's Companion, or Sunday Scholar's Reward*, 1824, 1.
13 'An editor's address' in *Boys of England*, 1866, 8, indicated this was the intended market. An 1880 advertisement in the *Publisher's Circular*, 21, revealed that *Union Jack* was expressly intended for shop assistants and factory workers.
14 The harshest critics were F. Hitchman, 'Penny fiction', *Quarterly Review*, 1890, 171, 152 and E. Salmon, 'What boys read', *Fortnightly Review*, 1886, 45, 255–6.
15 'Glaucus the Gladiator', *Boy's World*, 1885, 7, 571.
16 E. S. Turner's *Boys Will Be Boys*, London, 1948, still remains the standard work on the fiction in boys' magazines and is useful and enjoyable background to the history of boys' popular weekly magazines.
17 *Boy's World*, 1885, 594.
18 G. A. Henty, 'In times of peril', *Union Jack*, 1880, 1, 578.
19 'Notes from my log, or true stories of adventure and peril', *Boy's Own Paper*, 1892, 14, 118.
20 R. Rollington, 'The brothers; or, the strange revenge', *Boy's World*, 1885, 7, 763.
21 'A dreadful time', *Weekly Welcome*, 1887–8, 794–5.
22 'Elizabeth Ann Pascoe', *Child's Magazine and Sunday Scholar's Companion*, 1824, 11, 63–4.
23 'Juvenile Obituaries. Margaret Bedlington', *Youth's Instructor and Guardian*, 1824, 8, 9.
24 'Little Robert', *Children's Friend*, 1837, 14, 177.
25 'Notice of the death of William Shaw', *Little Gleaner*, 1877, 24, 171.
26 'Obedience', *Little Gleaner*, 1877, 24, 179.
27 'A solemn warning to youth', *Youth's Instructor and Guardian*, 1824, 8. 41.
28 'The last days of Eliza B. Jacob', *Child's Companion*, 1842, 148.
29 'Our cot – the story of baby Willie'; 'Uncle John's story', *Child's Companion, and Juvenile Instructor*, 1896, 39, 179–80.
30 'One of the unemployed', *Every Girl's Annual*, 1886, 198–9.
31 'The Angel's mission', *Juvenile*, 1853, 1, 146.
32 'Master Cruelty's bow and arrow', *Nursery and Infant's School Magazine*, 1831, 266.
33 'J. Twyman Hogue', *Little Gleaner*, 1866, 13, 19–20.
34 'Little Alfred', *Children's Friend*, 1893, 33.
35 'Sabbath Profanation', *Children's Friend*, 1837, 14, 205.
36 'Little Bobbie', *Little Gleaner*, 1892, 14, 113.
37 'Vanity', *Children's Friend*, 1893, 15.

38 'Juveniles speaking for themselves', *Juvenile*, 1853, 1, 134.
39 M. Sherborne, 'A Dark River', *Girl's Home*, 1910, 1, in which the heroine's baby dies in tragic circumstances, is typical of stories of this genre.
40 'Our cook's story', *Morning of Life*, 1876, 2, 18.
41 'Dress in season and in reason', *Girl's Own Paper*, 1887, 8, 820.
42 'Answers to correspondents', *Girl's Own Paper*, 1880, 1.
43 'Dress in season and in reason', *Girl's Own Paper*, 1888, 9, 281.
44 'Archie's Father', *Boys' and Girls' Companion*, 1886, 37, 11–12.
45 'The idiot boy', quoted in N. Temple, *Seen and Not Heard*, London, 1970, 205–6.
46 'Seven years for Rachel', *Girl's Own Paper*, 1884, 6, 356–8. The Ivorites were a group devoted to maintaining the ancient customs and language of Wales. Members were bound to offer financial assistance in times of difficulty and in this case were paying the funeral expenses.
47 *Child's Companion*, 1839, 75.
48 'The watershed of 1887–88', *A. I. Annual*, 1887, 1, 133.
49 'The death of Master Innocent Pleasure', *Nursery and Infant's School Magazine*, 1831, 257.
50 'The Indian Island', *Juvenile Forget-me-not*, 1833, 34, 92–3.
51 'A boy's dream', *Boy's Journal*, 1863, 1, 88.
52 'Seven years for Rachel', *Girl's Own Paper*, 1884, 6, 356–8. This story was serialized over several weeks.
53 'Master Lionel – that tiresome child', 1896, *Children's Friend*, 25, 63.
54 *Little Gleaner*, 1892, 14.
55 'The editor's word in season', *Morning of Life*, 1876, 2, 235.
56 'A minister's address', *Child's Companion, or Sunday Scholar's Reward*, 1824, 1.

9 VICTORIAN UNBELIEF AND BEREAVEMENT

1 A conference on this topic was held in 1986 at the University of Toronto under the leadership of Richard Helmstadter and Bernard Lightman. Useful general treatments include F. L. Baumer, *Religion and the Rise of Scepticism*, New York, 1960; A. O. J. Cockshut, *The Unbelievers: English Agnostic Thought, 1840–1890*, London, 1964; A. Symondson (ed.), *The Victorian Crisis of Faith*, London, 1970; F. M. Turner, *Between Science and Religion*, New Haven, 1974; O. Chadwick, *The Secularization of the European Mind in the Nineteenth Century*, Cambridge, 1975; S. Budd, *Varieties of Unbelief: Atheism and Agnosticism in English Society, 1850–1960*, London, 1977 and J. R. Moore, *The Post-Darwinian Controversies*, Cambridge, 1979.
2 Victor Turner's work has called attention to those transitional or liminal stages in each of life's important rites of passage, seeing such periods, during which social structure is replaced by disordered community, as 'inherently sacred'. These turning points in life – birth, initiation into adulthood, marriage, death, bereavement – are so

emotionally moving and important that they are in almost all societies treated religiously, that is viewed within the authenticating framework or structure of the sacred. See Victor Turner, *The Ritual Process*, Chicago, 1969, 6. 'Rites of passage' were viewed as fundamentally religious in Arnold van Gennep's original 1909 identification of the concept. For an extremely clear explication of V. Turner's work on liminality, communitas, and religion, see 'Appendix A' in Victor Turner and Edith Turner, *Image and Pilgrimage in Christian Culture*, New York, 1978, 243–55.

3 Mill began his essay on 'The utility of religion' by observing that only in his own time had there been much discussion of the 'usefulness' of religion. 'If religion, or any particular form of it, is true, its usefulness follows without other proof. . . . The utility of religion did not need to be asserted until the arguments for its truth had in a great measure ceased to convince . . . . In the present period of history, however, we seem to have arrived at a time when, among the arguments for and against religion, those which relate to its usefulness assume an important place. We are in an age of weak beliefs', *Three Essays on Religion*, London, 1885, 69–70.

4 For a helpful treatment of Victorian mourning customs see John Morley, *Death, Heaven, and the Victorians*, London, 1971.

5 R. W. Prothero Ernle, *Life and Correspondence of Arthur Penrhyn Stanley*, New York, 1904, II, 79.

6 On Carlyle see Fred Kaplan, *Thomas Carlyle*, Ithaca, 1983, 470 ff.; for Symonds see Phyllis Grosskurth, *John Addington Symonds*, London, 1964, 143; for George Eliot, see Gordon S. Haight, *George Eliot, a Biography*, Oxford, 1968, 517 ff.

7 See Peter Stansky, *William Morris*, Oxford, 1983, 88–9.

8 These reactions are identified by modern social scientists who specialize in 'grief theory' as being characteristic of people in a wide range of societies. See Sigmund Freud, 'Mourning and melancholia', *Collected Papers*, trans. Joan Riviere, New York, 1959, IV, 8, 152–72. Other helpful sources on the theory of 'grief work' include Erich Lindemann, 'Symptomology and management of acute grief', *American Journal of Psychiatry*, 1944, 101, 141–8; Geoffrey Gorer, *Death, Grief, and Mourning in Contemporary Britain*, London, 1965; Colin Murray Parkes, *Bereavement: Studies of Grief in Adult Life*, London, 1972; Paul Rosenblatt, R. P. Walsh, and D. A. Jackson, *Grief and Mourning in Cross-Cultural Perspective*, HRAF Press, 1976; and Paul C. Rosenblatt, *Bitter, Bitter Tears: Nineteenth-Century Diarists and Twentieth-Century Grief Theories*, Minneapolis, 1983.

9 E. Abbott and L. Campbell, *Life and Letters of Benjamin Jowett*, New York, 1897, I, 224, to F. T. Palgrave at the death of his mother; I, 283, to Sir Alexander Grant at the death of his father; II, 193, to Mrs T. H. Green at the death of her husband.

10 See Balliol College, Oxford, MS. 394 for the collected condolence letters sent to George Eliot. Jowett's is #11.

11 Imperial College, London, MSS, Huxley Papers, 19.162–8.

12 David L. Duncan, *Life and Letters of Herbert Spencer*, New York, 1908, II, 82.

13 Duncan, *Life and Letters of Herbert Spencer*, II, 82.

14 'Dreams and realities', in *An Agnostic's Apology*, London, 1893, 91–2.

15 Leonard Huxley, *Life and Letters of T. H. Huxley*, New York, 1901, I, 237. This was written in response to the Kingsley letter mentioned above.

16 Quoted in Haight, *George Eliot*, 515.

17 Herbert Spencer was one of her admirers who advocated burial in the Abbey. Imperial College MSS, Huxley Papers, 7.247.

18 For Carlyle, see Kaplan, *Thomas Carlyle*, 190 and 155; for Stephen, F. W. Maitland, *Life and Letters of Leslie Stephen*, London, 1906, 343; for Spencer, *Autobiography*, New York, 1904, II, 347; for George Eliot, Haight, *George Eliot*, 516.

19 Haight, *George Eliot*, 516.

20 Virginia Woolf, *Moments of Being*, Jeanne Schulkind (ed.), London, 1976, 40–1.

21 Gordon S. Haight (ed.), *The George Eliot Letters*, New Haven, 1978, VI, 93.

22 A. Sutherland Orr, *Life and Letters of Robert Browning*, Boston, 1906, 240.

23 Orr, *Browning*, 239.

24 James O. Hoge (ed.), *Life and Letters of Emily Lady Tennyson*, London, 1974, 357–59. Modern psychologists identify excessively extended mourning as 'pathological', expecting 'normal' grief to reduce in intensity within a matter of months and the most extreme anguish within weeks. See Erich Lindemann, 'Symptomology and Management of Acute Grief', *American Journal of Psychiatry*, 101, 141–8.

25 See Colin Murray Parkes, *Bereavement: Studies of Grief in Adult Life*, London, 1972, 80–1.

26 Jowett wrote in old age about the deaths of a number of his friends, 'They are with the unseen, in the hands of God, and I shall soon be with them. I do not expect ever to meet them again; that may afford comfort to some, but not to me, though I trust in God that with me, as with them, it may be well.' (*Life and Letters*, II, 280.) For the breadth of Stanley's views, see Prothero Ernle, *Life of Dean Stanley*, I, 486–8. Maurice, of course, was in constant theological trouble because of the heterodoxy of his views on eternal life – see Olive J. Brose, *Frederick Denison Maurice, Rebellious Conformist*, Athens, Ohio, 1971, *passim*. In writing to Huxley Kingsley asserted very little certainty in his own beliefs:

> I think it wise, & philosophical, to hold on to every atom of the old till the new has disproved it. I may be wrong: but you will agree that I have at least a method . . . . Meanwhile, pray understand that I do not complain of, or shame you . . . . You are probably right in not believing anything which you do not believe – for that is what it comes to. I do not believe that a man's opinions on such matters affect God's love toward him, & you

may disbelieve in a future state, & yet be, as I hope you will be, my
very good friend.

Imperial College MSS, Huxley Papers, 19.180–90.

27 'Dreams and realities', in *An Agnostic's Apology*, 111–12.
28 'An agnostic's apology', in *The Fortnightly Review*, XIX, June 1876, 241.
29 See I, 224 of W. M. Rossetti, *Dante Gabriel Rossetti, His Family Letters*, London, 1895.
30 Passages from the poem were recited at various agnostic funerals, including the poet's own, conducted once again by Dr Sadler. See the report of her funeral, including the full text of his sermon in *The Daily News*, 30 December 1880, 2.
31 Frederic Harrison, *Autobiographic Memoirs*, London, 1911, I, 213.
32 See Walter Simon, *European Positivism in the Nineteenth Century*, Ithaca, New York, 1963, *passim*.
33 Martha Voegler's 'The choir invisible: the poetics of humanist piety', in G. S. Haight and R. T. VanArsdel (eds), *George Eliot: A Centenary Tribute*, London, 1982, 66.
34 Useful books on the topic include Alan Gauld's *The Founders of Psychical Research*, New York, 1968; J. J. Cerullo's *The Secularization of the Soul*, Philadelphia, 1982; and Janet Oppenheim's extremely valuable *The Other World*, Cambridge, 1985.
35 Oppenheim, *The Other World*, 59, 109.
36 F. W. G. Myers, *Fragments of an Inner Life*, London, 1961, 14.
37 For an analysis of Myers and his relationship with Annie Marshall, see Gauld, *The Founders of Psychical Research*, 116–126, 130–3, 323–4.
38 See Derrick Leon's *The Great Victorian*, London, 1949, 120–1 and *passim*.
39 See Van Akin Burd (ed.), *John Ruskin and Rose LaTouche: Her Unpublished Diaries of 1861 and 1867*, Oxford, 1979; Ruskin's letters there and in various biographies, e.g. Leon's. See also Joan Evans and J. H. Whitehouse (eds), *The Diaries of John Ruskin*, Oxford, 1956–9, and Van Akin Burd (ed.), *Ruskin, Lady Mount-Temple and the Spiritualists*, London, 1982. Tim Hilton's excellent new *John Ruskin: The Early Years*, New Haven, 1985, does not cover the time period in question.
40 *LaTouche Diaries*, 134–5.
41 See John Ruskin, *Fors Clavigera*, New York, n.d., VII, 91–3.
42 *LaTouche Diaries*, 136.
43 Rossetti, *Dante Gabriel Rossetti*, I, 226.
44 Quoted from a letter of Rossetti's friend Bell Scott in Stanley Weintraub, *The Four Rossettis*, New York, 1977, 149.
45 Rossetti, *Dante Gabriel Rossetti*, I, 265, 273.
46 E.g., see Mrs Kingsley's biography of her husband, or that of Hallam Tennyson for his father.
47 Leon, *Ruskin*, 507.
48 *LaTouche Diaries*, 140–1.
49 Leslie Stephen, *The Mausoleum Book*, Alan Bell (ed.), Oxford, 1977, 53.
50 Basically he argued that the impact of a private person could often be more profound and longer lasting than that of a public figure

operating in the public sphere: 'I could not help thinking that a woman who was bringing up sons and daughters ready to quit themselves like brave men and women in the great struggle of life, might be doing something more really important than her conspicuous husband . . . ' When such domestic efforts were accomplished by a being of the 'rarest beauty' and 'a nobility of mind and character' their power could well continue indefinitely, certainly well beyond the lifetime of the blessed domestic caregiver. This talk was Stephen's public eulogy to his wife, and in it he claimed for her a kind of immortality. The talk was published in his *Social Rights and Duties*, London, 1896.

51 Leon, *Ruskin*, 351. The cases mentioned explicitly in this study provide good exemplars to illustrate this argument, but despondent, unreconciled attitudes toward death can easily be found in less dramatic cases in the lives of other Victorian unbelievers. Biographies of J. A. Symonds, Edmund Gosse, Henry Sidgwick, Herbert Spencer, Harriet Martineau, and George Grote, for example, are all useful for a broader understanding.

52 For the clearest examples of the contemporary discussion of these issues, see the various papers of the Metaphysical Society (available through the British Library) and Alan W. Brown's excellent study of that organization, *The Metaphysical Society*, Cambridge, 1947.

53 It is interesting to note that Rosenblatt in *Bitter, Bitter Tears*, 123–4, couches his analysis in terms of 'family systems', where resistance to change is a well-recognized phenomenon. In addition to the literature cited above at Note 8, see also two essays in Herman Feifel's *The Meaning of Death*, New York, 1965: David Mandelbaum's 'Social uses of funeral rites' and Edgar N. Jackson's 'Grief and religion'.

54 F. Kingsley (ed.), *Charles Kingsley*, London, 1877, II, 455–6.

55 For Spencer see N. and J. MacKenzie (eds), *Diary of Beatrice Webb*, Cambridge, 1983, II, 286; for Huxley, Leonard Huxley, *Life and Letters of Thomas Henry Huxley*, London, 1900, II, 62. Note that modern sociologists argue that finding a way to affirm an ongoing larger significance of life in the face of death is one of religion's universal and most important functions. See Peter Berger and Thomas Luckmann, 'Sociology of religion and sociology of knowledge', in Norman Birnbaum and Gertrud Lenzer (eds), *Sociology of Religion, a Book of Readings*, Englewood Cliffs, New Jersey, 1969, 410–18; also J. Milton Yinger, *Religion, Society, and the Individual*, New York, 1959, 222, ff.

56 For a useful modern treatment of the value of Christian teachings and ritual in dealing with grief, see E. N. Jackson, 'Grief and religion', in Herman Feifel (ed.), *The Meaning of Death*, 222 ff.

57 F. D. Maurice (ed.), *The Life of Frederick Denison Maurice*, New York, 1884, I, 405.

58 See especially Chapter 2, 'The control of anger and aggression', 29–48, in Paul Rosenblatt *et al.*, *Grief and Mourning in Cross Cultural Perspective*.

59 F. Kingsley (ed.), *Charles Kingsley*, II, 367.

60 *Life of Benjamin Jowett*, II, 20.

61 Parenthetically, I should probably mention here the Queen herself and her well known and undoubtedly extreme grief for the Prince Consort. She was certainly a believing Christian and by all of the standards used throughout this paper she was clearly extreme in her grief. I think, however, that her case was really unique; her position was so public that she had many more opportunities – perhaps obligations – for memorials and commemorative ceremonies than were available to her ordinary subjects. She, too, was thus to some extent without helpful formulae, and inventing her own traditions. In any case, although there is of course good evidence that her public grieving was ostentatious and prolonged, it is also possible to show that within a very short while within the privacy of the Household, she was able to perform her duties. See for example, Prothero Ernle, *Life of Stanley*, II, 61 ff.: within two weeks of Albert's death Victoria was arranging the details of a trip to the Middle East for the Prince of Wales.

62 Leslie Stephen's 1870 article in *Fraser's* entitled 'The Broad Church', eloquently presented the argument against what he and his fellow unbelievers saw as the hypocrisy of liberal Christianity. And the personal lives of Stephen, Henry Sidgwick, and others who resigned lucrative university posts because of their loss of faith, testified to the seriousness of the agnostics' intellectual commitment.

63 See James Turner's recent book on Anglo-American agnosticism with this title; Baltimore, 1985.

11 DEATH, GRIEF, AND MOURNING IN THE UPPER-CLASS FAMILY, 1860–1914

This essay is drawn from two chapters of my forthcoming book, *Death in the Victorian Family, 1850–1920*. The principles of selection of these families are explained in *Women, Marriage and Politics, 1860–1914*, Oxford University Press, 1986, 1–3.

1 R. W. Mackenna, *The Adventure of Death*, London, 1916; C. E. Lawrence, 'The Abolition of Death', *Fortnightly Review*, 1917; Edward Mercer, *Why Do We Die?*, London, 1919.

2 Bertram S. Puckle, *Funeral Customs: their Origin and Development*, London, 1926.

3 John Morley, *Death, Heaven, and the Victorians*, London, 1971.

4 Lou Taylor, *Mourning Dress: A Costume and Social History*, London, 1982; P. Cunnington and C. Lucas, *Costumes for Birth, Marriage and Death*, London, 1964.

5 David Cannadine, 'War and death, grief and mourning in modern Britain' in Joachim Whaley (ed.), *Mirrors of Mortality*, London, 1981, 187–242.

6 Geoffrey Gorer, *Death, Grief and Mourning in Contemporary Britain*,

London, 1965.

7 P. Ariès, *The Hour of Our Death*, London, 1981; D. Stannard, *The Puritan Way of Death: A Study in Religion, Culture and Social Change*, New York, 1977; Cannadine, 'War and grief', 189.

8 Cannadine, 'War and grief', 191.

9 The section on Queen Victoria is based on A. C. Benson and Viscount Esher (eds), *The Letters of Queen Victoria*, London, 1908, III; Christopher Hibbert (ed.), *Queen Victoria in Her Letters and Journals*, Harmondsworth, 1985; Elizabeth Longford, *Victoria R.I.*, London, 1964.

10 Longford, *Victoria R.I.*, 364–6, 378; M. Ponsonby, *A Memoir*, London, 1927, 47.

11 *Letters of Queen Victoria, III*, 476.

12 ibid., 477–8.

13 Longford, *Victoria R.I.*, 486, 489.

14 C. M. Parkes, *Bereavement: Studies of Grief in Adult Life*, London, 1975, 130–142; J. Bowlby, *Attachment and Loss, III. Loss: Sadness and Depression*, Harmondsworth 1985, 141–51. See Bowlby 106–11 for details of various studies. Results cannot be quantitatively precise, since 'no very systematic comparative data are available' (Parkes, 131).

15 Parkes, *Bereavement*, pp. 143–75

16 ibid., 133

17 Lucille Iremonger, *Lord Aberdeen*, London, 1978, 26–40, 43, 97–107.

18 Lord Elton, *Life of James Ramsay MacDonald*, London, 1939, 196.

19 D. Marquand, *Ramsay MacDonald*, London, 1977, 132–5.

20 Obituary of Dr J. H. Gladstone by W. A. Tilden, April 1905, MacDonald Papers, Public Record Office, PRO 30/69/861.

21 L. J. L. Dundas, Marquess of Zetland, *Life of Evelyn Baring, First Earl of Cromer*, London, 1932, 286–7.

22 Katharine Bruce Glasier to J. R. MacDonald, 9 December 1912, MacDonald Papers, PRO 30/69/734, ff. 21–4.

23 Count de Franqueville to Lord Selborne, 29 October 1916, MS Selborne 113, ff. 114–5, Bodleian Library, Oxford.

24 See e.g. Marquand, *MacDonald*, 133–4.

25 Mary Drew to A. J. Balfour, n.d. [before 6 May 1886], Balfour Papers, British Library, Add. MS 49794, ff. 179–80.

26 Edith Lyttelton, *Alfred Lyttelton. An Account of his Life*, London, 1917, 149–52.

27 ibid., 151–2, 156.

28 Edith Lyttelton, 'Interwoven', 1938, Chandos MS 6/1/J, Churchill College, Cambridge.

29 May Harcourt to Elizabeth Lady Harcourt, 23 August 1909, MS Harcourt dep. 648, ff. 28–9, Bodleian Library.

30 Marion Montagu to Margaret MacDonald, 5 February 1911, MacDonald Papers, PRO 30/69/905.

31 Harriet, Baroness de Clifford to Nina, Countess Minto, August 1877, Minto MS 12257, f. 149, National Library of Scotland.

32 Edith Lyttelton to A. J. Balfour, 23 August 1913, Balfour Papers,

Whittingehame MS 166.

33 Lady Wantage to Evelyn Lady Stanhope, 22 April 1905, Stanhope MSS, U1590, C 573/3, Kent Archives Office.

34 Kenneth Young, *Arthur James Balfour*, London, 1963, 5.

35 Journal of Mary Countess Minto, June 1914, Minto MS 12463, National Library of Scotland.

36 Mary Drew to Lord Rosebery, 20 April 1910, Rosebery MS 10015, f.205, National Library of Scotland.

37 See e.g. ibid.

38 Winifred Byng to Lord Carnarvon, 29 December 1887, Carnarvon Papers, British Library, Add. MS 61060.

39 See Parkes, *Bereavement*, 132.

40 Eveline Lady Portsmouth to Lord Carnarvon, 4 August 1878, Carnarvon Papers, British Library Add. MS 61050.

41 Violet Cecil to Edward Cecil, 24 July 1900, Cecil-Maxse MS U 1599 C705/1, Kent Archives Office.

43 Lavinia Talbot to Meriel Talbot, 21 July 1913, Talbot MS U 1612, Kent Archives Office.

43 Constance Flower to Mrs Marion Bryce, n.d. [1894], MS Bryce Adds. 42, Bodleian Library.

44 Mary Herbert to Mrs Marion Bryce, 15 July [1902], ibid.

45 Mary Bryce to James Bryce, n.d. [September 1903], MS Bryce Adds. 15.

46 Lavinia Talbot to Meriel Talbot, 21 July 1913, Talbot MS U 1612.

47 Lucy Cavendish to Edith Lyttelton, 13 December 1913, Chandos MS I, 5/5.

48 John Bailey (ed.), *The Diary of Lady Frederick Cavendish*, London, 1927, II, 329.

49 Lady Charlotte Phillimore to W. E. Gladstone, 10 February 1885, Gladstone Papers, British Library, Add. MS 44279, ff. 62–3.

50 Gertrude Gladstone to W. E. Gladstone, 19 October 1891, Glynne-Gladstone MS 22/8, St. Deiniol's Library, Hawarden.

51 Katharine Anne Elliot to Nina Countess Minto, 16 August 1865, Minto MS 12259, f. 1.

52 Lavinia Talbot to Meriel Talbot, 6 February 1910, Talbot MS U 1612.

53 Mrs John Sherwood, *Manners and Social Usages*, London, 1884, 125; Mrs Fanny Douglas, *The Gentlewoman's Book of Dress*, London, 1895.

54 Parkes, *Bereavement*, 188.

55 Elizabeth King to niece Margaret Gladstone, 13 October 1896, MacDonald Papers, PRO 30/69/887.

56 Agnes Anson to husband Fred Anson, 18 June 1888, Acland of Broadclyst MSS, Acland-Anson 2862M/F283a, Devon Record Office.

57 Elsa Bell to Molly Trevelyan, 11 February 1906, Trevelyan Papers, Newcastle University Library.

58 Victoria Dawnay to Mary Countess Minto, 12 November 1887, Minto MS 12427, f. 203.

59 Audrey Wallas to husband Graham Wallas, 6 May 1910, Wallas MSS, British Library of Political and Economic Science.

60 Clare Gittings, *Death, Burial and the Individual,* London, 1984, 25–6.
61 Lawrence Stone, *Crisis of the Aristocracy,* Oxford, 1965, 576, 784–6.
62 John McManners, *Death and the Enlightenment,* Oxford, 1981, 285.
63 Morley, *Death, Heaven and the Victorians,* 22, 83–5.
64 Lord Selborne, *Memorials,* London, 1853, I, 161.
65 *Lancet,* 20 January 1894.

12 THE LANCASHIRE WAY OF DEATH

1 These projects were financed by the SSRC (ESRC) and carried out under the aegis of the Centre for North West Regional Studies, University of Lancaster. The evidence collected was transcribed and indexed and is available for use by researchers both in the university library and in the Centre. The respondents were recruited in a variety of ways, but mainly from lists held by charities concerned with the elderly, from many and various personal contacts and from publicity in the media.
2 G. Duncan Mitchell (ed.), *A Dictionary of Sociology,* London, 1968, 147.
3 E. Chadwick, 'Supplementary report', in E. Royston Pike (ed.), *Human Documents of the Industrial Revolution,* London, 1966, 352–3.
4 Robert Roberts, *The Classic Slum,* 2nd edition, London, 1973, 87.
5 James Walvin, *A Child's World. The Social History of English Childhood 1800–1914,* London, 1982, chap. 2 'Death and the child' for an examination of this topic over a wider geographical area and longer time span.
6 Mrs A3B, born 1892. Father a labourer; mother a domestic servant; 9 children (7 survived). Mrs A became a domestic servant. The names given to the respondents are assumed ones as they were promised anonymity. The code number is the one used on their transcripts in the archive.
7 Miss T2B, born 1888. Father a flour mill manager; 13 children (1 died). It would appear that this family could not be described as working-class with father as a manager. However the family were not wealthy and lived in the poorest area of Barrow. After father died they became very poor, mother becoming a domestic servant and Miss T a laundry worker.
8 Mr B4P born 1896. Father a bleacher; mother a fowl dresser; 10 children. Mr B became a bleacher.
9 J. Hawkins Miller, 'Temple and sewer – childbirth prudery and Victoria Regina' in A. Wohl (ed.), *The Victorian Family: Structure and Stresses,* London, 1978, 27.
10 Lancaster Medical Officer of Health Report for 1917. 184 babies out of a total of 613 were delivered by one unqualified midwife.
11 I am very grateful to Ruth Richardson for first drawing my attention to those parallels in discussions many years ago. Her comments have always been full of insights. Some of them appear in Mary Chamberlain and Ruth Richardson, 'Life and death', in *Oral History,*

11(1), 31–43.
12 Mrs M3P, born 1898. Father a dockworker; mother a charwoman; 7 children (4 died). Mrs M. became a factory worker.
13 Mrs A3B, see above.
14 Mr F1P, born 1906. Father a poultry dresser; mother a washerwoman; 5 children. Mr F. became an electrician.
15 Mrs P1L, born 1898. Father a foreman in the linoleum works; mother no paid occupation; 5 children (1 died). Mrs P. became a clerk.
16 Mr T2P, born 1903. Father a labourer; mother a weaver; 7 children (4 died). Mr T. became a railway man.
17 Mrs B1P, born 1900. Father a moulder; mother no paid occupation; 19 children (including step and half brothers and sisters). Mrs B. became a weaver.
18 Mrs C5P, born 1919. Father a carter; mother a winder; 6 children (1 died). Mrs C. became a weaver.
19 Mrs S3L, born 1892. Father a labourer, mother a washerwoman; 2 children. Mrs S. became a winder.
20 Mrs S3L, see above.
21 Mr B1B, born 1897. Father a caretaker; mother a cook; 13 children (2 died). Mr B. became a baker.
22 Mrs W1B, born 1900. Father a moulder; mother no paid occupation; 10 children (2 died). Mrs W. became a shop assistant.
23 Mrs M1P, born 1913. Father a fitter and turner; mother a little child minding; 6 children (1 died). Mrs M. became a tenter (cotton worker).
24 Mr B1B, see above.
25 Mrs M6B, born 1896. Father a labourer; mother a dressmaker; 16 children (13 died). Mrs M. became a professional musician.
26 Mr B1B, see above.
27 Mrs A2B, born 1904. Father a labourer; mother a domestic servant; 4 children. Mrs A. became a shop assistant.
28 Mrs B1P, see above.
29 Mr B9P, born 1927. Father a waiter; mother a weaver; 2 children. Mr B. became a college lecturer.
30 This is an area of enquiry in a new ESRC project 'Familial and social change and continuity in working class families, 1940–1970', which began in November 1987.
31 Mrs G1B, born 1888. Father a fitter; mother no paid occupation; 16 children (5 died). Mrs G. became a clerical worker.
32 Mrs B1P, see above.
33 Mrs H4P, born 1903. Father a fitter but frequently unemployed; mother a weaver; 10 children (2 died). Mrs H. became a domestic servant.

BIBLIOGRAPHY

Anderson, M., 'The emergence of the modern life cycle in Britain', *Social History*, 10 (1), 69–87.

Ariès, P., *Western Attitudes towards Death*, trans. P. N. Ranum, Baltimore, 1974.

—*Essais sur l'histoire de la mort en occident du moyen age à nos jours*, Paris, 1975.

—*The Hour of Our Death*, trans. H. Weaver, London, 1981.

Beaty, N. L., *The Craft of Dying: A Study in the Literary Tradition of the Ars Moriendi in England*, New Haven and London, 1970.

Berger, P., and Luckmann, T., 'Sociology of religion and sociology of knowledge', in N. Birnbaum and G. Lenzer (eds), *Sociology of Religion: A Book of Readings*, Englewood Cliffs, New Jersey, 1969.

Boase, T. S. R., *Death in the Middle Ages: Mortality, Judgment and Remembrance*, London, 1972.

Brown, A. W., *The Metaphysical Society*, Cambridge, 1947.

Chamberlain, M., and Richardson, R., 'Life and death', *Oral History*, 11 (1).

Chaunu, P., *La Mort à Paris: 16ᵉ, 17ᵉ, 18ᵉ siècles*, Paris, 1978.

Clarkson, L., *Death, Disease and Famine in Pre-Industrial England*, Dublin, 1975.

Cunnington, P., and Lucas, C., *Costumes for Birth, Marriage and Death*, London, 1964.

Curl, J. S., *The Victorian Celebration of Death*, Newton Abbot, 1972.

Eassie, W., *Cremation of the Dead: Its History and Bearings upon Public Health*, London, 1875.

Erichsen, H., *The Cremation of the Dead*, Detroit, 1887.

Farrel, J. J., *Inventing the American Way of Death, 1830–1920*, Philadelphia, 1980.

Feifel, H. (ed.), *The Meaning of Death*, New York, 1959.

Fletcher, R., *The Akenham Burial Case*, London, 1974.

Gittings, C., *Death, Burial and the Individual in Early Modern England*, London, 1984.

Gorer, G., *Death, Grief and Mourning in Contemporary Britain*, London, 1965.

Harré, R., *The Social Construction of Emotions*, Oxford, 1986.

Haweis, Rev. H. R., *Ashes to Ashes, A Cremation Prelude*, London, 1875.

Hay, D., Linebaugh, P., *et al.*, *Albion's Fatal Tree*, London, 1975.

Hopkins, H., *The Long Affray*, London, 1985.

Jacobs, J., 'The dying of death', *Fortnightly Review*, new series, LXXII (392).

Kastenbaum, R. J., *Death, Society and Human Experience*, St Louis, 1972.

Laqueur, T., 'Bodies, death and pauper funerals', *Representations* 1(1).

Lebrun, F., *Les Hommes et la mort en Anjou aux 17ᵉ et 18ᵉ siècles*, Paris, 1971.

Lindeman, E., 'Symptomology and management of acute grief', *American Journal of Psychiatry*, 1944, 101, 141–8.

Loudon, J. C., *On the Laying Out, Planting and Managing of Cemeteries and on the Improvement of Churchyards*, London, 1843.

MacDonald, M., *Mystical Bedlam: Madness, Anxiety and Healing in Seventeenth-century England*, Cambridge, 1981.

McManners, J., *Death and the Enlightenment: Changing Attitudes to Death among Christians and Unbelievers in Eighteenth-century France*, Oxford, 1981.

McNeill, W. H., *Plagues and Peoples*, Oxford, 1977.

Mitford, J., *The American Way of Death*, London, 1963.

Morley, J., *Death, Heaven and the Victorians*, London, 1971.

Morris, R. J., *Cholera 1832*, London, 1976.

O'Connor, M. C., *The Art of Dying Well: The Development of the Ars Moriendi*, New York, 1942.

Oppenheim, J., *The Other World*, Cambridge, 1985.

Parkes, C. M., *Bereavement: Studies of Grief in Adult Life*, London, 1972.

Penny, N., *Mourning*, London, 1981.

Pincus, L., *Life and Death*, London, 1978.

Porter, R. (ed.), *Patients and Practitioners. Lay Perceptions of Medicine in Pre-industrial Society*, Cambridge, 1985.

Puckle, B. S., *Funeral Customs*, London, 1926.

Ragon, M., *The Space of Death: A Study of Funerary Architecture, Decoration, and Urbanism*, trans. A. Sheridan, University of Virginia, 1983.

Richardson, R., *Death, Dissection and the Destitute*, London and New York, 1988.

Robinson, W., *Cremation and Urn-Burial, or, the Cemeteries of the Future*, London, 1889.

Rosenblatt, P., Walsh, R. P., and Jackson, D. A., *Grief and Mourning in Cross-Cultural Perspective*, 1976.

Slack, P., *The Impact of Plague in Tudor and Stuart England*, London, 1985.

Stannard, D. E., *The Puritan Way of Death: A Study in Religion, Culture and Social Change*, New York, 1977.

Stannard, D. E. (ed.), *Death in America*, University of Pennsylvania Press, 1975.

Stone, L., *The Family, Sex and Marriage in England 1500–1800*, London, 1977.

Symondson, A. (ed.), *The Victorian Crisis of Faith*, London, 1964.

Taylor, L., *Mourning Dress: A Costume and Social History*, London, 1983.

Thompson, Sir H., *Modern Cremation, its History and Practice*, 3rd edn, London, 1899.

Tristram, P., *Figures of Life and Death in Mediaeval English Literature*, London, 1976.

Vovelle, G. and M., *La Vision de la mort et de l'au-delà en Provence après les autels des ames du purgatoire, XVe–XXe siècles*, Paris, 1970.

Vovelle, M., *Piété baroque et déchristianisation en Provence au XVIIIe siècle*, Paris, 1973.

—*Mourir autrefois: attitudes collectives devant la mort au XVIIe et XVIIIe siècles*, Paris, 1974.

Walker, D. P., *The Decline of Hell: Seventeenth-century Discussions of Eternal Torment*, London, 1964.

Walvin, J., *A Child's World: The Social History of English Childhood, 1800–1914*, London, 1982, chapter 2.

Whaley, J. (ed.), *Mirrors of Mortality: Studies in the Social History of Death*, London, 1981.

Wilson, Sir A., and Levy, H., *Burial Reform and Funeral Costs*, London, 1938.

Wrigley, E. A., and Schofield, R. S., *The Population History of England 1541–1871: A Reconstruction*, London, 1981.

Yinger, J. M., *Religion, Society and the Individual*, New York, 1967.

The CONTRIBUTORS

Lucinda McCray Beier is a Research Officer in the Centre for North-West Regional Studies, University of Lancaster. Her *Sufferers and Healers: The Experience of Illness in Seventeenth-century England* appeared in 1987, and she is now working on an ESRC sponsored project on 'Familial and social change and continuity in working-class families, 1940-1970'.

Diana Dixon is Lecturer in Library and Information Studies at Loughborough University of Technology. She is the author (with Lionel Madden) of *The Nineteenth Century Periodical Press in Britain: a Bibliography of Modern Studies (1976)*, and has written a number of articles on Victorian periodicals.

Martha McMackin Garland is Associate Professor of History at the Ohio State University in Columbus. Author of *Cambridge before Darwin: the Ideal of a Liberal Education, 1800-1860* (1980), she is currently working on a book tentatively entitled 'Victorian loss of Faith: the personal implications'.

Ralph Houlbrooke is Reader in History at the University of Reading. Author of *Church Courts and the People during the English Reformation, 1520-1570* (1979) and *The English Family, 1450–1700* (1984), he has also published various articles. At present he is working on a book provisionally entitled 'Death, church and family in England, 1450-1750'.

Pat Jalland is Associate Professor of History at Murdoch University, Western Australia. Her chief publications are *The Liberals and Ireland: The Ulster Question in British Politics to 1914* (1980), *Women,*

Marriage and Politics, 1860–1914 (1986), and (with J. P. Hooper) *Women from Birth to Death. The Female Life-Cycle in Britain, 1830-1914* (1986). She has also published many other essays and articles.

Anne Laurence is Lecturer in History at the Open University. Her *Parliamentary Army Chaplains 1642-57* will appear shortly. She has already published a number of articles.

Jennifer Leaney is working on a thesis on 'Homicide in mid-Victorian London' at Magdalen College, Oxford.

Jim Morgan is Head of Academic Standards at Leeds Polytechnic. He contributed a chapter on 'Demograpic Change, 1771 to 1911' to Derek Fraser (ed.) *A History of Modern Leeds* (1981) and is working on a thesis on 'The burial problem in Leeds in the eighteenth and nineteenth centuries'.

Roy Porter is Senior Lecturer in the History of Medicine (Wellcome Institute). His *Mind-forg'd Manacles: A History of Madness in England from the Restoration to the Regency* appeared in 1987. Among his many important publications *English Society in the Eighteenth Century* (1982) and *Disease, Medicine and Society in England, 1550-1860* (1987) are both connected in different ways with his chapter in this volume, as is *Patients and Practitioners: Lay Perceptions of Medicine in Pre-industrial Society* (1986), a book of essays edited by him.

Ruth Richardson is a Research Officer at the Institute of Historical Research, University of London. She is the author of *Death, Dissection and the Destitute: The Politics of the Corpse in Pre-Victorian Britain* (1988, paperback edition 1989). Dr Richardson's current work is on a major project indexing the Victorian journal *The Builder*.

Elizabeth Roberts is a Research Officer and part-time Administrative Officer at the Centre for North West Regional Studies, University of Lancaster. She is author of *Working-Class Barrow and Lancaster, 1890-1940* (1976), *A Woman's Place, An Oral History, 1890-1940* (1984), and numerous articles. She is currently working on an ESRC sponsored project on 'Familial and social change and continuity in working-class families, 1940-1970'.

INDEX